# The Writing of John Bunyan

The Bunyan Window in Bunyan Meeting Free Church, Mill Street, Bedford.
*By kind permission of Bunyan Meeting Free Church.*

# The Writing of John Bunyan

## TAMSIN SPARGO

## Ashgate

Aldershot • Brookfield USA
Singapore • Sydney

Published by
Ashgate Publishing Limited
Gower House
Croft Road
Aldershot
Hants
GU11 3HR
England

Ashgate Publishing Company
Old Post Road
Brookfield
Vermont 05036–9704
USA

The author has asserted their moral right under the Copyright, Designs and Patent Act, 1988, to be identified as the author of this work.

British Library Cataloguing in Publication Data

Spargo, Tamsin
  The Writing of John Bunyan
  1. Bunyan, John, 1628–88—Criticism and interpretation.
  I. Title.
  828.4'09

ISBN 1–85928–449–3

Library of Congress Cataloging-in-Publication Data

Spargo, Tamsin.
  The writing of John Bunyan/Tamsin Spargo.
    p.  cm.
  Includes bibliographical references.
  ISBN 1–85928–449–3
  1. Bunyan, John, 1628–88—Political and social views.
2. Christian literature, English—Puritan authors—History and
criticism.  3. Christianity and literature—England—History—17th
century.  4. Literature and society—England—History—17th century.
5. Power (Social sciences) in literature.  I. Title.
PR3332.S64  1997
828'.407—dc21                                         97–15586
                                                           CIP

ISBN 1 85928 449 3

This book is printed on acid free paper

Typeset in Sabon by Manton Typesetters, 5–7 Eastfield Road, Louth, Lincolnshire, UK.

Printed in Great Britain by the Ipswich Book Company, Suffolk

# Contents

# Acknowledgements

I would like to thank a number of people who have given me support, guidance and encouragement in completing this project, particularly Catherine Belsey, Fred Botting, Martin Coyle, John Drakakis, and Terence Hawkes. I am also grateful to the following for their helpful comments on the manuscript: Peter Childs, Joanna Croft, Elspeth Graham, Matthew Jordan, Stephen Knight and Kathleen McLuskie. A version of part of Chapter 3 appeared in Kate Chedgzoy, Melanie Hansen and Suzanne Trill (eds), *Voicing Women: Gender and Sexuality in Early-Modern Writing* (Keele University Press, 1996). A version of part of Chapter 4 appeared in *Textual Practice* 8.1 (Spring 1994). I am grateful to Keele University Press and Routledge for their permission to publish later versions and to Alec MacAulay and Caroline Cornish of Ashgate for their help in preparing this volume.

For my mother

# Introduction: Traces of Authority

In the context of the literary institution in the late twentieth century
'John Bunyan' is a name of considerable authority. It is the name of the
author of 58 texts, a name whose perceived authority guarantees the
special status of those texts.[1] It serves to differentiate between texts on
the grounds of authorship and to confer on certain texts the status of
products of that name. Generations of critics and literary historians
have operated as custodians of the name of John Bunyan, policing the
name within, and on behalf of, academic and cultural institutions. Texts
which once bore the name have been exposed as illegitimate claimants
and deleted from the Bunyan canon; shaky signatures on historical
documents have been denounced as differing too much from the standard form and rejected as evidence of authorship.[2] John Bunyan is a
name, a label, whose integrity is to be jealously guarded, a powerful
cultural signifier which is not to be associated with inferior material,
but which also functions, like William Shakespeare, as a popular signifier
of cultural achievement. *The Pilgrim's Progress* may no longer be a
popular best-seller in Britain, but the name of its author is still well
known. The name John Bunyan is respectable, yet popular. It is a name
deemed familiar enough to be featured on a regular basis in general
knowledge questions in the BBC's *Mastermind* quiz programme. It is a
name, however, whose meaning is neither single nor stable.

This study is an attempt to prise open the name of John Bunyan, not
in order to reveal the man behind the name, but to examine the operations of that name, to explore the discursive techniques which produced
the figure of this author, both in the seventeenth century and later, and
to identify the different meanings which have been ascribed to it in the
history of its production. Each of the chapters traces the faultlines and
power relations of authority at work in the writings of, and on, John
Bunyan. The texts examined include the familiar and the less well-
known works whose status has depended on the cultural and historical
contexts in which they were circulated, from the best-seller *The Pilgrim's Progress* to title-pages and prefaces, spelling guides and marginal
notes. Some of these texts bear the name(s) of this author, others are
associated with less authoritative names.

This study may be read as a 'Dear John' letter to the author, or as an
exercise in cultural materialism which examines the production and
reproduction of a particular figure of authority, the author, within
specific cultural formations at different historical moments. It does not
seek to claim Bunyan for any radical project, to redefine the author of

*The Pilgrim's Progress* as a revolutionary thinker or writer, nor to denounce him as a misogynist or quietist. It does not attempt to locate the 'true' John Bunyan but instead traces the textual and discursive construction of names and positions for writers and readers. Texts are sites of contestation that are inscribed by, and implicated in, the contradictory and discontinuous operations of power. Writers and readers, authors and critics are all involved in contests for meaning, in struggles to occupy positions of authority. This conflict over meaning is evident in the different understandings of the meaning of authority itself.

The relations, in Bunyan's writings, between different forms of authority, whether divine or secular, political or personal, have conventionally been explained by reference to a model of power which opposes the powerful and the powerless, the authorised and unauthorised. In this formulation, encapsulated in the phrases 'the authorities' or 'the powers that be', authority and power are properties, possessed or obtained, and exercised by, particular subjects or groups of subjects. This conception of power is, however, historically and culturally contingent. Although its own history is often veiled or effaced in the critical and historical accounts which deploy it, this model of power is, and always has been, open to question.

Versions of this understanding of power and authority are articulated in texts of the seventeenth century. The notion that power inheres in particular individuals underpins the idea of a patriarchal political and social order, expounded in a text such as Robert Filmer's *Patriarcha* (1680), which establishes a hierarchical system of analogous relations between those who wield power, fathers and monarchs, and those who are subject to it, children and subjects. In Bunyan's writings absolute power and authority are the properties of God alone and men and women are entirely subject to his decree. Yet relations of authority and subjection in this period were far from stable and the meanings of power and authority themselves are at stake and in crisis in the events and texts of the civil war, the revolutionary period, and its aftermath. Although some of the most dramatic changes in the period took place on battlefields, in Whitehall and on the scaffold, perhaps the most revolutionary changes occurred in a different battle, a battle of words.

Throughout the seventeenth century words are employed as weapons, as tools, but words can never be entirely under the control of their users. Attempts to legitimate conflicting political positions by harnessing the authority of words, even of supposedly divine origin, can never arrest the play of meaning. Scriptural texts such as 'the powers that be are ordained of God' (Romans 13.1) could be deployed in the period to support the *status quo*, but other texts offered material for radical critiques of existing political and social hierarchies. Single texts could be mobilised in support of radically opposed positions, as the meanings of individual words were open to contest. As Christopher Hill has argued, the Bible was one of the major battlefields of the seventeenth century.[3] But the deployment of the authority of scripture has repercussions which cannot be contained or controlled by any political project. The increasing insistence on the authority of this text involves an encounter with the textuality of authority.

A conventional model of power is, I would argue, inadequate to the task of exploring the multiple relations which are the conditions for the production of claims to authority. When the notion that power is the property of individual subjects is combined, as it almost invariably is, with an idealist, empiricist model of language, the effects are profoundly conservative. If language is viewed as the representation of a pre-existing realm of things and ideas and as under the control of an autonomous subject, then its role in the construction, reproduction and transformation of subjects and realities is occluded. The interrelationships of power and language may be more productively explored by employing, or deploying, a different understanding of both power and authority. Developing Michel Foucault's analysis of the operations of power, I suggest that authority does not inhere in any figure, whether that figure is God, the State or the individual human subject. Authority is an effect produced in differential relations of power and resistance; it is unstable, precarious and always contested. Whenever authority is on display it is also on trial. In this study I focus on a series of moments of crystallisation and crisis in the production of specific claims to authority. These are moments within the histories of specific discursive formations which both demand and produce particular figures of authority to underwrite or legitimate networks of unequal power relations. These are the histories of authorship, of individualism, patriarchy and imperialism: different and discrete histories which nevertheless intersect and overlap in the maintenance of specific social and cultural orders. Through textual analysis of specific instances of the operations of power in the production, reception and dissemination of Bunyan's writings, I investigate the intersection of political and cultural authorities from the seventeenth century to the twentieth century.

My engagement with questions of authority starts, perhaps inevitably, in the present, as an examination of the construction of John Bunyan as an object of knowledge in literary studies. John Bunyan is a name whose canonical status seems assured, its singularity paradoxically maintained through the continuing mobilisation of a regulatory polarity. The binary opposition of Conventicle and Parnassus, first defined by Coleridge, which identifies conflicting religious and aesthetic impulses within Bunyan's writings, accommodates and defuses the multiple and contradictory traces of authority and resistance within the texts. Conflicts and contradictions can be explained by reference to a founding tension in the consciousness of the author and so be divested of their disruptive force.

In Chapter 1 an examination of the forms of the name of the author on the title pages of Bunyan's texts reveals not a neat division into pastoral and aesthetic categories but rather a complex network of claims to different types of authority: pastoral, patriarchal, authorial and political. Bunyan's writings can be read as part of a battle of words about the true meaning of the Word. Located within a logocentric tradition in which God stands as transcendental signified, the original and originating meaning which holds in place all other meanings, these texts act as supplements to the Word. The authority of the Scriptures is presented as impeccable, but what is the status of Bunyan's supplementary texts? In the textual contest to assert the legitimacy of these texts, with rival writers, actual and implied, a number of different figures of authority emerge. In the later texts there is, I suggest, evidence of a claim to transcendence on the part of the writing subject which implicitly displaces God as sole source and guarantor of meaning. The figure of Bunyan presented in an advertisement published with *The Holy War* in 1682 closely resembles the figure of the creative writing subject celebrated and sustained by traditional, post-Romantic, literary criticism. Even in this text, however, the act of writing can be seen to expose the writing subject to the effects of difference, which render any claim to authority unstable. The textual construction of this meaning of authorship, however apparently authoritative, raises the possibility of other meanings.

Chapter 2 examines *Grace Abounding to the Chief of Sinners*. This is a text which has repeatedly been mobilised, within the literary institution and beyond, on behalf of a figure of authority whose historical construction has been frequently effaced: the individual subject. This section explores the critical attempts to restore the imaginary figure of Bunyan as autobiographical subject to presence and argues that this process has effaced the multiple relations of authority and resistance within the text. Bunyan's trial and imprisonment for unlicensed preaching are examined within the context of conflicting claims for interpretative authority. *Grace Abounding* is read as a claim to authority which escapes the carceral constraints on the body of the author but cannot evade the effects of difference.

Whilst the conflict between the State and nonconformists, exemplified by Bunyan's trial, has received considerable critical attention, other power struggles evident in Bunyan's writings have been effaced or marginalised. In accepting narrow definitions of the political, some critics have ignored crucial questions about authority and subjectivity raised in the texts. Whilst subject to the repressive power of the state as an unauthorised preacher, Bunyan is differently positioned in the social hierarchy of gender relations. Chapter 3 examines the complex effects of the encounter between patriarchal authority, located in the figure of Bunyan, and gendered difference in the seventeenth century. Here the fragility of Bunyan's pastoral and textual authority is revealed in an examination of female figures of resistance, whose exclusion from positions of authority in the seventeenth century has been mirrored in their (often literal) marginalisation within critical studies. In the context of female demands for a more active role in religious affairs, Bunyan's confident interdictions are countered by the production of a number of contra-dictions.

Finally, Chapter 4 explores the limits of authority in its encounter with cultural difference in a wider sense. It argues that much of Bunyan's cultural authority derives from his texts' mobilisation within overtly evangelical and implicitly imperialist frameworks. *The Pilgrim's Progress* is read as a key text in the history of Western imperialism, repeatedly reproduced in order to enlist different subjects within the discourses of salvation and civilisation. This section examines the methods used to define and fix the positions of reading subjects in, and of, Bunyan's texts, and identifies moments of resistance by those readers. It argues that any attempt to fix meaning is doomed to failure, and that the possibility of resistance to authority is essential to the construction of authority itself. Authority produces resistance, demands resistance, but can never control it.

# CHAPTER ONE

# The Name(s) of the Author

## I John Bunyan: the Authorised Version

On 31 August 1688 John Bunyan died after contracting a fever on a journey from Reading to London. Three hundred years later the anniversary of his death was marked by a number of celebratory and commemorative events and publications. A major conference was organised in Britain by the Open University and a number of texts featuring work by British and North American scholars on Bunyan were published in this year and soon after.[1] The organisation of the conference at the Open University, which was established to make higher education available to all, regardless of formal qualifications, could be seen to signal some continuity with the radical and populist impetus of some aspects of seventeenth-century nonconformist culture of which Bunyan was a part. The publication of a range of collections of essays signalled Bunyan's important status as an object of academic knowledge within a range of disciplines. In the context of the discursive construction of John Bunyan as an author, the most significant and revealing title among these collections, was *John Bunyan: Conventicle and Parnassus* (1988). The publication of this collection by Oxford University Press, who have published the standard scholarly editions of all Bunyan's major texts and more recently of his miscellaneous writings, could be read as reinforcing the respectable status of author and texts within literary studies in the late twentieth century; the choice of title suggests a critical continuity with the long and complicated history of attempts to assimilate Bunyan within the literary canon.

The editor, N. H. Keeble describes the project of the collection as an attempt to 'advance our understanding of Bunyan by adopting a variety of contemporary approaches to him, and to illustrate the many different kinds of interest which, after 300 years, he attracts'.[2] There are, indeed, a number of different critical methods and theoretical approaches represented in the text, from an examination of the relevance of deconstructive logics, to the study of Bunyan's allegories and glosses, to a study of the relationship between *The Pilgrim's Progress* and Restoration Latitudinarianism.[3] But whatever differences or conflicts of position emerge in this collection, the preface suggests that they have been harnessed together in order to produce a valuable contribution to a particular knowledge, whose object is the author as source and guarantee of the meaning of his writings.

The collection is presented as 'a comprehensive summary of the present state of Bunyan scholarship and criticism', addressing what Keeble describes as 'the crux of Bunyan studies', namely 'whether Bunyan's literary genius was inspired by, or throve at the expense of, his religious commitment'.[4] This, it is implied, underlies Coleridge's assertion that in *The Pilgrim's Progress* 'the Bunyan of Parnassus had the better of the Bunyan of the Conventicle'.[5] The polarity thus defined by the Romantic critic is offered in the preface as the central concern, 'implicitly or explicitly', of the contributors in the late twentieth century.[6] The assertion of the continuing dominance in modern critical studies of this opposition between aesthetic and religious imperatives is supported by reference to the challenge posed by the texts to those engaged in the pursuit of knowledge within specialised fields of academic enquiry: 'Historical and theological investigation of Bunyan's thinking must engage with dramatically and metaphorically charged sources, while the texts which literary study subjects to critical scrutiny are determinedly and relentlessly homiletic.'[7] This assessment of the difficulties posed for conventional academic disciplines by Bunyan's texts is revealing in the terms used to differentiate between historical or theological readings of the works on the one hand, and literary approaches on the other. While the former approach is described as an 'investigation' of 'sources' as a means of access to 'Bunyan's thinking', a process in which the metaphoric qualities of language may be seen to obstruct the path to a truth located in an individual consciousness, the latter is described as a process in which texts are 'subjected' to 'critical scrutiny', suggesting the rigorous activity of a literary mind for whom 'relentlessly homiletic' texts may be troublesome, and perhaps ultimately inappropriate, objects of knowledge.[8] But, although the academic disciplines are differentiated by norms of object and method, they can be seen to operate in the service of a knowledge which establishes clearly regulated differences only to collapse them in the person of its ultimate subject – the individual consciousness itself.

It can be argued that the unease which, on the evidence of Keeble's preface, the Bunyan texts appear to cause in those working within conventional disciplines may well be the result of the separation which has been demanded between literary texts and the culture of which they are constituent parts, a culture which must be seen to consist of a wide range of signifying practices. Bunyan's writings, as products of a period of conflict and change, are necessarily plural, bearing the marks of the struggles and discontinuities of the contest for meaning in the seventeenth century of which they were a part. This was a contest which resulted in the emergence of many values now assumed to be self-evident truths about the nature of language, power and subjectivity. Perhaps the most significant, and complicated, birth in this era was that of the individual subject of liberal humanism, the subject which was to rule supreme until dethroned and decentred by a series of interlocking, overlapping, and sometimes contradictory, developments in linguistics, sociology and psychoanalysis throughout the twentieth century. In the wake of this problematisation of the subject, the polarity of Conventicle and Parnassus can be seen to operate as a means not of exploring the differences and discontinuities within a body of texts ascribed to the same author, but rather of controlling and explaining those differences by appeal to, and in support of, the notion of the author as individual subject and source of meaning, and of the critic as individual subject in confident possession of the objects of knowledge.

Keeble is right to suggest that the opposition of Conventicle and Parnassus has been an important feature of Bunyan studies, but this opposition need not be understood as a founding tension in the consciousness of the author. It may instead be identified in the tensions and conflicts of the founding of a discipline. The John Bunyan whose death was commemorated in 1988 was the product not only of the seventeenth century, but of the discursive processes and cultural formations of the eighteenth, nineteenth and twentieth centuries, including those which contributed to the establishment of the discipline of literary studies.

The celebrations in 1928 of the tercentenary of the birth of John Bunyan were on a grander scale and more varied than those of 1988. There was a formal celebration in the Queen's Hall, with an address by the Archbishop-designate of Canterbury, as well as numerous other events whose location and participants could be read as less apparently at odds with Bunyan's political and theological leanings. It was also the occasion of a surge of writing on Bunyan; in their guide to publications on Bunyan, James F. Forrest and Richard L. Greaves list 130 books, essays, scholarly and newspaper articles and reviews published in this year. Among them were a tercentenary edition of John Brown's biography, *John Bunyan (1628–1688): His Life, Times, and Work*, edited by Frank Mott Harrison, George Bagshawe Harrison's *John Bunyan: A Study in Personality*, numerous popular biographies, several pictorial guides to Bunyan's Bedfordshire, including one which mapped the journey of *The Pilgrim's Progress* on to the physical geography of the county, and a facsimile edition of the *Church Book of Bunyan Meeting*.[9] In addition to the biographical, historical and explicitly religious material, the publications on Bunyan in this year indicate a growing desire to formalise author and texts as objects of scholarly literary critical attention or knowledge. While the newspaper articles repeatedly referred to *The Pilgrim's Progress* as a world classic, in a piece in the *Times Literary Supplement* Edmund Blunden noted the absence of a critical edition of Bunyan's works and in the *Bulletin of the John Rylands Library* James Rendel Harris called for the methods of 'higher criticism' to be applied to Bunyan's writings.[10]

These calls for the deployment of scholarly and critical processes and methods in the study of Bunyan were not the first indication of the writer's construction as an object of knowledge within the developing discipline of literary studies, or English literature. From the late-nineteenth century, although treated primarily as a religious writer in scholarly analyses, Bunyan had attracted the attention of some of the leading figures in the development of English literature as an academic discipline, including some whose work contributed to its distinctive 'civilising' or 'social mission' as it was defined against both Classics and philological textual studies.[11] In *The English Novel* (1894) Walter Raleigh rejected the idea that Bunyan was a novelist but praised his skills in narrative and character construction; Arthur Quiller-Couch edited his selected writings in 1908.[12] So, by 1928, Bunyan was already a respectable object of literary study. The case for Bunyan and his texts to be included within the canon of great English literature on artistic rather than historical grounds had been made by expert, if in some cases reluctantly professional, witnesses.

However, the literary eminence of author and texts was not beyond question. As the newspaper reports of this year testified, *The Pilgrim's Progress* was a best-seller throughout the world, but by 1909 it had already been suggested that few people actually read it.[13] The moral and artistic qualities of author and text, which were the subject of many adulatory contributions to the tercentenary events, were also subject to severe criticism. A notable exception to the celebratory tone of the majority of the publications of 1928 was Alfred Noyes's 'Bunyan – a revaluation', which criticised the author's Calvinist theology, derivative style and personal failings.[14] The vehemence of Noyes's attack provoked a slew of responses in defence of Bunyan's doctrinal, literary and personal merit, praising, among other things, Bunyan's genius and the relevance of his writings to those concerned with eternal values. Noyes's response, 'Rejoinder', rejected these assertions of the author's transcendence of personal, doctrinal and historical limitations, denouncing Bunyan's 'piteously crude mind, warped throughout his life by congenital defects'.[15] The debate initiated by Noyes's criticism was the most heated exchange since a controversy which lasted for nearly 30 years from 1858. The earlier debate was occasioned by an article in *Notes and Queries* entitled 'Was John Bunyan a gipsy?' in which James Simson repudiated George Offor's assertion that Bunyan was not a gypsy.[16] Both debates were about the status of the writer but were conducted in different terms and reveal different imperatives. The debate about whether or not Bunyan was a gypsy was concerned with both the writer's uncertain cultural and biological status, perhaps echoing seventeenth-century concern with his position as a tinker, and with the validity of the contributors' historical and scholarly research methods. In 1928 the disagreement concerned not the writer's genealogy as a historically situated subject but his moral and artistic merits as an author, and can be read, I suggest, as a product of the bid to appropriate Bunyan as author within the broadly humanist project of literary studies. The influence of this humanist disposition within literary studies is evident throughout a wide range of critical approaches to the texts, including this study. Even those critics who have defined their own positions, priorities and values in terms of opposition to dominant norms, both social and disciplinary, have continued to utilise and sustain the concept of the author as a special object of knowledge.[17] But too many other discourses have laid claim to Bunyan for this appropriation to ever be uncontested and complete. The maintenance of Bunyan as a literary author has demanded that his writing be divided into 'literary' and doctrinal or metaphoric and homiletic, those texts which are presumed to merit individual publication and those which are comprehended under the title of miscellaneous works. Whereas the former are guaranteed a respectable, if not central, position in the literary canon, as examples of the triumph of Parnassus, the latter, as the product of Conventicle are considered to be of greater interest to those working in other disciplines. As Roger Sharrock, General Editor of the Clarendon Press *Miscellaneous Works* noted, 'The reader of Bunyan's *Miscellaneous Works* is more likely to be a social or ecclesiastical historian, a theologian or a psychologist, than a literary student.'[18]

It is my intention to return to the history of the relationship between Bunyan and the discipline of literary studies later in this study, but I want to turn now to the relationship between the writer and his name in the seventeenth century.

## II   Bunyans Abounding: from Chief of Sinners to Nu Hony in a B

Difference invades the name of John Bunyan from the beginning. A survey of title-pages of the seventeenth-century editions of the texts which bear the name of John Bunyan reveals not one name of the author, but many different names. There are variations in the spelling of the name: John Bunyan, John Bunnyan, John Bunian. Whilst these differences may be read as examples of relatively non-standardised spelling in seventeenth-century writing and publishing, other differences may be of greater significance. If the figure of the author is, as Foucault (1977) argues in 'What is an author?', a function of discourse, then an examination of the variations in the form of the name of the author, John Bunyan, may indicate both the range of different discursive fields within which the individual texts operated and the complex interaction of those fields. It may also suggest that the binary opposition identified in Bunyan's writings between overtly doctrinal or didactic works and those which adopt and adapt fictional, allegorical or literary models, is the product not of a conflict or contradiction which can be located in the consciousness of their author, but of a taxonomy developed at a later historical moment. Certain forms of the name of the author may appear to point to particular literary or discursive structures that can be retrospectively identified with the Romantic categories that constitute the Conventicle/Parnassus opposition. But this retrospective identification has all too often served to obscure the greater complexity of seventeenth-century nonconformist writing practices and of the different meanings of John Bunyan as author within them. As I will argue, it is possible to identify a moment in Bunyan's writing which prefigures and contributes to the development of a model of the author as origin and owner of the text. But in the very act of claiming such a position, Bunyan's writing reveals its limits.

The fact that 58 published texts bear a version of the name John Bunyan appears initially to be evidence of one of the functions of the author identified by Foucault, who argues that 'the fact that a number of texts were attached to a single name implies that relationships of homogeneity, filiation, reciprocal explanation, authentification, or of common utilization were established among them'.[19] Certainly, from the publication in 1691 of *The Struggler*, the first attempt to produce a volume of collected works by Bunyan, to the 1980s which saw the first publication of a scholarly edition of the complete miscellaneous works, the name of the author would indeed appear to function in this manner.

To what extent, however, is this aspect of the author-function a purely retrospective process of categorisation enacted within the academic and publishing institutions for whom the name acts as label and guarantee of corpus or product? From 1691 on, the attachment of the name John Bunyan to a number of texts may well have implied that some at least of the relationships listed by Foucault had been established among them, but is there evidence that such relationships were perceived before the publication of the collected or complete works, before the death of John Bunyan and the birth of the author? I would suggest that it is possible to identify textual strategies which present relationships of filiation, established through reference to the name of John Bunyan, and that at a late stage in Bunyan's writing career this can be connected with the appearance of an author figure which anticipates that of Romantic and post-Romantic constructions of authorship. But this is only one of the author figures produced in the combination of writing and publication practices which led to the dissemination of texts under the name John Bunyan.

I wish to argue that throughout the 32 years of publication, from the first text to Bunyan's death, a number of different figures of authorship were established which have since been obscured by the post-Romantic preoccupation with the author as inspired 'literary' or 'artistic' creator. It is not my intention to champion these other figures, to suggest that they are somehow a better model of the writing process or the position of authorship. I do want to suggest that their existence may call into question the privileged position afforded to the Romantic figure of the author and point to some of the contradictions and faultlines which were already evident in its first appearances.

The privileged position of this figure within literary studies is ensured, in part, by the inclusion in the canon of only a very limited selection of Bunyan's texts. John Bunyan is known to most undergraduates as the author of a famous, but often unread, allegory, *The Pilgrim's Progress*, and by some as the author of an autobiography, *Grace Abounding*: both texts can easily be read as exemplary products of, and producers of, a creative authorial subject. The fact that only three texts, *The Pilgrim's Progress*, *Grace Abounding* and *The Life and Death of Mr Badman*, are available in scholarly paperback editions may well contribute to, as well as reflect the relative marginalisation of other texts which might prove more recalcitrant in a market which both serves and is underwritten by a Romantic model of authorship. A survey of the descriptions of the author on title-pages of the seventeenth-century editions may be a useful way of discovering some of the textual and discursive strategies which were employed to establish the name during Bunyan's lifetime and how these relate to broader issues of authorship and authority. It is important in this context to note that we cannot be sure who chose or wrote the descriptions which are the subject of this analysis. In the absence of any copyright legislation which named the writer as owner of his or her writing, published texts were the property of the publishers and there is considerable evidence that the division between publishers, printers and writers was not the same as it is today. In the period during which Bunyan was writing it was, for example, the printer not the writer of a text who was most vulnerable to prosecution for the publication of dissident material. Whilst the current understanding of the different roles played by those who are involved in the production of texts is in part an effect of the legislation introduced in 1710, it is also reinforced by the Romantic notion of the author as specially responsible, as creator in a unique sense of text and meaning, with publisher and printer relegated to positions as facilitators with economic rather than creative powers within cultural production. But when we read the title-pages of Bunyan's texts written over 200 years ago we cannot be sure who wrote them. Bunyan may be described as their author but if someone else, a publisher or printer, wrote that description, does that make him or her an author?

*Some Gospel-truths Opened*, the first text to be published as the work of John Bunyan, in 1656, is described on the title-page as 'Published for the good of Gods chosen ones, by that unworthy Servant of Christ, *John Bunnyan*, of Bedford, By the grace of God, Preacher of the Gospel of his dear Son'.[20] This description, the longest to appear on the title-page of any seventeenth-century text ascribed to Bunyan, introduces several key phrases or titles which are used to qualify or situate the name, John Bunyan, in later texts. In *A Vindication of the book called Some Gospel-truths Opened* (1657) and *A Few Sighs from Hell* (1658) the author is described as 'John Bunyan, Preacher of the Gospel of CHRIST'[21] and 'that Poor and Contemptible Servant of Jesus Christ, JOHN BUNYAN'.[22] *The Doctrine of the Law and Grace Unfolded* (1659) is 'Published by that poor and contemptible Creature, *John Bunyan of Bedford*'[23] and *Profitable Meditations* (1661) bears the inscription 'By *John Bunyan*, Servant to the Lord JESUS'.[24]

The majority of texts published from 1656 to 1666 are either combative texts, treatises in which Bunyan attacks the theological precepts or religious practices of different sects, notably the Quakers who had gained a considerable following in Bedford, or texts which are offered as written sermons. In both cases a stress on the writer's pastoral authority, on his status as minister would seem to be of paramount importance in establishing the authoritative status of the texts. The descriptive titles on the early works emphasise the dual status of the writer as abject sinner or contemptible subject and as divinely authorised minister. The often repeated word 'servant' suggests both positions, indicating at once a lowly status in relation to God and an active role in his service. References to Bedford, the location of Bunyan's ministry, reinforce the identification of the writer as minister, providing the reader with precise information about the geographical location of his ministry to support the implicit claim to a broader pastoral mission. Bunyan is located in Bedford, but 'God's chosen ones' may, like his readers, be elsewhere. The reader is thus assured that the hitherto unknown John Bunyan is a figure of some authority. The conventional assertions of unworthiness, the references to divine grace and claims to pastoral intent all imply that the writer is immersed in and authorised by what could be called a discourse of salvation. He and his texts are components in a divine strategy of addressing and enlisting sinners, a strategy which is described by deploying the familiar figures, terms and locations of pastoral ministry.

An exception to the deployment of this form of description can be found on the title-page of *Christian Behaviour* (1663), a guide to Christian conduct within the family unit. This text was published by Francis Smith, the radical Baptist printer who published almost all of Bunyan's writings up to 1678, including the aforementioned *Profitable Meditations* which was a verse dialogue between Christ and a sinner.[25] Even though this text departed from the treatise form, it bore the conventional pastoral description of 'Servant to the Lord Jesus'. Two years later, however, *Christian Behaviour* was described as written by '*John Bunyan*, a Prisoner of *Hope*'.[26] A new label is introduced here by Bunyan's imprisonment in November 1661 for preaching without a licence. Where in earlier examples Bedford, his pastoral location, reinforced his status as minister, here it is his status as prisoner which is emphasised. The description can be read as foregrounding his relationship to the representatives of the Law and of the Established Church who had denied his legitimacy as a minister, as a preacher of the Word. Bunyan here is not preacher but prisoner, his authority paradoxically that of one denied authority. He is still in Bedford but those who have imprisoned him have attempted to separate him from his congregation, to silence him. They, in turn, are challenged by the publication of this text, a written message by a prisoner 'of *Hope*'. The prisoner/author's '*Hope*' signals a possible end to his present situation, whether interpreted in a limited and specific sense as an end to his incarceration or as the freedom from worldly troubles afforded by ultimate reincorporation in divine being through salvation. In either case, the presence of this description on the title-page, and the publication of the text itself, constitute a direct challenge to the power of the persecuting authorities to silence its author.

The use of this description signals a clearly political dimension in the functioning of the name of John Bunyan produced in response to the change in his relationship with those in authority and of his own circumstances. The description of Bunyan as a prisoner was repeated in *Prison Meditations*, a short poem which was first published as an appendix to *Christian Behaviour*, but other texts published during the early and mid-1660s still describe the author as servant of Christ, including the two texts published by Joan Dover in 1665, *The Holy City* and *The Resurrection of the Dead*. The fact that these two forms of description coexisted while Bunyan was imprisoned points to the impact on publishing and textual strategies of a range of struggles for pastoral authority. In 1656 Bunyan was competing with rival ministers, many of whom had either official positions in the Established Church or longer histories of nonconformist ministry, but from 1661 he was in direct conflict with the representatives of state authority who had denied him a voice. The contemporaneous use of the figures of servant/ minister and prisoner indicate that we cannot think of discrete phases or stages in the construction of Bunyan as author, but rather of different forces at work on and in that construction. Although he had been active as a preacher up to his arrest, Bunyan was not appointed as official pastor of the Bedford congregation until January 1672, three months before his release from prison. But, as his account of his calling to the ministry indicates, Bunyan's sense of pastoral duty predated his appointment. In this context the need to claim a position of pastoral authority evident in the earliest texts is not displaced but rather given an additional impetus by his imprisonment.

Bunyan's enforced separation from his congregation affected his construction as an author in another way. In silencing an unlicensed preacher, those who arrested and imprisoned Bunyan contributed to his transformation into a writer. Deprived of the ability to minister to the Bedford congregation, being, as he wrote in *Grace Abounding*, '*taken from you in presence*', the preacher can only maintain sustained contact through the written word.[27] There is evidence that Bunyan was allowed to leave the gaol on a few occasions and even visited London, but the ultimate effect of the official prohibition on his oral ministry seems to have been to make him pursue his ministry in writing. The enforced use of the written word as a supplement or alternative to an oral ministry has profound effects from the 1660s onwards on the production of both texts and author.

The pastoral form of the name of the author outlined above was last used on the title-page of *Grace Abounding*, first published in 1666. Here a subtitle describes the text as 'A Brief and faithful relation of the exceeding mercy of God in Christ, to his poor servant JOHN BUNYAN'.[28] The title of the text and the name of the author are interwoven in a structural prefiguration of the avowed intent of the author, outlined in the preface, to publish this narrative in order that readers may be reminded of God's grace by '*reading his work upon me*'.[29] The author who has written this text 'by his own hand' and published it 'for the support of the weak and tempted People of God' is an active agent of the text's production.[30] However, as a subject produced by the workings of divine Grace, he is both the subject of this text and a text in his own right. In one textual moment three main techniques of nonconformist teaching, pastoral ministry, reading one's own life as an example of divine intervention, and writing, are held together in a precarious balance, a balance which cannot be sustained.

*Grace Abounding* stands as the culmination of the first stage in a ministry in which the production of author and texts has been firmly located within a predominantly pastoral framework of reference. The meanings of both Bunyan and his texts are signalled as decidable only by reference to the pre-existing theological and pastoral formations of nonconformist teaching and preaching, which are in turn largely derived from Puritan beliefs and practices of the earlier seventeenth century. The significance or meaning of Bunyan's status as 'author' of the texts written during this period is clearly to be read as being of no greater importance than his status as minister or preacher and as exemplary subject of divine authority. The claim that *Grace Abounding* is written 'by his own hand' indicates that the fact that this is a personal account matters, but that writing is not itself an activity which can confer authority on the writing subject. It is, rather, just one facet of a wider ministry, albeit one which, under certain circumstances, such as imprisonment, appears to offer a greater potential for communication than speech. The idea that writing could be viewed as a simple extension or continuation of oral ministry was, however, regarded as problematic within Puritan and nonconformist movements. The threat posed by writing as a supplement to divine truth, embodied in the Logos, is ever present to those ministers who attempted to re-present that truth through the medium of the written word.

The ambivalence of Puritan and nonconformist attitudes to the role of writing in the dissemination of divine truth has been explored by Lawrence A. Sasek in *The Literary Temper of the English Puritans*. Sasek examines the 'paradoxical situation' of Puritan ministers who, whilst insisting vehemently that the Bible was the one book necessary to salvation, 'continued to fill the bookshops with works of their own'.[31] He examines a number of prefaces and introductions to Puritan texts in which the authors repeatedly both apologise for, and attempt to justify, writing and publishing. A majority emphasise the subordinate role of the written text which is to be regarded as a poor substitute for the spoken word. William Whately, a Puritan preacher, offered the most succinct formulation of this attitude: 'Without question the word preached is more powerfully effectual to regeneration than the word read.'[32] Thomas Gataker, minister and classical scholar, similarly privileged the spoken word: 'The lifeless letter, for vivacity and efficacy, cometh far short of the living voice.'[33] Gataker's reference to the 'living voice' suggests that Puritan preference for a spoken ministry is based on the assumption that the physical presence of the preacher would reinforce the 'efficacy' of the sermon. The 'living voice' would have effective performance techniques at its disposal, such as variation of tone and inflection, rhythms and pauses, as well as the appearance and gestures of the speaker.

An emphasis on the particular effectiveness of the spoken word and of the speaker has been maintained in most evangelical, and political, movements up to the present day. Henry Abelove has drawn attention to John Wesley's skilful manipulation of the seductive appeal of his appearance, and appearances, in the Methodist movement which was the first national and international popular religious 'revival' after the subsidence of nonconformist fervour at the end of the seventeenth century.[34] American preachers and activists, from Billy Graham to the Reverend Al Sharpton, continue to exploit the power of visible and audible presence in the late-twentieth century, in 'live' appearances and on television, the medium whose diversity and reach, through cable and satellite, has for several decades provided a near approximation of presence. Television has allowed modern evangelists to deploy some of the same techniques used in live appearances in broadcasts which can reach global audiences.[35] It may bring its own problems but there is little evidence of the degree of anxiety about the effects of such techno-logical developments on divine truth that was evident in Puritan and nonconformist reactions to the possibilities and perils of print. Whilst today there seem to be few evangelists who advocate the use of the written word in the promotion of divine truth, in the sixteenth and seventeenth centuries writing began to emerge as a necessary medium for communication even though the anxiety it caused was considerable.

Most early Puritan writers betray an unease about the use of the written word, treating it as a substitute for an oral ministry which they have been forced to abandon. Sasek notes that a number of writers defended their writing by pleading illness or incapacity which prevented them from preaching, from being present. Some did write in defence of the pastoral efficacy of the written word, notably Richard Sibbes, William Greenhill and later, and most vehemently, the near contemporary of Bunyan, Richard Baxter, whose position typifies later nonconformists for whom writing, during the Restoration, often served as the only means of continuing a ministry, albeit within the constraints of renewed censor-ship. Read in the context of these concerns, Bunyan's own writings reveal shifting attitudes towards the relationship between preaching and writ-ing, between the exploitation of the metaphoricity of writing and the maintenance of the full meaning and truth of the Word. They also reveal the position of author, as writing subject, to be an unstable one, both in relation to God and the Word and to a series of other subjects.

Although this book is not primarily concerned with the nature of Bunyan's theological precepts or positions, it may be useful at this point to outline one crucial strand of his representation of the relationship between God, knowledge and language. In Bunyan's texts God's word is offered as synonymous with truth and it is through knowledge of God's truth in his words, the Scriptures, that the fallen may be saved, restored to their rightful place in the full presence of God. God is seen to operate as transcendental signified, original and originating meaning which holds in place all other meanings, available to men and women through the double process of redemption implied in the Logos: the Word of God incarnate in the figure of Christ the saviour, visible signifier of God the signified, who offers the Second Covenant, and inscribed in the Scriptures as redemptive texts whose divine authority, and authorship, acts as a guarantee of truth. In this duality we can glimpse a parallel with the opposition between the 'living voice' and presence of oral ministry and the perils of writing. Salvation through Christ, the Logos incarnate, is not simple or easy but it is, to put it crudely, direct. The Scriptures are written texts and Bunyan, like many of his contemporaries, is forced to engage in some complicated textual manoeuvring in order to differentiate these divinely authored, and so truthful, writings from the less reliable and possibly deceiving texts of fallen humanity.

In *Light for them that sit in Darkness*, a treatise published in 1675, three years after his appointment as minister and in the interval between his first and second periods of imprisonment, Bunyan made the following assertion:

> From these Texts it is evident that in every Generation or Age of the World, God did give his People a Promise; a remembrance; and so ground for a believing-remembrance that he would one day send them a Saviour: for indeed the Promise is not only a ground for a remembrance, but for a believing-remembrance: what God saith is sufficient ground for Faith, because he is Truth and cannot lye or repent.[36]

What God says is true because God is truth, or as Bunyan wrote more succinctly in *Come, & Welcome, to Jesus Christ* (1678): 'Now I say, his word is truth, and he is full of truth, to fulfill his truth even to a Thousand Generations.'[37] God is thus eternally and utterly truthful. But men and women, separated from God by the Fall, can only hope to be restored to eternal life in, or as part of, his presence by truly knowing his truth as it is made available to them both in the figure of Christ whom they must believe *in* and in his Word which they must believe or understand. True knowledge of God, the prerequisite of salvation and the eventual dissolution of the corrupted human self in the full presence of the Creator, can only be achieved through access to the Word. But by the seventeenth century absolute confidence in the self-evident meaning of the Word, of the Scriptures, was no longer possible.

In the wake of the Reformation and the dethroning of the Catholic Church as sovereign in the field of authoritative interpretation of God's true meaning(s), the contest between different Protestant groups to substantiate their conflicting truth claims took the form of a bitter battle of words about the Word, a battle which was complicated by Puritan emphasis on individual Bible reading as opposed to earlier stress on clerical exegesis. Throughout his life Bunyan was involved in a contest for meaning, which involved a struggle to achieve an authoritative position as interpreter of the Word, with and against other Christians including not only those within the Established Church but also rival groups who like Bunyan and his congregation defined themselves in opposition to an orthodoxy which they believed to be unchristian or even anti-Christian. As the titles suggest, Bunyan's first two texts, *Some Gospel-truths Opened* and *A Vindication of the book called Some Gospel-truths Opened*, are typical examples of this combative writing, in which Bunyan engages in fierce debate with Quaker opponents about the meaning of the Scriptures.

Bunyan's anxiety about how to guarantee the authority of an interpretation of the Word and about the possibility of inscribing the Word in the words of man, in short about his status as a reader and writer in the service of God is evident in *Light for them that sit in Darkness*. He opens by stressing the '*simplicity*' of the Scriptural writings of St Paul and attributes failure in correct interpretation to '*the Unaptness of the Minds even of the Saints themselves to retain it without commixture*'.[38] The reference to '*commixture*' seems to ascribe to the text an elemental purity which unapt minds cannot retain because they have mixed it (up) with something else. This is, in turn, the result of '*not-having, or (having) not-retaining, the true Knowledge of the Person of the Lord Jesus Christ*'.[39] So failure to understand the Scriptures is a reflection of a failure to know Christ. This true knowledge of Christ, the key to correct interpretation, is only available to those who '*get and retain the true Knowledg of themselves, and the due Reward of their Sins by the Law*'.[40] Bunyan's argument seems to circle around the unacknowledged necessity of gaining knowledge, partly at least, through reading, or being read, the Scriptures: God may move the individual sinner in mysterious and apparently extra-textual ways but how except through access to the Scriptures is one to gain knowledge of '*the Law*'? The logically unsatisfactory and depressing conclusion of the argument is that incorrect interpretation is a symptom of individual inadequacy on the part of readers from whose '*Sense, and Reason, and Unbelief, and Darkness, arise many imaginations, and high thoughts which exalt themselves against the Knowledg of God*'.[41] If the Scriptures are open, albeit through no fault of their own, to incorrect interpretations by ungodly and godly alike, what chance does Bunyan's own writing have of promoting divine truth?

Bunyan stresses that he has been *'plain and simple in my writing'*, echoing the *'simplicity'* of St Paul, because *'the Sin against the Holy Ghost, is in these days, more common than formerly, and the Way unto it more beautified with colour, and pretence of Truth'*, adding that *'by some there is cried a kind of* Hosanna *to them that are treading these Steps to Hell'*.[42] The plainness and simplicity of his writing is thus a token of the urgency of its task to continue the redemptive project of the Scriptures, but it is also a mark of difference between a text whose doctrine offers *'the Way of Salvation'* and the *'Fables, Seducing-Spirits, and Doctrines of Devils'*, *'the plausible Pretences'* which will ensnare the careless reader.[43] The insistence on the simplicity of the Scriptures and of Bunyan's own 'little book' would seem to suggest a desire to eliminate the dangers of complexity or plurality of meaning inherent in writing which could obstruct the clear path to salvation offered to the faithful reader. The negative reference to *'Fables'* can be connected to the lengthy justification of the allegorical method employed in some of Bunyan's later writings, notably *The Pilgrim's Progress*, which I shall examine in due course, but at this stage in his career Bunyan is at pains to point out the difference between his simple, faithful book and the seductions of writing.

Bunyan confidently assures the reader of the origins of his text: *'Reader, let me beseech thee to hear me patiently; read, and consider, and judg. I have presented thee with that which I have received from God, and the Holy Men of God, who spake as they were moved by the Holy Ghost do bear me witness.'*[44] But the reassurance that God is the first, true author of this text, with the divinely inspired Holy Men as witnesses to Bunyan's authority as its human transcriber, is immediately followed by a statement that indicates the participation of the text in a contest for legitimation of different interpretations of the meaning of God's word: *'Thou wilt say, all pretend to this: Well, but give me the hearing, take me to the Bible, and let me find in thy Heart no favour, if thou find me to swerve from the Standard.'*[45] The assumed challenge to the reader, which introduces the idea of conflicting claims to interpretative authority, recalls, by use of the word *'pretend'*, the *'plausible Pretences'* associated earlier in the preface to the text with the *'pretence of Truth'* which characterises *'the Sin against the Holy Ghost'*. The staging of the reader's challenge is immediately preceded by a paragraph in which the betrayal of Christ by the hypocritical is denounced in a series of phrases which operate by contrasting their pretended and actual attitudes. They *'pretend they love him, when they hate him; pretend they have him, when they have cast him off; pretend they trust in him, when they bid defiance to his Undertakings for the World*.[46] Throughout this passage Bunyan mobilises the pejorative sense of the word 'pretend' which, in conjunction with its sense as a claim, either to truth or to a position of authority, as in pretender to a throne, succeeds in undermining the challenge in the very act of representing it.

Returning to his defence of his own special relationship with God the one true creator/author, Bunyan asks the reader to '*receive my Doctrine*', appealing from a position '*in Christ's stead*'.[47] By implication, in contrast to those rival claimants whose profession of divinely authorised positions as interpreters masks their denial of Christ's sovereign position and saving mission, Bunyan is to be read as, temporarily at least, occupying that position, continuing that mission. This is followed by a further declaration of the impeccable sources of the text, this time not God but scriptural truth, contrasted with the writings of man: '*I have not writ at a venture, nor borrowed my Doctrine from Libraries. I depend upon the sayings of no man: I found it in the Scriptures of Truth, among the true sayings of God.*'[48] Here the contrast with human libraries and sayings partly obscures the slip which has taken place from divine truth to scriptural truth, insisting on an opposition between human and divine rather than that between divine presence and divinely-authored writing which is implicit in the anxiety about interpretation.

Throughout the text, Bunyan makes repeated use of metaphors of speech and hearing. The reader is asked to '*hear me patiently*', to '*give me the hearing*'; the godly who misinterpret are '*dull of hearing*', unable to apprehend the '*true sayings of God*' or of those who '*spake as they were moved by the Holy Ghost*'.[49] Whilst it is possible to conclude that Bunyan is merely alluding to, and using the rhetoric of, his preaching in order to establish the continuity of his mission, the attempt to describe the process of reading divinely inspired texts in terms of hearing the spoken word may be another sign of the anxiety about the status and impact of written language Bunyan shared with his fellow Puritan and nonconformist ministers and writers. Similarly the efforts to differentiate between authoritative, divinely inspired writings as the inscription of truth and other non-veridical forms of writing, indicate that this text may be an attempt to deal with fears about the potential '*most dangerous and damning Miscarriage*' of the '*Great Truth*' of God.[50]

The privileging of metaphors of speech and hearing here can be read as an example of the phonocentrism which Jacques Derrida has identified with logocentrism and its debasement of writing. In what Derrida terms 'the epoch of the logos', the processes of writing and reading are seen to be preceded by a truth or meaning which pre-exists signification, constituted by and within the Logos of the creator God.[51] The signified is thus defined by an immediate relationship with the Logos and one of mediation with the signifier. Derrida asserts that within the discourses of logocentrism which oppose the writing of truth and 'bad writing (writing in the "literal" [*propre*] and ordinary sense, "sensible" writing, "in space")' the metaphors employed can be seen to confirm the privilege of the Logos.[52] The meaning of writing within such discourses is identified as 'a sign signifying a signifier itself signifying an eternal verity, eternally thought and spoken in the proximity of a present logos'.[53] Writing is thus at a further remove from truth than speech.

But if, as Derrida also notes, 'There is not a single signified that escapes, even if recaptured, the play of signifying references that constitute language', if meaning is, as he argues, a product of difference and deferral, then the full meaning and truth which is implied in the concept of the Logos is itself always subject to those forces and cannot be represented or re-presented within language in its imagined original and authoritative fullness or singularity.[54] In the preface to *Light for them that sit in Darkness*, it is possible to see an implied recognition of and attempt to escape the vertiginous displacements and discontinuities of meaning which are the inevitable products of signification. This recognition can be read as occasioned by the post-Reformation struggle for authority. The answer, but of course not the solution, to the dangers posed by writing is, in this text, an absolute insistence on the pre-existing, external nature of truth, located primarily in the voice of God, whose transcendent presence is affirmed in the voices of those men who are inspired by the Holy Ghost. It is the breath of transcendent presence in the voice of divinely inspired writing which is seen to guarantee its truth.

When Bunyan enlists the voice of presence to establish the authority of his text, he urges the reader who challenges that authority by suggesting that other authors make similar claims to his to '*take me to the Bible*'.[55] The Bible here stands as the Logos enscripted, divine presence made textually available, as Christ is the Logos incarnate, and is invoked to suppress the challenges of difference. But the Bible itself is a text and, whatever the status of the author and of its supposed origin, it is subject to the processes of reading, of interpretation, to the effects of difference without which its own meanings could not exist. Bunyan may urge the reader to compare his text to the Bible and reject it '*if thou find me to swerve from the Standard*', but controlling interpretation by reference to a standard can only temporarily halt the play of deferral and detour which even insistence on a metaphysical, transcendent truth cannot arrest.[56] Applying the standard of the Bible may allow the reader to make judgements about the claims to interpretative authority in Bunyan's writing but the standard itself is open to question.

The challenge posed to divine truth by writing is not the only threat to established authority evident in this text. As I noted earlier, knowledge of God and knowledge of the self are seen to be mutually interdependent in *Light for them that sit in Darkness*. Those believers who have deviated from the true knowledge of God inscribed in the Scriptures have done so because they do not possess true knowledge of themselves as sinners. Those who have '*had some Knowledg*' of the reason of Christ's '*Coming into the World, with his Doing, and Suffering there*' but have lost it, have done so '*because they first lost the Knowledg of themselves, and of their Sins*'.[57] So whilst God as transcendent truth, pre-existing and comprehending signification, must stand as the ultimate object of knowledge in the discourse of salvation, another object of knowledge is acknowledged whose position in the broader hierarchy of knowledge in this period was potentially disruptive: the knowing subject.

Self-knowledge, the knowledge of one's condition as a sinner, which involves a recognition of self-presence, is seen to be a necessary precursor to knowledge of the full presence of God. This is a point developed more fully in *Instruction for the Ignorant*, published in the same year as *Light for them that Sit in Darkness*. Written in the form of a catechism or dialogue, this text poses a series of questions about the difficulty of knowing God and offers answers which are accompanied by scriptural references. Knowledge of God is stated as the precondition of worshipping him in spirit and heart, but obtaining that knowledge is no easy process. The questions raise the problems of conflicting interpretations of the nature of God:

> Q. *But do not every one profes they know God?*
> A. Yes; But their supposed knowledge of him varieth as much as doth their faces or complexions, some thinking he is this, and some that.[58]

A list of misconceptions and 'false Opinions' of God follows, which prompts the ensuing dialogue:

> Q. *How then shall I know when I have the true Knowledg of God?*
> A. When thy Knowledg of him and the holy Scriptures agree.
> Q. *The Scriptures! do not all false Opinions of him, flow from the Scriptures?*
> A. No, in no wise; 'tis true, Men father their errors upon the Scriptures, when indeed they flow from the ignorance of their hearts, *Ephes. 4.18.*[59]

As in *Light for them that Sit in Darkness* anxiety about the Scriptures as a source of conflict over meaning is revealed and then deflected as false interpretation is attributed to the failure of the reader, here the 'ignorance of their hearts', there the '*Unaptness of the Minds*'.[60] The questioner's search for the basis of knowledge is a frustrating one. Having been assured that the truth of one's knowledge of God is to be confirmed by reference to the Scriptures, this knowledge is in turn subject to further confirmation:

> Q. *But how shall I know when I have found by the Scriptures, the true knowledg of God?*
> A. When thou hast also found the true knowledg of thy self, *Isa. 6.5. Job. 42.5.*
> Q. *What is it for me to know my self?*
> A. Then thou knowest thy self, when thou art in thine own eyes, a lothsome, polluted, wretched, miserable Sinner, and that not any thing done by thee, can pacifie God unto thee, *Job. 42.5. Ezek. 20.43,44. Rom. 7.24.*[61]

The apparent circularity of the logic of this model of self-knowledge, and its relation to the knowledge of God which is the way to salvation, is best understood if its theological premises are read within the contexts of the doctrine of predestination and of its underpinning logocentrism.

There is no direct challenge to the ultimate authority of divine presence implied in the concept to self-knowledge as advocated in this text. Self-knowledge is offered not as a substitute for, but as a component of, knowledge of God. The knowledge of one's self which is the guide to true knowledge of God is already ordained, just as in predestinarian theology one's status as saved or reprobate is pre-ordained. The doctrine of predestination, to which Bunyan subscribed, is a form of determinism which holds that God has already decided who is to be saved, the elect, and who is to be damned, the reprobate. The process of seeking self-knowledge advocated in Bunyan's texts connects with a range of practices through which the individual subject is located in relation to this scheme of predetermined fates. Predestination doctrine does not allow for the possibility of the individual altering the elect or reprobate status assigned by God, but in practice the individual could and should look for signs of his or her status. As numerous historians and critics have noted the concept of predestination could easily lead to despair which was counted as a potentially damning sin, but the doctrine offered believers some hope of finding hints, if not evidence, that they might be saved. The techniques of self-examination, of continually analysing one's own relationship to God, exemplified by Bunyan in *Grace Abounding*, were practical ways of ensuring that the possibility of election or salvation, if ordained, was not thrown away. The true meaning of an individual's status was perpetually deferred, would only become known at the moment of the Last Judgement, but a desire to know could itself be read as a positive sign. The Bunyan whose agonised self-searching is the subject of *Grace Abounding* and Christian whose 'travail', implying both labour and journey, is charted in *The Pilgrim's Progress*, can never be confident that they are elect, but their endeavours are offered as a model for Christian practice which contrasts directly and sharply with the blithe disregard of self-knowledge displayed by the self-seeking reprobate Mr Badman in *The Life and Death of Mr Badman*.

The self-knowledge advocated by the text is thus of a particular kind and implies a specific understanding of self-presence. Self-presence, which must be recognised in its fallen state of difference from the full presence of God before its reabsorption, has always already been comprehended within that full presence, it has no independent or autonomous status or meaning. To know one's self is to recognise the differences introduced into the relationship between God and man in the Fall and, through that recognition, to move towards the reconciliation of the divine in the human with the divine in itself. The model of an implied mutuality of knowledge of God and self-knowledge demands a recognition of difference which is limited by reference to a metaphysical framework which relies on the existence of a transcendent signified. The potentially dangerous supplementarity of self-knowledge must, like that of writing, be controlled by the establishment of a hierarchical structure which guarantees the absolute authority, the transcendence of divine presence in an anterior, or exterior, relation to the processes of signification.

Although the form of self-knowledge demanded by the text does not overtly challenge the metaphysical framework which holds it in place, the hierarchy of objects of knowledge within that framework was subsequently to be radically changed. In Bunyan's early writings the emphasis on the self-as-sinner can be read as an implicit acknowledgement of the rise of a new figure, one which would eventually displace God as the ultimate object of knowledge: the individual human subject. Texts like *Light for them that sit in Darkness* and *Instruction for the Ignorant* acknowledge and mobilise the stress on self-examination and individual relationship to the divine which was a vital component of Puritan and nonconformist theology and practice but insist on the pre-ordained, predestined limits of the authority of the self. They can thus be read as participating in the transition from a metaphysics grounded in a theological conceptualisation of presence to one which is recognisably modern, namely humanism. What their tensions and tortuous turns of argument reveal is that the transfer of power and authority from God to the individual human subject which is one of the distinguishing features of the birth of modernity was far from smooth and can be traced as productively in those texts which explicitly resist such a transfer as much as in those texts which celebrate it.

Knowing, whether knowing God or knowing one's self, is, in these texts, the key to achieving salvation, to escaping the limits of human subjectivity and becoming reincorporated in the pure being of the divine. But the acquisition of knowledge, as the texts cannot help but confirm, implicates the subject in the discursive struggles of his or her own material context. The reader who is urged to listen to the voice of God inscribed in the Scriptures for confirmation of his or her own position in relation to God is inevitably involved in an encounter with the differences produced in any act of signification. Bunyan's early writings may, in common with those of his Puritan predecessors and nonconformist contemporaries, attempt to control the destabilising effects of the written dissemination of meaning by differentiating between fallen writing and that which approximates the clear, true voice of God, but they cannot escape their own material status as writing or the discursive struggles for meaning and authority in which they are implicated.

Bunyan, and his publishers, may be at pains to present the author as servant of God, deploying the figure of preacher or minister to claim a position of authority denied by the established church and state authorities. But neither author nor publisher has total control over the meanings of any text, including the meanings of the name of the author.

### III   The fame of the author?

Sasek's analysis of Puritan attitudes to writing reveals one intriguing exception to the general marginalisation of writing and authorship within the pre-Restoration Puritan tradition. Prefaces and introductions to *posthumous* publications, he notes, frequently emphasised not only the value of the written works as a means of communicating divine truth, but also the value of the writer. In Sasek's words, 'the emphasis on the man himself, almost as a personality, in the prefaces tended to elevate some writers into classics, into important literary figures, and to sanction within the framework of puritanism a genuinely literary fame'.[62]

Although I have reservations about the aptness of the phrase 'genuinely literary fame', it is certainly possible to identify the mobilisation of the name of 'John Bunyan' within a near approximation to a framework of literary repute in the publication of his writings immediately after his death. The publication in 1692 of 'A Continuation of Mr. Bunyan's Life', to accompany *Grace Abounding*, would certainly appear to fit into the pattern of celebration of the author's 'personality', suggested by Sasek. The proposal for publishing *The Struggler*, Charles Doe's edition of the complete works of Bunyan, to be funded by sub-

scription, similarly foregrounds Bunyan's eminence as pr
writer, with particular emphasis on his status as author of *T*
*Progress*, and presents its aim as being 'to preserve his la
name'.[63] The publication, to be illustrated with engravings
thor's image, is, significantly, presented as a response to an ...aurdi-
nary case. This is not presented as a standard procedure, but as an
exceptional action prompted by an 'extraordinary' case: 'The chief
reasons we argue from are not common rules, that therefore every good
minister's endeavours ought to be printed in folio. But this case is
extraordinary, as an eminent minister, made so by abundance of gospel
grace, who has also writ much, which hath gone off well.'[64]

The success of Bunyan's writing is thus cited as one of the reasons for
this publication. An account of Bunyan's life and 'labours' is included in
the proposal, which includes a section on the writing of *The Pilgrim's
Progress*. This book, it argues,

> hath done the superstitious sort of men and their practices more
> harm, or rather good, as I may call it, than if he had been let alone
> at his meeting at Bedford, to preach the gospel to his own auditory,
> as it might have fallen out; for none but priest-ridden people know
> how to cavil at it, it wins so smoothly upon their affections, and so
> insensibly distils the gospel into them, and hath been printed in
> France, Holland, New England, and in Welsh, and about a hun-
> dred thousand in England, whereby they are made some means of
> grace, and the author become famous; and may be the cause of
> spreading his other gospel-books over the European and American
> world, and in the process of time may be so to the whole uni-
> verse.[65]

Here one text is presented as both conferring fame on its author and
creating interest in his other texts. *The Pilgrim's Progress*, it seems, is
pivotal in evangelical marketing strategies. It is the supreme success
story in nonconformist attempts to harness the power of the written
word, and the printing press, to extend an evangelical ministry beyond
the geographical constraints of the author's physical location. Doe stresses
the effects of the text on its readers throughout the world but also
acknowledges its effect on the author who has 'become famous'. I want
to suggest that if we trace the effects of the publication of this text on
the marketing of the author even before his death, we may find evidence
of some of the ways in which the processes of writing and publication
not only confer fame on the author but also begin to destabilise the
relationship between Bunyan as writer and God as original author, and
to upset the precarious balance between the intended communication of
singular truth and the dissemination of uncontrollable meaning.

The publication of *The Pilgrim's Progress* in 1678 can be read as
occasioning a change in the form of the name of the author which

culminates in the posthumous editions of his writings. First editions of
eight texts attributed to Bunyan, published after *Grace Abounding* and
before *The Pilgrim's Progress, Part One*, are extant, including *Light for
them that sit in Darkness, Instruction for the Ignorant* and *Come &
Welcome, To Jesus Christ*.[66] Of these editions six bear the simple name
John Bunyan on the title-page, one, *Come & Welcome, To Jesus Christ*,
is offered as the work of J. Bunyan and another, *A Confession of my
Faith*, has no author's name on the title-page but bears the initials J. B.
at the end of the prefatory letter. *The Pilgrim's Progress, Part One* is
attributed to John Bunyan, with no reference to the author's position
either as sinner or minister. Only three of the texts published after
*Grace Abounding* make any reference on the title-page to Bunyan's
pastoral activity, the first two describing the author as 'JOHN BUNYAN
of *Bedford*', and the third, published the year after his death, as 'that
Eminent Preacher, and Faithful Minister of Jesus Christ, Mr. JOHN
BUNYAN of *Bedford*'.[67] All three texts, *The Jerusalem Sinner Saved, or
Good News for the Vilest of Men* (1688), *A Discourse of the Building,
Nature, Excellency and Government of the House of God* (1688) and
*The Acceptable Sacrifice* (1689) were published by George Larkin,
publisher of *Grace Abounding*. No title-page makes reference to Bunyan
as author of *Grace Abounding*, whereas after the publication of *The
Pilgrim's Progress, Part One*, four texts published by three different
individuals all describe the work as written by the author of *The Pilgrim's Progress*.

In 1680 *The Life and Death of Mr Badman*, published, like *The
Pilgrim's Progress*, by Nathaniel Ponder, is the first text to be attributed
to Bunyan as author of the latter text. Two years later, *The Holy War*,
the next text to be published, this time by Dorman Newman, is similarly attributed. Whilst both of these texts share the fictional or narrative model employed in *The Pilgrim's Progress*, the two other texts
which bear this form of the name of the author are treatises which have
apparently little in common with it, and have not been included in the
literary canon of Bunyan's writings: *A Discourse upon the Pharisee and
the Publicane*, published in 1685 by Jo Harris, and *The Advocateship
of Jesus Christ*, published in 1688 by Dorman Newman.

Whilst Newman, as publisher, with Benjamin Alsop for the first
edition and alone for the second, of *The Holy War*, might be seen as
attempting to capitalise on the success of the earlier texts he had published, Harris had published no other Bunyan texts. The form of the
name of the author in this context would seem to suggest that the
market potential of 'John Bunyan' could be underwritten by the name
of the text. The authority or worth of the author of new texts is here
guaranteed by reference to an earlier text. A new name of the author is

thus produced through the discursive procedure of linking two texts, of conferring on the later text the established authority of the earlier text. The Bunyan who stands as author of the texts written after 1678 is in a sense the product of the success of *The Pilgrim's Progress*. But there is no evidence on the title-pages that the name 'John Bunyan' in and of itself is being offered as guarantee of these texts, as it has been in conventional literary studies. The name of the author still requires a suffix in the form of the name of one text, *The Pilgrim's Progress*. No suggestion is made that the texts have a shared origin in a figure of the author, represented by his name.

In textual material accompanying one of these texts there is, however, evidence of an attempt to establish an intimate connection between the form of the name of the author, 'John Bunyan, the Author of *The Pilgrim's Progress*', and the writing subject. This text can be read as a claim to authorial authority and is a clear example of the type of text identified in a recent study as being at the heart of the development of the figure of the author. In *Pretexts of Authority: The Rhetoric of Authority in the Renaissance Preface* Kevin Dunn examines the institution of authorship which emerged from authoritarian models of textuality which developed through and with humanism. Dunn argues that it is in the Renaissance and, more particularly, in the Reformation, that the authority of the author is established and institutionalised within the highly developed market culture of the seventeenth century. He offers a useful revision of Foucault's argument that texts, books and discourses 'really began to have authority ... to the extent that authors became subject to punishment, that is, to the extent that discourses became transgressive'.[68] Dunn modifies this analysis, arguing that since discursive transgression and its punishment antedate the development of authorship as an institution in the European tradition 'texts, books, and discourses begin to need authors when their transgression itself seeks institutionalization. In other words, it is when the subversive discourse finds itself on the brink of empowerment, of articulating something more than a negative critique of the reigning orthodoxies, that the authority of the author becomes necessary'.[69] This revised model can be productively applied to Bunyan whose punishment, his lengthy incarceration, was indeed for discursive transgression, but of a spoken rather than written kind. His enforced separation from his Bedford congregation may have contributed to his development as a writer, to the production of texts which bore his name, but the construction of John Bunyan, author, cannot be simply attributed to the punitive actions of the State.

Dunn is particularly interested in the moment when 'the writer attempts an ideological separation of himself and his work from the market that created both in order to establish the work as inimitable artifact rather than commodity and himself as author rather than crafts-man or chapman'.[70] The terms employed here might seem to fit overtly literary or fictional writing or the texts of humanism more closely than the didactic, combative or 'saving' texts of religious writing in the period. But Dunn himself focuses on texts which he locates at the 'edges' of the institution of authorship, on the writings of Luther and Milton as well as of Descartes and Bacon, refusing to accept the exclu-sive model of humanism as a separate tradition.

Whatever their misgivings about the effects of writing, Puritan and later nonconformist groups exploited the opportunities offered by the press, as N. H. Keeble has argued, both to overcome the isolating and, literally, silencing effects of persecution by ecclesiastical and civil au-thorities and to reach a wider audience in the form of a readership. Keeble quotes Richard Baxter's succinct formulation of the role that written publication might have in nonconformist strategies, '*Preachers* may be silenced or banished, when *Books* may be at hand', but notes that this knowledge was shared by those who wished to deprive radical and dissenting religious groups of any means of communicating with each other or with wider audiences.[71] In the mid- and late-seventeenth century, nonconformist writing, like any other type, was implicated in the market and in the processes of regulation which were instituted after the Restoration in the form of censorship and licensing of publica-tions. There is not enough space here to chart the changing conditions, the periods of harsh repression interspersed with those of greater leni-ency, of the publishing industry in the period of Bunyan's career. The complex systems of regulation and the struggles by nonconformist writ-ers and printers to deal with them are described and analysed in detail in Keeble's study. It is interesting to note, however, in the light of Dunn's argument that authorship becomes important when subversive discourses are on the brink of empowerment, that *The Pilgrim's Progress*, the text which seems to have contributed most to the construction of Bunyan as author, was the only text he wrote which was granted an official licence, which is noted on the title-page, and could thus be seen as having been given in some sense a seal of approval by those who censored written discourse. Whilst this does not in itself constitute a singularly important moment in the construction or production of Bunyan as author and we do not know whether licence applications were made for other Bunyan texts, it can be read in conjunction with the subse-quent marketing of texts under the name of Bunyan as the author of *The Pilgrim's Progress*, as an example of the ways in which radical and nonconformist writers and printers adapted to the legal and economic constraints and possibilities of the market.

Dunn's examination of the work of Martin Luther, whose influence on Bunyan's theological position and self-presentation has been firmly established, focuses on the interrelationship in his 'self-authorizing personal narrations' of a pull towards a medieval corporate voice and the subversive individualism of Renaissance discourses which Dunn connects with the attempted resolution of the bifurcated forces of divine inspiration and personal agency in St Paul.[72] In the work of both writers theological and material contexts are interconnected in the rhetorical attempt to negotiate an authoritative position which will communicate rather than challenge the ultimate authority of God. Dunn's reading reveals that both writers deployed an image of the body of the writer in this attempt. Paul, writing to the embattled early Christians, employs the image of his own, irreducibly human, suffering body, marked by the visible traces of martyrdom, produced through battles with his persecutors, to establish a position of authority which imitates Christ's suffering without threatening to efface it. Luther, writing in the mid-sixteenth-century context of the struggles between Reformed and Catholic positions, presents himself, as Bunyan will later in *Grace Abounding*, as a text written by God, a body of writing, but also as a writer forced through the exigencies of his own material circumstances to add to this divinely authored corpus his own narrative which negotiates the contradictions of inner and outer experiences.

The rhetorical strategies employed later by Bunyan can be read as displaying continuity with those of both Paul and Luther. Written in the contexts of a different struggle for authority within a competing network of religious groups, and of a more fully developed publication market, the otherwise parallel situation of Bunyan's text is inflected by a further, and more troubling or destabilising, force unleashed by a stress on writing in a literal or graphic sense.

When *The Holy War* was published by Newman in 1682, the association of its author with *The Pilgrim's Progress*, signalled on the title-page, was reinforced by '*An* ADVERTISEMENT *to the* READER', printed at the end of the text. There are still traces of the instability in the name of the author in this text, even as his reputation, guaranteed by connection with his most successful text, is consolidated. Later editions of *The Pilgrim's Progress*, published before *The Holy War*, included a portrait of Bunyan as the sleeping man, presumably dreaming the dream which became the narrative of the text. The inclusion of an image of the body of the author could be connected with the deployment of figures of the body in Dunn's analysis of Paul and Luther; it certainly suggests that a connection is being forged between text and author through the representation of what is claimed to be his 'real' appearance. In this later text two portraits are included which bear strong similarity to the earlier engraving, and which can be read as both consolidating his status as author and revealing its fragility. One engraving shows Bunyan as a type of Mansoul, adapting the earlier image's insertion of the body of the author into the narrative of the text; the other, which shows the author without the context of the text, is described as a portrait of 'John Bunnyon'. The difference in spelling of the names of the author on title-page and engraving may seem trivial, but read in the light of 'An ADVERTISEMENT to the READER', it may be seen to be of considerable significance.

The advertisement is a defence of Bunyan's authorship of the earlier text, undersigned by the author, here written as 'JOHN BUNYAN'. Presented, like the text's prefatory address to the reader, in verse form, this stands not only as a refutation of implied accusations that Bunyan has profited by other writers' labours but also as a claim to a position as originator of the text's 'matter in this manner'. This contrasts with his earlier arguments about the nature of his position as writer both in the early treatises and in *The Pilgrim's Progress* whose allegorical mode itself marked a departure from the 'simplicity' claimed for Bunyan's previous experiments with written ministry.

In the preface to *The Pilgrim's Progress, Part One*, the defence of allegorical method as a means of contributing to the '*advance of Truth*' implies a position for the author which is almost passive.[73] The author '*fell*' into allegory and '*things*', which might be interpreted as ideas or words, of unspecified origin, '*multiply*' in the writer's '*crown*' and are '*set down*'.[74] This preface has long been regarded as the supreme articulation of a model of inspired writing which marks Bunyan as a predecessor of the Romantics. Its image of the writer falling 'suddenly into an Allegory'[75] when writing another text, of being moved to write, would find echoes in the writings of many of the major figures of Romanticism and is a key contributor to the development, through Coleridge's reading of the text, of the figure of Bunyan as an exceptional and inspired writer and of his text as 'literary' in a sense which exceeds its qualification as such through formal characteristics. But the privileged position which would be given by the Romantics to the imagination is here occupied by 'things' which as yet lack a name and which Bunyan treats with some caution: '*Nay then, thought I, if that you breed so fast,/ I'll put you by your selves, lest you at last/ Should prove* ad infinitum, *and eat out/ The Book that I already am about.*'[76] If this is inspiration as we have learned to recognise it through the lens of Romantic models of writing and of post-Romantic literary criticism, it is, as yet, a troubling force for a nonconformist writer when faced with the task of transmuting it into text.

Nonconformist commitment to 'experimental faith' as opposed to rationalist philosophy and to the acquisition of knowledge of the truth of God and one's own relation to him through attentiveness to the workings of the Holy Spirit rather than formal education, can be read as diverging from the increasingly rationalist mainstream cultural tradition of the period. It is possible to argue, as some have done, that some nonconformist models of composition, with their stress on divine revelation, most strikingly formulated by the Quakers as 'the light within', differed markedly from traditional seventeenth-century models, such as those of Davenant, Hobbes and Dryden, which insisted on the priority of judgement over imagination or fancy in the writing process.[77] But the model of divine inspiration which was associated with dangerous enthusiasm by those working in the Classical and later Augustan traditions was not accepted by all nonconformists without qualification. Bunyan's fears about the deceptions of 'Reason' in Light for them that sit in Darkness, were, as we have seen, matched by an equal unease about 'imaginations' which 'exalt themselves against the Knowledg of God': inspiration could be satanic as well as divine and Bunyan's vehement denunciation of the Quakers insists that their claims to inspiration are deluded. A key difference between Bunyan's position and that which he ascribed to the Quakers was their respective attitudes to the Scriptures. As he notes in the fifth edition of Grace Abounding in 1680, they claimed that 'the holy Scriptures were not the Word of God', whereas their divine origin and the need constantly to judge oneself according to them was central to Bunyan's theology.[78] In the light of this difference, it may be possible to interpret the meaning of the 'things' which might breed 'ad infinitum' in the preface to The Pilgrim's Progress differently. In contrast to the extreme stress on unmediated revelation by the Quakers, Bunyan stressed mediation and the materiality both of Christ's sacrifice and of the Scriptures. Whilst Bunyan, as I have argued, was equally at pains to assert the difference between truly inspired writing and seductive texts, he is anxious to differentiate his position, and his model of inspiration, from that of the Quakers. I believe that it is also important to acknowledge the historical and textual differences between his model and that of the Romantics. From a fully materialist perspective which does not accept the model of inspiration, whether divine or human in origin, the 'things' might be read as something far more substantial or material: as the language which allows thought, as words. Both Christian metaphysics and humanist literary criticism have privileged those aspects of writing which can be seen as anterior to it – God, the muse, the human mind – but we should be wary of conflating the models of inspiration which they deploy and of effacing the differences not only between mainstream and

nonconformist traditions but within the latter. I want to argue that
Bunyan's later writing can be read as constructing a position for the
author which may ultimately challenge the idea that God is the source
and guarantee of all meaning, but that this position is itself ultimately
revealed as contingent, as the product of, and vulnerable to, the effects
of writing.

The writer here is presented as a channel for divine truth, his mode of
writing as authorised by scriptural precedent already signalled on the
title-page by the citation of Hosea 12.10, 'I have used Similitudes', and
the text's didactic potential as its ultimate justification. Authorial intent
is, however, less clearly defined. The description of the writer's decision
to '*set down*' the breeding '*things*', whose appearance interrupted the
writing of another book, is followed by a passage in which the initial
emphasis on the passivity of the writer is modified:

> Well, so I did; but yet I did not think
> To shew to all the World my Pen and Ink
> In such a mode; I only thought to make
> I knew not what: nor did I undertake
> Thereby to please my Neighbour; no not I,
> I did it mine own self to gratifie.
> Neither did I but vacant seasons spend
> In this my Scribble; Nor did I intend
> But to divert my self in doing this,
> *From worser thoughts, which make me do amiss.*[79]

In this passage, the writing of *The Pilgrim's Progress* is presented as a
means of self-gratification which is also a method of self-government.
Writing is a diversion, in the sense both of a pleasurable activity and of
an activity which displaces '*worser thoughts, which make me do amiss*'.
The effects of self-policing and self-production evident in the practice of
writing an account of one's spiritual progress or condition, of which
*Grace Abounding* is an example, can be connected with the attempt to
contain self-knowledge within a theocentric metaphysical model displayed in *Instruction for the Ignorant*, but the stress on writing is
problematic. The writer still stands as a channel for the transmission of
divine truth and as a subject-space which can be occupied by good or
bad thoughts. Writing is presented as a positive means of diversion, of
keeping the subject from 'worser thoughts', but writing involves occupying a position, or positions, which are not entirely under the control
of the writer. In the interaction between text and reader, the 'I' of the
writer, whose domination of the passage quoted above catches the eye
of the reader, may eventually challenge the singularity and transcendence of God as sole origin and guarantee of meaning. In the changing
discourses of authorship from the seventeenth to the twentieth century

only one author will be allowed to claim *The Pilgrim's Progress* as his product and property. Very few readers today would say that that author was called God.

An examination of the advertisement to the reader which accompanies *The Holy War* may indicate, however, that this is not a smooth transition from one figure of ultimate and absolute authority to another as the development of a humanist approach to issues of cultural production and the Romantic model of authorship might imply. The advertisement begins by relating accusations that *The Pilgrim's Progress* 'is not mine':

> Some say the *Pilgrim's Progress* is not mine,
> Insinuating as if I would shine
> In name and fame by the worth of another,
> Like some made rich by robbing of their Brother.
> Or that so fond I am of being Sire,
> I'le father Bastards: or if need require,
> I'le tell a lye in Print to get applause.
> I scorn it; *John* such dirt-heap never was,
> Since God converted him. Let this suffice
> To shew why I my *Pilgrim* Patronize.[80]

The conjunction of 'name' and 'fame' here immediately introduces the concept of reputation as bound up with the establishment of the name of the author. The accusations against Bunyan, as reported, appear to hinge on a perceived dislocation between the name of the author and the product, the text, attributed to that name. Bunyan, it seems, is accused of claiming the name and fame of an author, which is not legitimately his, being rightly the property of a 'Brother'. It is important to note that there is no suggestion that he is seeking to usurp the position of God as universal Father: the generating, creating force of the divine is occluded or effaced here by the struggles for the right to claim legitimate paternity by the rival Brothers writing and publishing in the seventeenth-century market.

The initial refutation of these accusations foregrounds the name of the author on a literal level: 'I scorn it; *John* such dirt-heap never was,/ Since God converted him.'[81] The shift from first person to third in this sentence would appear to objectify the name of the author, to introduce a distance between the writing subject and the subject written about, an effect reinforced by the fact that the name is printed in italics. Yet the use of the forename alone simultaneously suggests a relationship of familiarity between writer and name, which reduces the distance between subject and object without collapsing the difference. The combined impact of these textual strategies may serve to designate the name as a distinct object, but one which can be claimed by a rightful owner.

The central claim of this address to the reader is an apparently confident assertion that *The Pilgrim's Progress* is the product of Bunyan's 'own heart':

> It came from mine own heart, so to my head,
> And thence into my fingers trickled;
> Then to my Pen, from whence immediately
> On Paper I did dribble it daintily.[82]

The text is presented here as originating in the core of the writer's corporeal being and as following a progress through other parts of his body, 'head' and 'fingers', through 'my Pen' and on to paper. Head, fingers and pen are all links in a chain which leads from heart to paper, from point of origin to destination, a chain in which bodily parts and inanimate object are all bound to their owner, the dribbling author. Ink thus becomes a secretion of the body of the author, a fluid channel for the transmission of the text from the innermost part of the body, the heart, to the external surface of the paper. The body of the author stands here as the point of origin of the text rather than as a channel for the transmission of material which has its origin in divine being. Through the use of the metaphoric chain of heart to paper, the process of literary production from conception to inscription has been internalised, located in the operations of the body of the author, which stands defined against exterior and anterior forces, both divine and worldly. There is a striking connection here with the rhetoric of the writer's body traced by Dunn, but the crucial difference is that this is not a suffering body as in Paul's case, or the historically situated body of Luther, but emphatically a *writing* body.

There is an oblique qualification of the apparent exclusion of divine input in the process of the production in the next section:

> Manner and matter too was all mine own,
> Nor was it unto any mortal known,
> 'Till I had done it. Nor did any then
> By Books, by wits, by tongues, or hand, or pen,
> Add five words to it, or wrote half a line
> Thereof: the whole, and ev'ry whit is mine.[83]

The assertion that no 'mortal' knew of the substance or style of the text may signal divine knowledge of the writer's intentions, but agency here is clearly both human and individual. If there is a divine input in the creative process it has been transmuted into human activity: the breath of divine presence must be transformed into writing by the human body. Whereas, in the opening section, divine agency in the production of Bunyan as a subject is located in the past, when 'God converted him', here the possibility of divine agency in the production of the text is subsumed within a model of creation/creativity which foregrounds the process of writing in order to guarantee the authorship, the author-ity, of the writer. This strategy is in marked contrast to the earlier texts such as *Instruction for the Ignorant* and *Light for them that sit in Darkness* which deployed metaphors of speech and hearing in order to privilege divine truth and to differentiate between divinely sanctioned and 'fallen' texts, and can be read as a response to the changed context of later seventeenth-century writing and publishing practices. Writing had become the one sure way of continuing an evangelical mission, and writing entailed addressing not only readers as potential souls to be saved, but also those who would deny the authority of the writer. In the earlier texts Bunyan defended himself, his own writings, and the Scriptures against those who challenged their veracity; here he defends his own status as author.

In the advertisement the text is presented as the product and, in a sense, the property of the author, who later reinforces his claims to ownership of *The Pilgrim's Progress* by a parallel statement of his relationship to the text which the reader is in the process of reading:

> Also for *This*, thine eye is now upon,
> The matter in this manner came from none
> But the same heart, and head, fingers and pen,
> As did the other. Witness all good men;
> For none in all the world without a lye,
> Can say that this is mine, excepting I.[84]

The repetition of the pattern, heart, head, fingers and pen, once more locates the origin of the text in the writing body of the author. Writing is, in a sense, like getting something out of the writer's system. This text, like *The Pilgrim's Progress*, is claimed as the sole product and property of the writing subject. But has the gap between the writing subject and the name of the author opened up in the original accusations been bridged?

In a final move to close that gap, the writer may be read as attempting to guarantee the legitimacy of the writing subject, the name of the author and the text, by presenting them as being inextricably linked in a system of mutual reciprocity. Just as the passage opened with a double move which both objectified the name of the author and claimed kin on the part of the writing subject, so this text ends with the writing subject re-creating the name of the author, quite literally. The verse is presented to the reader as a text which offers a succinct formulation of his claims to be the legitimate source of the works which bear this name and of the legitimate right of those texts to bear that name:

> I write not this of any ostentation,
> Nor 'cause I seek of men their commendation;

I do it to keep them from such surmize,
As tempt them will my name to scandalize.
Witness my name, if Anagram'd to thee,
The Letters make, *Nu hony in a B*.[85]

The writer writes his own name differently, playing with its capacity to
be something else. This self-advertisement may be read as the culmination of a series of claims to transcendence on the part of the writing
subject, in which the dismissal of counter-claims by rival writers is
paralleled by an implicit displacement of God as sole source and guarantee of meaning. Yet the textual play, by means of which this apparently confident assertion of control over the meaning of the name of the
author is achieved, foregrounds the fragility of this imaginary moment
of resolution. '*Nu hony in a B*' is a rearrangement of the ten letters
which, on the title-pages of *The Pilgrim's Progress* and *The Holy War*
and at the foot of this advertisement, are arranged as 'John Bunyan', the
established name of the author. The apparent control of the meanings
of the name of the author by the writing subject, who dismantles and
reconstitutes his own graphic identity, is displayed in an attempt to
master and limit the arbitrary system of differences by which the name
is formed and reformed. The temporary displacement of 'John Bunyan'
by '*Nu hony in a B*' may be read as a move which paradoxically
reinforces the imaginary identification of the writing subject with the
'real' name, 'John Bunyan'. Yet this apparent mastery of difference is at
the level of the grapheme: the re-placement of 'John Bunyan' as '*Nu
hony in a B*' demands the substitution of the letter 'i' for the letter 'j'.
The typographic interchangeability of these two letters is itself culturally contingent; even though decades earlier the two letters were indis-
tinguishable typographically, by this time they were only rarely
interchanged. This anagram would not be acceptable in a twentieth-
century crossword and the spelling of 'Nu' and 'hony' is eccentric even
by seventeenth-century standards. Bunyan's inscription of an imaginary
identity is achieved precisely at the level of written signification: a
name, a subject, is formed and re-formed by an assemblage of graphic
fragments. Difference thus establishes the possibility of identity: it acts
as a hinge which both connects and separates units of signification,
temporally and spatially.

The graphic construction of '*Nu hony in a B*' as a different meaning
of the name of the author may serve to reinforce other meanings ascribed to 'John Bunyan' in this advertisement, such as creative writing
subject, but it also raises the possibility of other meanings, other positions. Just as 'John Bunyan' can be rearranged as '*Nu hony in a B*', so it
could be rearranged today as 'U ban Johnny'. The writing subject's
apparent mastery of the written subject is thus exposed as itself an

effect of linguistic difference at the level of the grapheme and of historical contingency in the production of meaning.

In order to sustain the imaginary identity and transcendence claimed
on behalf of the writing subject, the alternative meanings and position
which may be allotted to the writing subject must be excluded or
subordinated within a hierarchical system of relations. In the six years
between the publication of *The Holy War* and Bunyan's death in 1688,
14 texts were published in his name.[86] Apart from two texts which refer
to Bunyan as author of *The Pilgrim's Progress* and two which locate
him as 'John Bunyan of Bedford', these texts bear the simple form of
the name, 'John Bunyan', or, in the case of *A Book for Boys and Girls*
(see Bunyan, *Misc. Works, Vol. VI*), published in 1686, 'J.B.'. There
seems, initially, to be little material here for an examination of the
discursive construction of different forms of the name of the author
which might challenge the ascendancy of that of 'Author of *The Pilgrim's Progress*' as suggested by the advertisement. The texts themselves, however, may suggest that, whatever the apparent stability of the
form of the name of the author, the authority of the position of the
writing subject is far from absolute.

In 1683 there was clearly no need to establish the authority of John
Bunyan as minister or author in order to legitimate *A Case of Conscience Resolved* (see Bunyan, *Misc. Works, Vol. IV*) as a written intervention in a debate on the role of women in nonconformist religious
activity, as there was when his first text was published in 1656. Yet
both texts rely on an implied differentiation which privileges his position and values and reveal a continuing need to reassert their validity.
Although the position of John Bunyan, author, within a nascent discourse of literary reputation, as identified by Sasek, may have become
by this time relatively secure, the different positions of John Bunyan,
writer of combative texts which participated in the religious and social
conflicts of the late seventeenth century, were far from secure.

The authority of Bunyan's claim to a position, such as that of pastoral father of his congregation, for example, mobilised to great effect in
the framing of *Grace Abounding* in 1666, is later challenged, both by
rival claimants to such a position, such as William Kiffin, and by those
who would challenge the hierarchical structure upon which the position
itself depends, such as women. Such conflicts may be read as occasioning and informing *A Case of Conscience Resolved* which, published two
years after *The Holy War*, interrogates and modifies the pastoral/pater-
nal position occupied by Bunyan in earlier texts. Texts such as *A Case
of Conscience Resolved* make explicit the strategy of exclusion by which
Bunyan, as author, attempts to defend his position of authority. They
also, as I shall argue in a later chapter, reveal the concomitant effects of

textual and cultural difference, which undermine such strategic attempts to limit them. An examination of such effects within these texts, conventionally categorised as examples of the influence of Conventicle rather than Parnassus and therefore marginalised within traditional literary criticism, may suggest that this categorisation itself depends on a strategy of exclusion which has dominated Bunyan studies and guaranteed it an apparently secure position within an increasingly fragile hierarchy of conventional literary criticism.

In my examination of these texts, I propose to explore not only the positions constructed for the author, John Bunyan, but also those allotted to, or denied to, a number of other figures whose names are conventionally placed in a subordinate or marginal relationship to the name of Bunyan in a discursively produced hierarchy of authorship and authority. Elizabeth Bunyan, presented during her husband's lifetime as dutiful wife and mother, occupies a very different position in a text written by Bunyan but published only after the death of the author. Bunyan's account of Elizabeth's forceful intervention on his behalf, in which she challenges the political and linguistic legitimacy of state authority, effectively subverts Bunyan's own prohibition on women taking an active role in political, public affairs. The 'Agnes Beaumont Affair', traditionally presented as a footnote to the text of *Grace Abounding*, raises questions not only about the discursively constructed subordination of women within Bunyan's writings, but also about the marginalisation of female authors and their texts within traditional literary criticism. After an incident in which John Bunyan and Agnes Beaumont, a member of his congregation, incurred the wrath of her father, Bunyan is accused of witchcraft and womanising and Beaumont is charged with patricide. Bunyan's response is to defend his pastoral, and patriarchal, authority by locating the threat of seduction within a dangerous female sexuality. Beaumont survives her ordeal to write a different story, *The Narrative of the Persecution of Agnes Beaumont*, which foregrounds the struggles of a daughter to negotiate the conflicting claims upon her of rival father figures. In so doing she begins to chart a different space, of writing, yet neither Beaumont, as author, nor her text, has been allotted any position in literary studies other than a marginal one.

Other texts, such as *The Pilgrim's Progress, Part Two* and *A Book for Boys and Girls*, appear initially to operate a system not of exclusion but of inclusion. The prefaces to both texts recognise the cultural differences of their readers and attempt to subsume those differences within a hierarchy which binds them in subordination to an authority located in the divinely legitimated author. It is these texts which, together with *The Pilgrim's Progress, Part One*, *The Life and Death of Mr Badman*, and *The Holy War*, are customarily categorised as Bunyan's 'literary' works, although *Grace Abounding* is frequently cited in literary histories as an influential text and *A Book for Boys and Girls* offered a marginal position as an example of inferior poetry. I intend to examine these texts, not as late examples of Bunyan's 'literary genius', but as texts in which the drive to enlist the maximum number of reading subjects within a discourse of salvation, by addressing readers in terms of their cultural differences, ultimately discloses the imaginary nature of the position of control over the texts' meanings, claimed by the author. These texts were produced and published both in England and further afield, targeted through price and content at an ever larger market of different types of reader.

The popularity of *The Pilgrim's Progress* with various types of reader is evidenced not only by the references in Bunyan's later writings but also by its publication in a range of differently priced editions. The unabridged text would, like *Grace Abounding*, have cost between 1*s.* and 1*s.* 6*d.*, but in 1684 a 22-page edition was published, presumably to appeal to those whose purchasing power extended only as far as chapbooks or pamphlets. *A Book for Boys and Girls*, which I read as the culmination of Bunyan's drive to enlist reading subjects, was sold for 6*d.*[87]

In a final twist to the story of the forms of the name of the author in the seventeenth century and of the role of writing in the construction and destabilisation of the position of author, *A Book for Boys and Girls* reveals an explicit acknowledgement by Bunyan of literacy as the basis of knowledge. The text includes not only a preface in which adult men and women are positioned as children to be coaxed by Bunyan into a recognition of their real positions in relation to divine truth, but also a guide to spelling which makes explicit the need for individual subjects to read which had been the source of such anxiety and cause of considerable rhetorical manoeuvring in Bunyan's early writings. Just as the anagram of '*Nu hony in a B*' revealed the limits of authorial mastery, so the system Bunyan employs to teach his readers how to spell can be read as revealing that signification cannot be controlled by any single subject. *A Book for Boys and Girls*, I shall argue, introduces a different framework of signification in which meaning is not located in the figure of an anterior, transcendent author, human or divine, but is produced in the process of reading. Meanings thus produced, be they of words within texts, or of the positions discursively allotted to the author or the readers, can be neither single nor absolute. The construction of figures of authority produces positions of resistance from which the basis of that authority can be challenged. Reading subjects, in the seventeenth century and later, allotted subordinate or marginal positions within the hierarchical frameworks which appear to maintain other subjects, including the author, in privileged positions, may, in the act of reading, contest the meanings which support such frameworks.

The name of the author may still be a powerful signifier within the discourse of literary criticism but, as a signifier, its meanings cannot be controlled. This instability may, in turn, suggest that the framework of power relations implicit in a literary critical discourse, in which one particular function of the name of the author is privileged, is itself neither natural nor permanent.

CHAPTER TWO

# 'I being taken from you in presence': *Grace Abounding to the Chief of Sinners* and claims to authority

## I Presence Restored?

*Grace Abounding to the Chief of Sinners* occupies a unique position within the traditionally agreed canon of texts by John Bunyan. In a literary criticism which takes as its supreme object of knowledge the individual human consciousness, any text which can be read as autobiographical is assured of a double significance. It may be read as itself offering the most immediate access to the originating consciousness of the author, whilst providing an authoritative source of legitimation for other more overtly fictional, less apparently personal, texts. A succinct formulation of this approach within Bunyan studies is provided by one of its earliest advocates, George Offor: 'The *Grace Abounding*, or Life of Bunyan, is a key to all the mysteries of *The Pilgrim's Progress*, and *Holy War*.'[1]

Whilst the majority of critics have acknowledged that *Grace Abounding* is an example of *spiritual* autobiography, the meagre historical and social information on the life of Bunyan it provides has been pounced on to flesh out the image of an author who might otherwise remain an elusive figure, eclipsed by his writings. The need to establish a credible founding subject behind and beyond his texts, produced in the image of the reader, has led generations of critics to scour *Grace Abounding* for the true meaning of the Bunyan deemed to lie beneath the surface of the 'I' of the text. There have been, of course, a great many, different, true meanings.

The efforts to restore the perceived subject of *Grace Abounding* to presence have taken a number of forms. Some critics, following clues in the text, have attempted to piece together a socio-historical identity for the author which might in turn explain or elucidate his writings. This process, given the paucity of factual references in the text, has proved in most cases to be a frustrating one. Those passages which appear to refer to a level of concrete experience outside the text are, for the most part, extremely vague, leaving the critic who wishes to decide meaning by reference to the 'real-life' author no choice but to look to alternative documentary evidence. This is, in the case of Bunyan, an extremely limited archive. One example of the undecidability of such references in *Grace Abounding* is the passage on his providential escape from death whilst serving as a soldier. This is a single paragraph added to the third edition, together with other references to escapes from drowning and from an adder, and interpreted in the text as evidence of God's mercy:

> 13. This also have I taken notice of with thanksgiving; when I was a Souldier, I with others were drawn out to go to such a place to besiege it; but when I was just ready to go, one of the company desired to go in my room, to which, when I had consented he took my place; and coming to the siege, as he stood Sentinel, he was shot into the head with a Musket bullet and died.[2]

The identity of the army in which the writer was serving is not specified, but a number of critics and biographers have attempted to uncover the truth of Bunyan's military service and, by extension, of his political sympathies. The majority have accepted the scant documentary evidence available as proof that Bunyan served in the Parliamentary forces garrisoned at Newport Pagnell, but this apparent fact of the life of the author has proved of little help in determining his political beliefs or in resolving the often contradictory political meanings which are evident in the texts.[3] The knowledge that John Bunyan served in the Parliamentary army cannot explain the shifting, discontinuous meanings of concepts of authority, obedience and power in his writings. Nor, as the numerous attempts to glean biographical evidence from the texts testify, can a reading of those meanings grant access to the mind of the author.

Other critics have offered alternative, yet equally reductive, readings of the true Bunyan by employing the textual material of *Grace Abounding* to produce psychoanalytical portraits of the author, which seek to resolve the problems of the text by reference to a founding conflict located within the unconscious of the writer. A typical example of this method of reading presents *Grace Abounding* as an attempt 'to settle ego disturbance', to resolve an 'intra-psychic conflict' which lies behind the text and which the critic holds to be the result of the 'loss or alienation of parental affection'. The reading of *Grace Abounding* is offered within a framework which takes the symbols of cross and sepulchre within Christian writings to be a 'reconciliation of father and mother, the formative male and female impulse'.[4] Setting aside any criticism of these extraordinarily sweeping definitions of male and female 'impulse', it is possible to argue that this reading fails to recognise that the subject it has placed on the analyst's couch, is not an individual human being, conscious or unconscious, but a text.

Whilst such readings appear to challenge the notion of conscious authorial control, by locating the meaning of the texts in an extra-linguistic unconscious, they relegate their only source material to a secondary, mediating role, retaining as absolute object of knowledge a source of meaning which is deemed to pre-exist signification. The 'I' of the text must remain firmly tied to an 'I' behind or before the text. The written 'I' of *Grace Abounding* is thus offered as a means of access to the writing 'I' which, in turn, is offered as explanation for the text, an explanation which also serves to guarantee the authority of the reading. Readings which locate the source of meaning in the conscious or unconscious thought of the author rely on a conception of the originating subject which cannot be retrospectively identified in its fully authoritative position within the Bunyan texts. The 'I' which conventional literary criticism has attempted to restore to presence, whether it be John Bunyan, Parliamentary soldier and radical, or John Bunyan, disturbed ego, starved of parental affection, can neither explain nor contain the shifting and conflicting meanings of subjectivity evident in *Grace Abounding*.

First published in 1666, *Grace Abounding* was written at a time when the subject of liberal humanism was emerging, not fully-formed and sovereign, but produced in conflict with other competing models of subjectivity. Whilst this text has been repeatedly interpreted as a contribution to our knowledge of this subject in its most authoritative guise, that of the creative or creating author, *Grace Abounding* may instead be read as contributing to an exploration of the contingent meaning of an apparently self-evident subjectivity. As a text which constituted an intervention in the struggle to define the meanings of authority, authorship, knowledge and power, *Grace Abounding* may be read as participating in the foundation of a recognisably 'modern' subjectivity.

It is something of a commonplace in traditional critical assessments of *Grace Abounding* to emphasise the particular vividness of the portrayal of the narrator's anxiety as a departure from the norm in the established tradition of spiritual autobiography, treating the text as a moment of triumph of the creative individual consciousness, embodied in the author, over the generally impersonal, dehumanising constraints of a doctrine or discourse. But to read the apparent concentration on self-examination in *Grace Abounding* as evidence of the presence of a single, sovereign identity within, or behind, it is to ignore the complex range of different subject positions and discursive relations established. An examination of the interrelationship of these positions and relations may well indicate some similarity between an emerging subjectivity and that of liberal humanism, but, by attending to the contradictions and discontinuities within the meanings of that subjectivity offered here, it may serve to defamiliarise those all too often taken for granted today.

A close reading of this text must involve an encounter with a complex network of relations of authorship, authority and power which appear to resist any attempt at resolution by reference to a unified or unifying subject. What emerges in *Grace Abounding* is not a clear authorial persona but a number of conflicting positions within a range of discourses which the 'I' of the text can be seen to occupy. Certainly Bunyan here is author, but he is also text; he is Minister, but also Chief of Sinners; he is Father and Servant, preacher and writer, interpreter of the Word and product of the Word. *Grace Abounding* may be read as making a number of claims to authority. One of these claims bears a close resemblance to that which lies at the heart of conventional literary criticism, namely that it is the creative, meaningful individuality of the author which guarantees the limits of meaning of a text. The repeated reassurances in the frames of the text that these writings are indeed 'written by his own hand' or 'written by himself' indicate that the concept of an individual author whose authorship of a text must be firmly established was amongst the meanings available in the mid-seventeenth century. Successive additions to the text of *Grace Abounding*, of which six editions were published during Bunyan's lifetime, would seem to support this assertion.

The emended editions which survive have the phrase 'Corrected and much enlarged by the Author' added to the title-page. A seventh edition, published in 1692, includes an essay, generally attributed to George Cockayne, a fellow minister, entitled 'A Continuation of Mr. Bunyan's Life; beginning where he left off, and concluding with the Time and Manner of his Death and Burial; together with his true Character, &c.'.[5] This essay by a 'true Friend, and long acquaintance of Mr. Bunyan' is offered as an account of his last days of 'Pilgrimage on Earth', a reference perhaps to his most popular text both then and now. It is suggested that this is an account which 'for want of time; or fear some over censorious People should impute it to him, as an Earnest covering praise from Men; he has not left behind him in writing'.[6] Reference is made to Bunyan's writings, although only five are named, *Of Prayer by the Spirit, The Holy City, Resurrection, Grace Abounding* and *The Pilgrim's Progress, Part One*, and the essay is followed by a postscript which ends with the remark that after Bunyan's death, 'his Works, which consist of Sixty Books, remain for the edifying of the Reader, and the Praise of the Author'.[7]

Such passages may be read as indications of the increasing emphasis on the proprietorial relationship between author and text, a relationship stressed yet more clearly in prefaces to the later works in which Bunyan is anxious to differentiate between his own texts and 'impostors'.[8] Bunyan is clearly to be understood as the author of these texts in the sense of having written them, but is he presented as being the author of their meanings? The final words of the addition to *Grace Abounding* quoted above may hint at a notion of immortality through writing which conflicts with the meaning of immortality offered within the discourse of salvation supported by the narrative as a whole, thus raising the problem of the relationship between writing and believing and the subject positions available within alternative discourses. So whilst there are indications that the concept of authorship bore some of the meanings ascribed to it today, it would seem unlikely that the meaning of the term 'author' can be read here as identical with that offered by liberal humanism.

For many critics the increased emphasis on individual experience suggested by the conventional reading of *Grace Abounding* as spiritual autobiography is evidence of the need to make public a personal state, to make external an essentially interior reality. Yet are they in effect reading a text which exists only in their readings? The term 'autobiography' does not appear in *Grace Abounding*, even with the qualifying term 'spiritual' which has been employed subsequently to explain the text's failure to satisfy expectations created by the contemporary meaning of autobiography.

In *British Autobiography in the Seventeenth Century* Paul Delany offers his definition of autobiographical texts as '(1) *primarily* written to give a coherent account of the author's life, or of an extensive period or series of events in his life, and (2) composed after a period of reflection and forming a unified narrative'.[9] Delany's definition of 'religious autobiography' or 'spiritual autobiography' (the two terms appear to be interchangeable in his text) both relies on, and modifies, his definition of autobiography in general. Such texts are defined as 'records of the progress of a soul'.[10] Delany sees the unprecedented production of both secular and spiritual autobiographies during the seventeenth century as the product of '[s]ome deep change in British habits of thought' and attributes this, in part, to the 'unprecedented general social mobility' during the Civil War and its aftermath.[11] He suggests that '[t]o undertake an autobiography, the writer must have a sense of his own importance', although, as his survey of a wide range of such texts reveals, this sense of 'importance' takes a number of very different forms.[12] Whilst Montaigne may argue 'I write not my gests, but my selfe and my essence', apparently presenting the reader with a glimpse into a human subject whose essence is his property, the stress in many 'autobiographies' by members of religious sects is not on an individual or essential self but on the typicality of the author's status and experience, which are presented as *exempla*.[13] In such cases the 'importance' of the author would seem initially to reside not in his or her individuality but in the subject-author's textual status as example.

Delany suggests that the great outburst of autobiographies among the sectaries from 1648 'formed part of an extraordinary welling-up of popular expression, a nationwide extension and democratization of spiritual fellowship', made possible by the breakdown of government control of the press after 1642 and the failure to enforce the Licensing Act of 1643.[14] He contrasts the number and variety of autobiographical texts produced before 1660, including material by Ranters and antinomians such as Abiezer Coppe and Lawrence Clarkson, with the more conventional texts of the post-Restoration period, including *Grace Abounding*. Delany's survey of the earlier material would seem to support his argument that the production of such texts may be linked to political and social changes during this period although his decision not to examine prophetic texts by women may suggest that his model of autobiography as 'unified narrative' is somewhat exclusive. Indeed an examination of the nature and reception of these prophetic texts by female authors might challenge Delany's somewhat idealistic representation of the era of 'spiritual fellowship', as I shall argue in a later chapter. The linguistic subversiveness of much radical writing during the period of 1640–60 is not examined in detail in Delany's study, nor are the different models of subjectivity which operate in the texts of various religious groups. Delany, in effect, employs an overall model both of autobiography and of subjectivity which is ultimately exclusive and rationalist.[15] He does, however, acknowledge that religious autobiographies of the period deviated from this model: 'Seventeenth-century autobiography in Britain, far from being a lyrical expression of "renaissance individualism", was the servant of didactic, historical, or controversial purposes.'[16]

More recent studies by Nigel Smith (1989), Christine Berg and Philippa Berry (1981), amongst others, have done much to reassert the importance of the radical religious writings during the period between Civil War and Restoration which Delany's survey underplays. Smith's study, *Perfection Proclaimed: Language and Literature in English Radical Religion 1640–1660*, suggests that whilst many radical texts shared the concern with language, rhetoric and literal scriptural interpretation of traditional Puritanism, such writings often deviated from the conceptual and textual norms of orthodox religious thought and writing. Prophetic writing, in particular, is seen to have exploited the traditional Puritan endeavour to identify the workings of the divine within the individual human being in such a way as to dismantle a series of oppositions which more traditional texts sought to maintain:

> Versions of self were created which moved increasingly towards the merging of the individual with the Godhead, the ultimate claim for perfection. As experience gave way to prophecy so the distinction between expression and behaviour disappeared: writing, speech, and gesture combined in imitations of Old Testament prophetic

behaviour. The complications this created, both inside and outside the text, with regard to the dramatic or theatrical way in which existence was conceived, were considerable. An inner world of archetypes, confident in its glorification, was created across the tumultuous central twenty years of the century. Undoubtedly the language of radical religion was founded upon irrationality in theory and in practice as the difference between the internal and the external, the literal and the figurative, disappeared. Self, church, and Godhead became one.[17]

Smith argues that 'the proliferation of extreme theories of divine language and signification' did not continue in the more restrictive climate of the Restoration, although he does make a persuasive case for the continuing influence of radical writings in later religious and political movements.[18] Certainly, a text such as *Grace Abounding* may seem initially to bear little resemblance to the linguistically and conceptually transgressive texts of the earlier period, yet an examination of the text may reveal the ultimate instability of its apparently less subversive models of authority and subjectivity.

In his examination of *Grace Abounding* Delany acknowledges the conventional reading of the text as based on an account of spiritual experiences required for admission to a local communion, and suggests that the published text is a revised version which 'was no longer primarily a credential of godliness, but had now become a spiritual handbook and personal apologia designed for the edification of fellow Christians'.[19] *Grace Abounding* is seen to conform to the basic pattern of 'ministerial' autobiography, with three parts, describing the author's 'conversion, calling, and ministry'.[20] Delany argues that the conversion narrative is paramount in Bunyan's text, with the material on calling and ministry being presented in 'sketchy' form in the 'Brief Account of the Author's Call to the Work of the Ministry' and 'A Brief Account of the Author's Imprisonment'.

Roger Sharrock's introduction to the Clarendon Press edition of the text includes a list of contents of the first edition which appears to support this argument. Sharrock divides the text into groups of paragraphs as follows: Before Conversion: 1–36; Conversion: 37–252; Calling: 253–305; Ministry: 319–39. Sharrock suggests that the emphasis on conversion is 'most personal and least influenced by traditional precedents' and that 'the uniqueness of Bunyan's treatment lies in its psychological penetration and freedom from rationalization into stock Calvinist formulae'.[21] This celebration of *Grace Abounding* as an example of the triumph of the personal and individual over the formulaic or conventional seems to rest on a somewhat fragile base. Bunyan's stress on his lengthy period of despair, in paragraphs 132–252, is selected as evidence of his emphasis on 'inner conflicts' and hence of his departure from traditional forms, yet such passages are shown to be typical of texts of the period, with examples cited from the works of Vavasour Powell, John Crook, T. A. and A. I.[22] The nature and order of Bunyan's related experiences are viewed as conforming precisely to accepted seventeenth-century norms, yet he is presented as somehow exceeding such constraints through the operation of an 'inner need':

> This imperious inner need, ultimately stronger than the motive of religious propaganda, has imparted a continuous rhythmical flow to the whole work so that it reads like a single sentence, torrential but not confused, having its changes of tone and tempo that are nevertheless obedient to the overriding music of the whole; the music is that of a speaking voice: it is as if the confession is delivered in a continuous intimate speech to a friend.[23]

Whilst this analysis appears to invoke a model of subjectivity which closely resembles the tortured and creative author privileged in modernist criticism, the textual effects, presented as the product of this 'imperious inner need', may not be reduced to such a model. Sharrock subsequently, and tellingly, refers to Bunyan as uniting 'the emotional fervour of the extreme sectaries with a firmer Calvinist framework than they adhered to' and acknowledges that 'the mental conflicts depicted in *Grace Abounding* [ ... ], though they are real states of the soul, grow out of quibbling misunderstandings about texts'.[24] The critic who appears to invoke a twentieth-century model of unified subjectivity thus implicitly, and grudgingly, acknowledges both the impact of texts which offer competing models of subjectivity on the Bunyan text and the overtly textual and linguistic level at which the author-subject's attempt to secure a legitimate position or identity takes place.

Delany suggests that '[a]utobiography had a direct and truthful quality which could be relied on to make a strong appeal to the unconverted'.[25] The records of sales of such texts would seem to support the argument for their popularity, yet was their 'truthful' quality the reason for their popularity? Did such texts offer the truth of an individual human experience, as modern autobiography purports to, or did they perform a more complex role both for writers and readers? A number of more recent analyses of *Grace Abounding* have, in different ways, begun to explore the complex interrelationship of models of subjectivity, authority and textuality both within the text and within the discursive frameworks which legitimated its production and circulation. Whilst these texts may be seen to display a shared refusal to explain the text by reference to a pre-existing and controlling author figure, the differences between readings point to different agendas, priorities and critical positions.

## II   Rereading the subject of *Grace Abounding*

The textual status of the 'experience', and of the subject, presented in *Grace Abounding* are examined in Jeremy Tambling's analysis of the text in *Confession: Sexuality, Sin, the Subject*, in which he offers a reading of the text as a form of confessional narrative. In contrast to Sharrock's reading, Tambling's focuses on the text as *producing* rather than reflecting the subject. *Grace Abounding* is read as the inheritor of a Puritan tradition of internalised confession which substitutes the study, or private space, for the public confession-box, and the processes of writing and reading for the spoken confession. The text's 'obsession with the self' is thus 'the desire to internalise the confessional, to be what is expected of it' and the central technique in the production of the subject is seen to be 'to wrest from textual sources a set of happenings that can be claimed to be authentic'.[26] The self which Tambling identifies in *Grace Abounding* is, as he states, 'quite un-Rousseau-like', yet the text is poised 'at the beginning of the change of description from the idea of the person to the individual'.[27] Tambling employs Foucault's reading of the nineteenth-century practices of the social sciences in which the 'daily characteristics of the prisoner' were logged in a practice which entailed, in Foucault's words:

> the examination as the fixing ... of individual differences ... the pinning down of each individual in his own particularity ... [which] indicates the appearance of a new modality of power in which each individual receives as status his own individuality, and in which he is linked by his status to the features, the measurements, the gaps, the 'marks' that characterize him and make him a 'case'.[28]

Tambling suggests that this is 'the moment that the word "autobiography" appears', ascribed an 'ontological status differentiating it from biography when the issue of the aut(h)o(r) becomes apparent'.[29] The writers of earlier texts, which have subsequently been categorised as autobiographical, are seen, in Tambling's analysis, to be engaged in a different practice:

> Bunyan has no sense of the difficulty involved in describing himself as though he were a character and not himself. The self is not seen as the occluding difficulty which creates a blindness-and-insight situation in any attempt to give its narration of itself. The question of who or what is the I that can so speak of the self, that part-taken-as-a-whole, is not addressed.[30]

The subject of *Grace Abounding* is thus not the individual subject as reliable, or unreliable, source and guarantee of meaning, but rather the nexus of various textual practices which connect human experience with divine reality. In Tambling's reading, *Grace Abounding* is 'a history of interpellation', in which Bunyan responds to voices from the pulpit, from heaven, and interprets voices and signs as 'a person of the book'.[31] Bunyan's search for a conclusive sign of salvation is seen as a process of interpretation in which contradictory scriptures are harmonised, a process which is then reinscribed as experience, 'making it seem that he is the voluntary subject who willingly submits himself to the discourse of the other'.[32] This process of resolving contradictory texts is seen to demand the elision of differences and the maintenance of an appearance of passivity, of submission to scriptural authority, on the part of the interpreting subject-writer. Tambling cites as an example the passage by Bunyan in which two conflicting texts are seen to 'struggle strangely in me for a while' which ends with one text emerging victorious, a victory interpreted by Bunyan as mercy defeating judgement:

> He must show that the struggle of texts is resolvable; if he cannot, he will not appear as the unitary (Christian) subject he longs to be (and which the act of writing finally makes him). To appear this complete subject, he must misinterpret and misread. He ultimately chooses to accept the god of mercy over the Old Testament God of judgement, but writes in such a way that it appears that the struggle was not his, but that he was only the passive agent in it.[33]

The passivity of Bunyan's apparent position within this textual struggle is revealed as illusory in Tambling's final example in which Bunyan describes his battle of interpretation with Satan:

> If ever Satan and I did strive for any word of God in all my life, it was for this good word of Christ; he at one end and I at the other. Oh, what work we did make! It was for this in *John*, I say, that we did so tug and strive; he pull'd and I pull'd; but, God be praised, I got the better of him.[34]

Satan, Tambling argues, may be read as the 'repressed' that 'would read differently, interrupting the monological power of the text' and whose defeat amounts to 'the silencing of precisely that part of the self that cannot be interpellated, that cannot be made part of the confessional, unitary self'.[35]

Tambling's analysis of *Grace Abounding* as a confessional text, rather than as 'autobiography' is persuasive, yet his stress on what he terms 'the genesis of secrecy', on the importance of the private space as the primary location of interpellative power, leads to a (deliberately) partial reading of the text. Tambling emphasises the 'private space where the book is read' as a significant departure from earlier public confessional practices. Bunyan's account of his own reading of Luther's commentary on Paul's epistle to the Galatians is cited as an example:

> I found my condition in his experience, so largely and profoundly handled, as if his Book had been written out of my heart; this made

me marvel: for thus thought I, this man could not know anything
of the state of Christians now, but must needs write and speak the
Experience of former days.[36]

The experience which Bunyan longs for, Tambling argues, is textual and
Luther's book 'itself commenting on a master-text, contains a power of
address the more potent for seeming to be heart-to-heart'.[37] Bunyan, as
reader, in 'the space of the silent study', becomes 'the confessant as he
takes Luther to be describing him and his experiences'.[38] In Tambling's
analysis this is 'literary criticism and the practice of reading literature as
commonly practised, where the wonder is held to be that timeless texts
speak to our condition', whereas 'what actually speaks is the reader as
confessant, whose experience is formed by an ideology of literature'.[39]
Bunyan's 'desire to *see* some man's experience' is seen to trust 'the
materiality of print in the face of its labile character as writing'.[40]

Whilst this is a convincing reading of the status of the text in *Grace
Abounding* and of its relationship to a developing approach to reading
'literary' texts, including *Grace Abounding*, the sliding from 'private
space' to 'silent study' in Tambling's analysis is problematic. Although
the notion of private reading is clearly important within seventeenth-
century nonconformist practices, as within earlier Puritan practices, and
may have contributed to the development of the concept of reading as a
process of connecting two individual subjects, the seventeenth-century
meanings of 'private space' may not be identical with those of later eras.
Certainly the spaces of reading and interpretation referred to by Bunyan
in *Grace Abounding* bear little resemblance to Tambling's 'silent study';
Bunyan, the reader, the listener and interpreter, is more often located on
a road or under a hedge than in a study, silent or otherwise, and these
are spaces offered by him to his readers as the locations for receiving
divine communications. Bunyan's list of such places in his preface to
*Grace Abounding* may hold a key to their status. The list includes both
literal places and Scriptural locations: the '*hedge*', '*Hill* Mizar', '*the
Close*', '*the Milk-house*', '*the Stable*', '*the Barn*'.[41] These locations would
seem to stand as common ground between writer and readers, as spaces
which defy definition as either personal or public and which are to be
read as the contemporary versions of scriptural 'types'. The process of
interpretation is thus again paramount in the definition of legitimate
space as it was in the definition of a legitimate subject position; scriptural precedent, correctly interpreted, becomes the means of categoris-
ing a location as spiritually, and, I would argue, politically, significant.
The space of writing in, and of, *Grace Abounding* is the prison cell, a
space which might appear to bear some resemblance to the 'silent
study', particularly in post-Romantic images of Bunyan's Bedford cell.
It is a space which is designed to remove the subject from the public

domain, yet it is a space which is itself defined as public, as I shall argue in the next section.

Tambling's apparent elision of private space and silent study may derive from his location of *Grace Abounding* within a history of confessional texts. Tambling does acknowledge that the text might also have functioned in different ways, as a challenge to a secular royalist and reactionary authority, written by Bunyan as 'a prison-house protest against the authority that has silenced him', and as a means of validating a call to the ministry.[42] These functions of the text are, however, seen as subsidiary in Tambling's account. The conventional nature of the textual techniques of *Grace Abounding* is similarly acknowledged, yet not given particular attention, in Tambling's analysis.

In an article published in 1984, Peter J. Carlton examines the role in *Grace Abounding* of what he refers to as 'disclaiming locution'.[43] This term, derived from the psychoanalytic theory of Roy Schafer, is employed to describe the use of statements such as 'that sentence fell with weight upon my soul' in order to present the writer-subject as a 'passive locus for the activity of alien agents' and to present the subject's actions as experiences.[44] Carlton's reading of the role of such statements in the text prefigures Tambling's reading in many ways. Both readings hinge on the passage in which Bunyan's choice of one scriptural passage rather than another is presented as a passive acceptance of divine agency through the Word as evidence of the imaginary nature of this authorial or subjective passivity; both acknowledge that the emphasis on, and meaning of, experience, differs in texts produced within the various sections of the Puritan and dissenting movements. A significant difference in their readings is identifiable as the emphasis placed by Carlton on the role of authority and convention in the production and function of the texts.

The conventions of Puritan and dissenting writing are, in Carlton's analysis, a substitute for the objective religious authority which had been rejected or lost after the Reformation. 'Disclaiming locutions' are seen to fill 'the void left by that loss' and, by 'constituting certain thoughts and feelings as happenings, such statements transformed mental events into direct communications from God, making them implicitly authoritative'.[45] The Puritan insistence on the scripture as sole, non-contradictory, authority is seen by Carlton to have involved a *contestation* of objective religious authority in the form of ecclesiastical hierarchy and a link is established between the convention of 'disclaiming locution' in texts such as *Grace Abounding* and an established tradition of polemical Puritan writings on scriptural authority. The technique is also related to the Puritan 'pastoral method' in which metaphors and figures of the Christian soul assaulted by alien forces abound in sermons and treatises.[46]

The proliferation of conversion narratives which abide by certain established conventions, including that of 'disclaiming locution', is seen as a result of the application of techniques employed in polemical and pastoral writings to subjective experiences in order to afford them an objective or authoritative status. This legitimation could only be achieved through 'rigorous adherence to a communally sanctioned form'.[47] Texts such as *Grace Abounding* may thus be seen to contest ecclesiastical authority, whilst conforming to 'the authority of convention'. Inspiration, according to this model, is not a quality which denotes authorial transcendence of the constraints of convention, which would seem to be its meaning in many evaluations of Bunyan's achievement in *Grace Abounding*. It is, rather, a quality whose presence can only be ascertained in statements or texts which conform to a conventional model; inspiration is thus a discursively constituted quality, as it is, albeit differently, within conventional literary criticism.

The argument that the experience presented in narratives such as *Grace Abounding* is legitimated, even constructed, by a specific cultural framework is extended by John Stachniewski in *The Persecutory Imagination: English Puritanism and the Literature of Religious Despair*. Stachniewski, like Tambling, employs Foucauldian analysis of techniques of 'subjectification' in his examination of the pervasiveness of Calvinist paradigms of election and reprobation within the texts of English Puritanism. Preachers and books, fathers and their surrogates, are seen by Stachniewski to employ what Foucault termed 'dividing practices', both in 'their constant discursive segregation of the godly from the ungodly and, more subtly, by inducing the replication of that division within the inner consciousness'.[48]

The concept of God is, in Stachniewski's model, 'a communal construct from which the individual could not easily escape' and the 'conceptual frames' of conversion narratives are seen to operate with a prescriptive force.[49] In this context, *Grace Abounding* is read as a textual record of the 'persisting doubleness of the experiential paradigm', as a struggle between the elect and reprobate positions outlined in Bunyan's *A Map, shewing the order and causes of Salvation and Damnation* (1663?).[50] Reprobation, or exclusion, with its concomitant effects of isolation and alienation, socially and theologically, is seen to act as a constant threat, to be countered by sign of election, of belonging to the community of the saved. Presented as a 'transcript' of experience, the text is seen both to accomplish and attest to release from the despair which accompanies fear of reprobation, and to integrate its subject-author into the community of the elect. Bunyan's attempts to decide whether individual scriptural texts place him as elect or reprobate are accompanied by a series of engagements with language and authority, both spiritually or theologically and materially or culturally. His swearing and cursing when young is seen as evidence of 'self-assertive authority', produced in defiance of the ultimate authority of God, of the law, and as an effect of his own material and spiritual lack of status. This rebellious phase is followed by his 'outward Reformation', in which he borrows the language of godliness, but has yet to occupy a subject position within it. Only in the encounter with the poor Bedford women is Bunyan presented as truly acquiring language, as becoming inscribed as a subject within the discourse of salvation. This symbolic rebirth is seen, paradoxically, to be accompanied by an increased anxiety about language as the subject must become speaker: 'I could not now tell how to speak my words, for fear I should mis-place them.'[51] The authority conferred on Bunyan by the 'discourse originating from God's Word', a product of his 'submission to an authority higher than the great ones of the world', will be tested in encounters with other authorities, differently constituted and sustained, in which the meaning of his authority will be challenged.

A parallel, but differently accented, analysis of competing authorities in *Grace Abounding* is developed in Felicity Nussbaum's article, '"By these words I was sustained": Bunyan's *Grace Abounding*'.[52] Nussbaum reads *Grace Abounding* as a text of self-presentation which sets 'two impulses – one towards the universal allegorical ideal and the other towards the particularized individual – in continual conflict'.[53] Two ways of conceptualising the self are seen to compete with and complement each other, as Bunyan tests the limits of 'divine patriarchal authority' and 'substitutes his own personal authority for God's'.[54] Nussbaum supports her argument by citing the passages added to the third and fifth editions of the text, passages which 'intensify the separation between the protagonist and the narrator in their emphasis on his loneliness, isolation, and the length of time the process of conversion required'.[55] The structure of *Grace Abounding* is seen not as the 'unified narrative' required by Delany, but as a series of sections with tentative resolutions which describe 'a self in process rather than a stable or unified identity'.[56]

Central to Nussbaum's reading of *Grace Abounding* is her assertion that Bunyan is claiming a position of authority:

> Bunyan uses the early conversion to create a temporal and spatial arena for the exploration of a series of possible selves which test the patriarchal authority of God. At the same time that Bunyan explores the possibilities of rebellion against God, of Bunyan the father rather than God the father, the autobiographical text begins to compete for authority with the Scriptural texts. After finding God in the early conversion, he then tests the limits of his own newfound authority. The period of temptation allows for both a

mask and a purge; it provides a crisis of authority, but also a safe and secure position from which to struggle, for the narrator, the protagonist, and the reader know the outcome from the beginning of the text. We are certain that the conclusion will find the transgressor safe in the abounding grace of the authority of God. The autobiographer will achieve his goal of becoming God's child and becoming the father of the reader.[57]

Bunyan, the protagonist, is seen to 'rebel "within" authority', to confront the limits of divine authority in a text which both competes with and complements the Scriptures. In the struggle between competing figures of authority in *Grace Abounding* it is words which are seen to 'take on an authority that God, Christ, and Esau, on the one hand, and the self, on the other, cannot assume'.[58] Scripture is seen to contain elements of both the ideal and the particular and to provide the material for Bunyan's production of his competing and complementary text. Bunyan questions the authority of the Scriptures, as he does that of God, wondering 'whether the holy Scriptures were not rather a Fable and cunning Story, then the holy and pure Word of God?', yet assumes that capturing experience in writing will preclude further uncertainty: 'Well, I would I had a pen and ink here, I would write this down before I go any further, for surely I will not forget *this* forty years hence; but alas! within less then forty days I began to question all again.'[59] Bunyan's own writing, in the form of *Grace Abounding* may be read as ultimately competing with Scriptural authority, as Scriptural texts form a subtext within Bunyan's text. Nussbaum extends this argument in her chapter on *Grace Abounding* in *The Autobiographical Subject: Gender and Ideology in Eighteenth-Century England*, suggesting that:

> Through religious discourse, Bunyan is recruited and recruits into being the sovereign Subject of ideology, the Subject in whom all subjects partake. The words of Scripture serve as a corollary text while the autobiographical 'self' competes as a substitute textual authority, a devotional guide that replaces the Scriptures and the Absolute Subject.[60]

These rereadings of the subject in, and of, *Grace Abounding* engage in different ways with the question of authority within the text. It is to the framing of the text, to the presentation of the narrative within a specific textual framework, and to its articulation of a claim to authority within a framework of pastoral power relations, that I shall turn in the next section.

## III   Authority on trial

The preface to *Grace Abounding* takes the form of an address, itself
prefaced by the following title: 'A PREFACE: Or brief Account of the
publishing of this Work: Written by the Author thereof, and dedicated
to those whom God hath counted him worthy to beget to Faith, by his
Ministry in the Word.'[61] An uncertain relation is suggested here between the author, writer of the text as 'Work', and the Minister, elected
by God to 'beget' others to faith through the Word. The preface is
dedicated not to a patron as benefactor nor to a general readership, but
to 'those whom God hath counted him worthy to beget to Faith'. The
grammatical structure of this dedication is such that it could be addressed to those already converted but also to those who have yet to
receive the Word. No limit is specified to Bunyan's intended addressees,
nor is it clear whether his 'Ministry in the Word', past, present, or
future, will take the form of the written or the spoken word. The phrase
'brief Account of the publishing of this Work' could be taken to mean a
factual description of the production and distribution of a written text
or an evaluation of the process of making a text available publicly. Only
one phrase in this title appears to carry a single meaning: 'Written by
the Author thereof', which recalls the statement on the title-page of the
first edition in which the text as a relation of the experiences of John
Bunyan is described as 'written by his own hand'.[62] Yet this apparently
unequivocal assertion of authority will itself be complicated, if not
undermined, in the address which follows, an address which reveals an
extremely complex interrelationship of different meanings of authority,
knowledge, power and subjectivity.

The address opens as follows:

> *Children, Grace be with you,* Amen. *I being taken from you in
> presence, and so tied up, that I cannot perform that duty that from
> God doth lie upon me, to you-ward, for your further edifying and
> building up in Faith and Holiness, &c., yet that you may see my
> Soul hath fatherly care and desire after your spiritual and everlast-
> ing welfare; I now once again, as before from the top of* Shenir *and*
> Hermon, *so now from* the Lions Dens, and from the Mountains of
> the Leopards (*Song* 4. 8), *do look yet after you all, greatly longing
> to see your safe arrival into* THE *desired haven.*[63]

This opening passage would seem at first glance to answer some of the
questions prompted by the title to the preface. The address would
appear to be that of a minister to his congregation, an attempt to
continue in his duties towards them whilst he is unable to be with them
'*in presence*'. It has already been established on the title-page that
Bunyan is in prison. As *A Relation of the Imprisonment of Mr. John*

*Bunyan*, also called *A Relation of My Imprisonment*, written by Bunyan but not published with this text (*Grace Abounding*) until 1765, indicates, Bunyan was arrested and imprisoned in 1660 for preaching without a licence, under the provisions of the Elizabethan Act against Conventicles (35 Eliz. cap.1, An Act for Retaining the Queen's Subjects in their Due Obedience).[64] The passage establishes a type of relationship between minister and congregation, 'father' and 'children', which was commonplace in nonconformist, as in other, Christian discourse. This figure of the familial relationship between minister and congregation which implies both material and spiritual dimensions and a dialectic of power and duty, both between and within the individual members of the group, can be read as connecting with a particular form of what Michel Foucault termed 'pastoral power'.

In the essays 'Politics and Reason'[65] and 'The Subject and Power'[66] Foucault argues that Christianity initiated a new set of power relations whose particular characteristics are as follows:

> 1) It is a form of power whose ultimate aim is to assure individual salvation in the next world. 2) Pastoral power is not merely a form of power which commands; it must also be prepared to sacrifice itself for the life and salvation of the flock. Therefore, it is different from royal power, which demands a sacrifice from its subjects to save the throne. 3) It is a form of power which does not look after just the whole community, but each individual in particular, during his entire life. 4) Finally, this form of power cannot be exercised without knowing the inside of people's mind, without exploring their souls, without making them reveal their innermost secrets. It implies a knowledge of the conscience and an ability to direct it.[67]

The language of the prefatory address would certainly seem to indicate a relationship between Bunyan and his readership within the framework of pastoral power. The ultimate aim is clearly to ensure salvation: '*my Soul hath fatherly care and desire after your spiritual and everlasting welfare*'. The exercise of such power as is implied by the authoritative position granted by God is viewed as a 'duty' to be fulfilled even at great personal cost. Most significantly it is a relationship which demands continual scrutiny of the individual soul:

> *My dear Children, call to mind the former days, the years of ancient times; remember also your songs in the night, and commune with your own heart, Psal. 77. 5,6,7,8,9,10,11,12. Yea, look diligently, and leave no corner therein unsearched, for there is treasure hid, even the treasure of your first and second experience of the grace of God toward you. Remember, I say, the Word that first laid hold upon you; remember also your terrours of conscience, and fear of death and hell: remember also your tears and prayers to God; yea, how you sighed under every hedge for mercy.[68]*

It is this process of self-examination which Foucault locates at the heart of the 'pastoral modality of power', a self-examination whose end is not, significantly, the discovery of the truth of the self identified with subsequent techniques of self-analysis, but rather the acknowledgement of the necessity of total obedience to the will of the shepherd. This submission is not the result of rational decision on the part of an individual subject, nor of a legal compulsion; it is the only tenable position for the subject within the discourse of salvation whose aim is the 'mortification' of the self, the renunciation of worldly presence in order to attain an eternal position within the full presence of God.

In an essay called '*Grace Abounding* and the new sense of the self', Roger Pooley has suggested that Bunyan is 'demanding a space in which he can exercise pastoral power, leading others into his interpretations'.[69] Pooley interprets Bunyan's challenge to the authorities, related in *A Relation of My Imprisonment*, as deriving not simply from a notion of 'individual freedom confronting state power' but 'from another conception of power, more overarching yet more tricky to interpret than the rule of law'.[70] This suggestion would appear to be supported by the text. Bunyan, as 'father', acknowledges a '*duty that from God doth lie upon me*' to guide his 'children' into 'THE *desired haven*'. The preface clearly locates the rewards of suffering elsewhere, as in the final words 'The Milk and Honey is beyond this Wilderness: God be merciful to you, and grant that you be not slothful to go in to possess the Land.'[71]

It is in the temporal interval on earth before this repossession of a divine home, I would argue, that the public places which Tambling subsumes under the category of 'silent study' are presented as having a special significance. Mundane, marginal locations such as the hedge, the barn and the stable, which stand literally and metaphorically outside the limits of conventional ecclesiastical territory, are to be restored to a central position within a different map of the realm of the spirit. The prison cell in which Bunyan writes is similarly reinterpreted, relocated within this map, as a space saturated not by state power but by divine power, or grace. This redefinition of the meaning of space, achieved through the identification of literal locations with scriptural types, provides a new map of the 'real world' which challenges the validity of existing maps or interpretations. Although it lacks the clear binary structure of Bunyan's published map of salvation and damnation, which presents two parallel linear paths which individual subjects are destined to follow, this fragmentary map begins to challenge the accepted meanings of what constitutes a powerful or authoritative position, both in terms of location and relation.

Some attention has been paid to Bunyan's status as a dispossessed subject, whose family had once occupied a more secure social position, and who had resorted to an itinerant occupation as a tinker. Stachniewski, in his analysis of the alternation between the assumption of reprobate and elect identities in *Grace Abounding*, suggests the existence of a 'collective imagination' which 'registered a congruence between the Calvinist God and arbitrarily discriminatory market forces'.[72] He traces the interconnection, throughout the text, of scriptural and commercial-legal metaphors of birthrights, of selling Christ, and suggests that there is a 'social basis' for Bunyan's 'vulnerability to a reprobate identity'.[73] The young Bunyan is deemed to have lacked 'a strategy for relativizing the dominant ideology' and, consequently, to have 'internalized the worthlessness ascribed to him' as a poor, uneducated subject.[74] His subsequent inscription as a subject within a redemptive discourse is seen to afford a relative freedom from the dominant ideology and to provide a different position from which to view his social status. It also, I would argue, provides a vocabulary and a redefinition or realignment of exist-ing meanings, which affords him an *authoritative* position within a different framework of power relations. This pastoral framework does not confront the state directly, but rather threatens to destabilise the oppositions between public and private, legitimate and illegitimate, powerful and powerless, upon which it rests.

Bunyan's claim to an authoritative position as father and minister within the prefatory address is reinforced by a number of scriptural quotations and references in the first person which were originally attributed to Solomon, Paul and Samson. Bunyan is also linked by analogy with Moses and with the greatest of human shepherds within the Christian narrative, David. References to the lions' den, the '*Philistians*' who '*understand me not*' and to '*the Wilderness*' may be interpreted either as allusions to the world which is to be renounced or as veiled or coded references to the persecuting authorities against whose established regime of pastoral power the dissenting sects defined themselves. The fact of Bunyan's imprisonment for preaching the Word without licence, under the provisions of an act originally designed to counter the activities of conventicles deemed to pose a threat to the state power embodied in the sovereign person of Elizabeth I, may indicate that the practice of preaching and interpreting the Scriptures without the constraints of the authorised church was interpreted as offering an unacceptable challenge to the existing social and political structure.

Bunyan's repeated protestations of loyalty to the throne and state-ments condemning subversive or revolutionary political activity have been the subject of much critical debate, often in order to identify his overall political sympathies. In *Of Antichrist, and His Ruine*, probably written in the early 1680s and first published in 1692, Bunyan presents a forceful condemnation of those around the King who promote 'wicked Antichristian Penal Laws' and 'the abominable filthiness of that which is Antichristian-Worship',[75] whilst declaring his own loyalty to the King and calling on his readers to pray for the King:

> Let the King verily have a place in your Harts, and with Heart and Mouth give God Thanks for him; he is a better Saviour of us than we may be aware of, and may have delivered us from more Deaths than we can tell how to think. We are bidden to *give Thanks to God for all Men*, and in the first place, *for Kings, and all that are in authority*.[76]

> Pray for the long Life of the king. Pray that God would always give Wisdom and Judgment to the king. Pray that God would discover all Plots and Conspiracies against his Person and Government. Pray also that God would make him able to drive away all Evil and evil Men from his presence; and that he may be a greater Countenancer than ever, of them that are holy and good, and wait and believe, that God has begun his quarrel with *Babylon, Antichrist*, the mother of *Antichrist*, the Whore; would in his own time, and in his own way, bring her down by the means which he has appointed.[77]

Loyalty to the monarch is offered as a Christian duty, established in the Scriptures, for kings are to be God's agents in the destruction of Babylon and Antichrist. Individual monarchs may appear to have done more to further this divine plan: 'noble' Henry VIII, 'good' Edward VI and 'brave' Elizabeth I are all praised by Bunyan for 'casting down' Antichristian laws and worship. Yet even a monarch who appears hostile to the 'church of God' is to be prayed for, rather than condemned. No reference is made to Charles II (or to James II who may have succeeded to the throne at the time of writing) by name, but warnings against blaming the King for the persecution of the godly clearly differentiate between the current monarch who is 'a better Saviour of us than we may be aware of' and his, named, predecessors:

> Take heed, I say therefore, of laying of the Trouble of the Church of God at the doors of Governours; especially at the doors of *Kings*, who seldom trouble Churches of their own Inclinations; (I say, *seldom*; for some have done so, as Pharaoh:) But I say, lay not the Cause of your Trouble there; for often-times they *see* with other Mens Eyes, *hear* with other Mens Ears, and *act* and *do* by the Judgments of others: (Thus did *Saul*, when he killed the Priests of the Lord; and thus did *Darius*, when he cast Daniel into the Lyons Den:).[78]

Here, as later in the treatise, reference to the contemporary political situation is combined with indirect allusion to Bunyan's own suffering at the hands of the authorities, suggested by the reference to the 'Lyons

Den' which Bunyan had offered as his place of writing in the preface to *Grace Abounding*. Scriptural analogies locate both monarch and subject within a narrative whose divine author has pre-ordained the role and status of each character, a narrative which allows Bunyan simultaneously to condemn Antichristian and Babylonian persecution and to distance himself from those who explicitly attributed such actions to the person of the monarch. Bunyan sums up his position as follows:

> I do confess my self one of the old-fashion Professors, that *covet to fear God, and honour the king.* I also am for *blessing* of them that *curse* me, for *doing good* to them that *hate* me, and for *praying* for them that *despitefully use me, and persecute me*: And have had more Peace in the practice of these things, than all the World are aware of. I only drop this, because I would shew my Brethren that I also am one of them; and to set them right that have wrong Thoughts of me, as to so weighty Matters as these.[79]

This opaque statement of the author's position in relation to the 'weighty Matters' of obedience to God and King, which is presented to 'my Brethren' as a proof of being 'one of them' and as a counter to 'wrong Thoughts of me', implicitly acknowledges the force of persecution in shaping the lives of the persecuted, but turns a position of passive subjection into active subjection. What form the 'wrong Thoughts' had taken remains uncertain, but in the context of a treatise which calls for the destruction of Antichrist and in so doing calls for obedience to a monarch frequently associated with 'Antichristian' activities, it seems likely that Bunyan had been associated with plots against the king.

*Of Antichrist, and His Ruine* and *Grace Abounding* stand near the end and the beginning, respectively, of Bunyan's pastoral ministry, yet both texts involve a series of negotiations with competing models of authority. By the 1680s Bunyan had achieved relatively authoritative positions as both minister and author, but in the 1660s his authority was, literally, on trial. The disruptive power of the sects lay not in encouraging individuals to disobey an unjust or persecuting ruler, but rather in insisting that ruler, judge and tinker alike are all required to act in obedience to an absolute authority whose true meaning is inscribed not in any constitution or law of man but in the living Word, the Scriptures as the visible and audible transcription of the ever, and everywhere, present deity.

It is the emphasis on the Scriptures as sole material means of access to God's truth which enables nonconformists such as Bunyan to claim interpretative authority on a par with the Established Church. When challenged by the justices at the Bedford quarter sessions in 1661 for refusal to conform to the practice of using the Book of Common Prayer, Bunyan returns to the Bible to defend his position:

> I said that those prayers in the Common Prayerbook, was such as
> was made by other men, and not by the motions of the Holy
> Ghost, within our Hearts; and as I said the Apostle saith, he will
> pray with the spirit and with understanding; not with the spirit and
> the Common Prayerbook.[80]

> I said, shew me the place in the epistles, where the Common
> Prayer-book is written, or one text of Scripture, that commands me
> to read it, and I will use it. But yet, notwithstanding, said I, they
> that have a mind to use it, they have their liberty; that is, I would
> not keep them from it, but for our parts, we can pray to God
> without it.[81]

Similarly, it is to the Scriptures that Bunyan looks for justification of his
claim to the right to preach, to follow a calling from God, when
challenged by Justice Kelynge who, Bunyan reports in 'A Relation of
My Imprisonment', 'asked me where I had my authority?'. Bunyan
responds by citing Scriptural exhortations to those who have received
'the gift' to exercise it, to '*speak* as the oracles of God'. Kelynge attempts to limit the application of the Scriptures in order to exclude
Bunyan and to reinterpret gift as material calling, in Bunyan's case, 'the
gift of tinkering'. Bunyan refuses to accept this different interpretation
and is returned to prison, under threat of banishment or death. As
Stachniewski notes in his reading of this passage, the justices, who share
Bunyan's basic Protestant commitment to the authority of the Word,
must acknowledge the base of his claim to authority, if not the actual
claim, which is rejected as being couched in alien language, 'pedlers
French'. When the justices fail to induce Bunyan to accept their interpretation of his position, they are presented as being 'reduced to exple-
tives' and his claim to spiritual authority, despite protestations of due
obedience, provokes the repressive reaction of institutional power.[82]
The passage ends with a claim that the encounter and the imprisonment
served only to reinforce Bunyan's assurance of his divine calling: 'So
that I found *Christ's* words more than bare trifles, where he saith, he
*will give a mouth and wisdom, even such as all the adversaries shall not
resist, or gainsay*. And that his peace no man can take from us.'[83] In a
parallel textual move, the justices are later renamed by Bunyan as 'the
*Adversaries* of *God's Truth*'.[84]

It may be argued that the Established Church had failed to maintain
control of the meaning of the Word, of truth, resorting in many cases to
enforcing the silence of dissenting voices by banishment or death having
failed to achieve what Foucault has defined as essential to the operation
of power in contrast to force, namely causing an individual with the
potential to resist to behave in a certain way. If a relation of power may
be defined as the ability of one party to subjugate, to govern or direct

another, then the failure of the attempt to obtain Bunyan's agreement to follow a certain course of action, attending officially sanctioned church services and abandoning his own ministry, can only result in what may be termed the operation of force, the prolonged incarceration of the body and removal of the troublesome subject from the public sphere. The results of such an action reveal both the limitations of the attempts to silence by force, but also the complex relationship between different models of power and their implications for the development of alternative subjectivities. There is apparently incontrovertible evidence that in the early stages of his imprisonment Bunyan was allowed to attend the meetings of dissenting sects both locally and in London and that when his confinement was more rigidly maintained from 1664 to 1668 the influx of nonconformist prisoners provided him with a captive audience. The years of imprisonment were also to prove Bunyan's most prolific writing period.

The writing of *Grace Abounding* in prison may indeed constitute an attempt to continue a 'Ministry in the Word' which had proved to be an unacceptable challenge to church and state, yet the very fact of writing has effects which explicitly and implicitly disrupt any single purpose or effect which might be ascribed to the text. The text may be read as a defence of Bunyan's claim to authority as interpreter of the Word, but this can only be maintained by analysing the effects of the Word upon him as well as his continual efforts correctly to interpret his position in relation to individual scriptural statements and thus within the discourse of salvation as a whole. Bunyan's position must shift between active interpreter of the Word and obedient subject of the Word, between spiritual father of his children and child of God the Father. He is in effect writing a text in order that his own life may be read as God's text: '*Wherefore this I have endeavoured to do; and not onely so, but to publish it also; that, if God will,others may be put in remembrance of what he hath done for their Souls, by reading his work upon me.*'[85]

The insistence on God as the one true author stands alongside a series of statements which seem to betray an uncertainty about the role and authority of the text's human author. While it is confidently argued that it is the operation of God through the Word which has constructed Bunyan as an authorised text in which others may read the true meaning of the relationship of man to God, Bunyan the author of *Grace Abounding* can be allowed only an uncertain and incomplete authority. In transcribing his experience of the power of the Word, Bunyan is offering an example to others of '*the great grace that* God *extended to such a Wretch as I*'.[86] The text is to act as a supplement to the Word, not as a substitute. But as with all supplements there is a risk of supplanting the original. It is possible to identify in the preface to *Grace*

*Abounding* an anxiety about the process of relating the effects of the Word in other words:

> *I could have enlarged much in this my discourse of my temptations and troubles for sin, as also of the merciful kindness and working of* God *with my Soul: I could also have stepped into a stile much higher than this in which I have here discoursed, and could have adorned all things more then here I have seemed to do: but I dare not:* God *did not play in convincing of me; the* Devil *did not play in tempting of me; neither did I play when I sunk as into a bottomless pit, when* the pangs of hell caught hold upon me: *wherefore I may not play in my relating of them, but be plain and simple, and lay down the thing as it was: He that liketh it, let him receive it; and he that does not, let him produce a better.*[87]

The association of *'higher'* style and adornment with playing and the assertion of the need to be *'plain and simple'* in relating *'the thing as it was'* would seem to suggest a desire to eliminate the dangers inherent in representation. This echoes an anxiety about the process of signification, the plurality inherent in the metaphoric qualities of language, which is evident in many other texts of the period. But here it is closely linked to a number of potentially conflicting claims on the part of the author. Bunyan is claiming interpretative authority, asserting the legitimacy of his divine calling to preach the Word and, as the final sentence of the above passage indicates, in so doing he is producing a text which must itself participate in a contest to establish its own legitimacy of meaning. Bunyan does not, and cannot, claim to be the source or guarantee of that meaning, but just as he must adopt the position of spiritual father in order to assume authority as a minister, so he must adopt the position of author of this text, attempting to control the meanings contained within it, to express *'the thing as it was'* without adornment or invention. He must, in effect, try to control the deferring, differentiating effects of language, to imitate in the words of man the assumed singularity and transcendence of meaning of the Word of God. The possibility of incorrect interpretation, of misreading, which informs the narrative section of *Grace Abounding* is the cause of a profound anxiety about the narrator's spiritual condition. Yet in offering that narrative as a representation of his struggle to achieve true knowledge of his position within the discourse of salvation, Bunyan must run the risk of inviting similar misreadings. Chief amongst these in recent years has been the tendency, identified earlier in this chapter, to read the text as the story of an inner life, a glimpse into the tortured soul of the author.

*Grace Abounding* may then, in conclusion, be read as a text which actively engages with the problems of authority, interpretation and knowledge within a logocentric framework of metaphysics, a text whose avowed intent to bear witness to the absolute authority of the transcendental signified must continually be frustrated by the deferring, differentiating processes of its own written materiality. In writing the narrative of God's capacity to write the life of his subjects, to produce men and women as texts which bear the imprint of the Logos, Bunyan cannot exclude the potential disruption to the clear hierarchy of authority implied by his own writing. Just as the attempts to silence Bunyan by incarceration failed to contain the voice of dissent in seventeenth-century England, so the author's attempt to arrest the production of meaning is inevitably doomed to failure. Authority is always on trial.

# CHAPTER THREE

# Authority, exclusion and resistance: from interdiction to contra-dictions

## I  Interdiction

In the seventeenth century the voices of dissent, raised against the established order and in opposition to dominant meanings, were raised neither in unison nor in harmony. Bunyan's attempts to establish an authoritative position from which to promote his reading of God's true meaning necessarily involved a struggle on behalf of that reading which opposed its meanings to those produced not only within conformist writing, but also within the texts of different dissenting groups. The meanings promoted, explicitly or implicitly from different positions of resistance to what is retrospectively identified as the dominant social, political and religious order, can be read as neither identical nor continuous. Whilst certain shared beliefs and discursive strategies may indicate common ground between different sectaries or different writers during this period, it is evident that the differences and divisions so often overlooked in general accounts of seventeenth-century nonconformity were not only an inevitable component of dissent but formed an essential impetus to the production of texts and, ultimately, of meanings. The combative production of texts in defence of a particular range of meanings from a position of apparent nonconformity towards dominant systems of meanings may, therefore, result in very diverse writings. Some of these texts may appear to have more in common with the official opposition, the state and ecclesiastical authorities, than with other nonconformist groups whose meanings might prove a greater immediate or ultimate threat. Bunyan's writings are no exception. Whilst few, if any, of his combative texts have been afforded canonical status, they offer a revealing insight into the strategies of exclusion which underpin the construction of an authoritative position both textually and discursively.

In his introduction to *Volume IV* of the Oxford University Press edition of the *Miscellaneous Works*, which contains six combative texts written between 1672 and 1685, T. L. Underwood offers a succinct formulation of the significance of what he terms 'tract warfare'. Engagement in controversy was an essential component of Bunyan's ministry, he argues, 'for it was required for the protection of the flock, the

defence of the preacher's legitimacy, and the preservation of the faith –
ministerial obligations which Bunyan took very seriously'.[1] Underwood
also notes the contradiction between Bunyan's description of his attitude towards such controversies in *Grace Abounding* and the evidence
of his involvement offered by the tracts themselves. In *Grace Abounding* Bunyan declares:

> I never cared to meddle with things that were controverted, and in
> dispute amongst the Saints, especially things of the lowest nature;
> yet it pleased me much to contend with great earnestness for the
> Word of Faith, and the remission of sins by the Death and Sufferings
> of Jesus; but I say, as to other things, I should let them alone,
> because I saw they engendered strife, and because I saw they nei-
> ther, in doing nor in leaving undone, did commend us to God to be
> his.[2]

In fact, as Underwood notes, Bunyan was engaged in a range of textual
battles over major doctrinal matters and 'things controverted' throughout his life. Controversy provided the occasion of Bunyan's first publications and continued to inform his writings, either explicitly or implicitly.
Whilst the texts vary in vehemence and acrimoniousness, they conform
to a general pattern which seeks to undermine the authority of the
opponent's claims and, ultimately, of his position, by challenging the
legitimacy of the opponent's interpretation of the Word. The writer
attempts to establish the truth of his position on a contentious issue by
amassing scriptural evidence to support it and by highlighting errors or
inadequacies in the opponent's interpretation of the Word. The opponent's quotations are systematically reinterpreted from the writer's position and frequently mobilised to mean exactly what the original
interpreter did not want them to say.

Bunyan's disputes with individual, named and anonymous, opponents have been examined in some detail by a number of historians and
critics, and his pamphlet wars with Quakers such as Edward Burroughs
and the Latitudinarian, Edward Fowler, have received considerable critical attention.[3] Bunyan's disputes with the latter are particularly vitriolic
in tone and are marked by an exchange of personal denunciations by
both writers. The characterisation of the opponent as ignorant, incom-
petent or devilish, as in the Bunyan/Fowler exchanges, is clearly part of
a strategy intended to undermine the rival's authority. As the title of a
tract published anonymously in response to Bunyan's *A Defense of the
Doctrine of Justification, by Faith* in 1672, *Dirt Wip't Off*, indicates,
textual mud-slinging was an integral part of seventeenth-century controversial writing. Underwood describes the 'acrimonious denunciations of opponents as the agents of the devil, and the professions of
innocence and claims of being victimized by unprovoked attack' as

'part of the rough and tumble nature of religious controversy'.[4] The apparently personal, if formalised, nature of these attacks may, however, obscure greater battles taking place within the texts. In 1685 Bunyan describes his motivation in writing *Questions about the Nature and Perpetuity of the Seventh-Day Sabbath* (see Bunyan, *Misc. Works, Vol. IV*) as a sense of shame in the face of growing factionalism amongst believers:

> The truth is, one thing that has moved me to this work, is the shame that has covered the face of my Soul, when I have thought of the Fictions and Fancies that are growing among Professors: And while I see each Fiction turn it self to a Faction, to the loss of that good spirit of Love, and that oneness that formerly was with good men.[5]

If 'oneness' is to carry the dual meanings of unity and singularity which the opposition with factionalism implies, it can surely only be located in an imaginary past, as the promised dissolution of difference in the unique indifference of divine being can only be located in an imaginary future. At the moment, and through the medium of writing, Bunyan can only assert the legitimacy of his desire for such 'oneness' by means of an implied distinction between his writings, presented in the name and service of 'truth' and the 'Fictions and Fancies' which are defined as the cause of factionalism.

This attempt to outline an opposition between Bunyan's writings and unreliable 'Fictions and Fancies' may be compared to the more apparently unstable opposition drawn between similar categories in the preface to *The Pilgrim's Progress, Part One*. In the preface Bunyan's defence of his allegorical method depends on the assertion of a difference between his 'Fable' or 'Fancies' and a category of text proscribed for evangelical use in Scriptures. Bunyan, the preface asserts, is offering 'Truth within a Fable', as opposed to the 'old Wives Fables' which St Paul advised Timothy 'to refuse'.[6] In order to assert the difference between his fable and the 'old Wives Fables' Bunyan argues that Paul does not forbid the use of 'Parables', thus claiming a connection between his method and that of the writers of the Scriptures.[7] The letter from St Paul to Timothy which Bunyan cites in fact proscribes 'profane and old wives' tales'.[8] It may, therefore be significant that it is only the latter type of proscribed material to which Bunyan makes reference. The connection between unreliable fables and female authors may already have been a conventional one, but in the context of Bunyan's claims to authority it is an association upon which much depends.

Five years after *The Pilgrim's Progress, Part One* and two years before *Questions about the Nature and Perpetuity of the Seventh-Day Sabbath* Bunyan published a combative treatise which makes explicit an attempt to exclude an entire category of subjects from any position of authority within public, religious and political affairs. An examination of this text may indicate both the continuing fragility of Bunyan's position as an authoritative voice of dissenting truth and the strategies by which he attempted to exclude other dissenting voices whose truth-claims threatened to undermine his own. The named opponent in this text is Mr K., but the voices are female.

A Case of Conscience Resolved, published in 1683, is Bunyan's first and last explicit acknowledgement of the demands made by women in the seventeenth century for a position from which to speak in the public domain of religion. Published one year after The Holy War, in which female characters exist only as names in passages which outline the genealogy of male characters, and one year before The Pilgrim's Progress, Part Two, whose protagonists are female, this text may be read as a failed attempt to exclude women from a subject position which might threaten the fragile security of Bunyan's own position. It may also suggest that questions of the representation of women in Bunyan's writings are of far greater importance than generations of Bunyan critics have allowed. Whilst the role of women within church structures and as writers of religious and secular texts during this period has been examined in a variety of different ways and from a number of different positions by critics and historians,[9] the place of woman or women within Bunyan's writings as read by the majority of Bunyan scholars is a marginal one. I wish to argue that an examination of a text such as A Case of Conscience Resolved may raise important questions not only about the status and subject positions explicitly or implicitly afforded to women within Bunyan's writings, but also about the values and priorities of a criticism which has repeatedly denied the importance of such questions.

It is widely accepted that the Protestant emphasis on the direct rela-tionship between the individual and God and the obligations that were placed on each believer to examine, and testify to, their spiritual condi-tion opened up a space for female participation in religious movements as it did for unordained male believers, and that the greater emphasis on grace in Puritan and later in dissenting and nonconformist move-ments offered more opportunities for women than did the Anglican and Presbyterian churches. The frequently cited episode in Grace Abound-ing in which Bunyan encounters 'three or four poor women sitting at a door in the Sun, and talking about the things of God' presents the women's discourse on 'the work of God on their hearts' as having a profound effect on the hearer who is made aware of the gap between his own 'brisk' talking and his real spiritual condition.[10]

The women are presented as moved to speech by the operations of divine grace:

> And me thought they spake as if joy did make them speak; they
> spake with such pleasantness of Scripture language, and with such
> appearance of grace in all they said, that they were to me as if they
> had found a new world, as if they were a people that dwelt alone,
> and were not to be reckoned among their Neighbours, Num. 23.9.[11]

The emphasis on the role of grace is crucial in nonconformist challenges, or modifications, to the traditional Pauline injunction on women
to be silent; claims to be acting as a conduit or mouthpiece of God
frequently stood as the foundation of women's, as of unordained men's,
encroachment on a field of oral or written ministry from which they
would normally be excluded. In this scene, as Keeble has noted, Bunyan
'has attended a critically awakening sermon; and those who have assumed the dominant role of preachers to him are women'.[12]

This episode could be read as implicitly aligning Bunyan with the
dissenting group with whom he most frequently and vehemently clashed
in his combative writing, namely the Quakers, whose doctrinal, if not
always practical, position on the status of women as active agents of
divine communication is conventionally accepted as more radical than
that of other sectaries such as Baptists or Congregationalists. The experiential theology of Quakerism attracted many women during the years
after the revolution who played an active role in preaching the group's
particular message.[13] The representation of the Bedford women in *Grace
Abounding* appears to endorse the idea that women could be recipients
and communicators of divine grace as Quaker doctrine claimed but as
the story behind, and textual and discursive strategies disclosed by, *A
Case of Conscience Resolved* reveal, the actual position of women
within nonconformist movements, including Quakerism, was complex
and shifting. Whilst the theological or doctrinal frameworks of nonconformity may have offered possibilities for women which contradicted
the apparently repressive gender politics of traditional scriptural interpretation of women's ordained inferiority, the responses of nonconformist groups, and particularly of male preachers, to female activity
were not always consistent with these frameworks. As various sectaries
struggled to assert their own authority against conformist and nonconformist 'rivals' in the years following the Restoration, the status of
women became a key discursive battleground for preachers and writers
who sought to define their own position in a rapidly changing social
and cultural context. In the middle to late seventeenth century the need
to occupy a position of respectability led Quaker leaders to dissassociate
themselves from the more radical and enthusiastic aspects of their movement, which involved a repositioning of male and female believers
within a family model. This process was already under way when
Bunyan wrote *A Case of Conscience Resolved*, but in his text Quakers,

linked, as elsewhere, with Ranters, figure as a threat not only to his own authority but to the safety of the female believers of his own congregation.

The female activity which is the spur for this text seems initially to be unlikely to provoke such a hostile response from the author of *Grace Abounding* who had openly testified to the importance of women's speaking in his own conversion. The women in Bedford were sitting alone in the street talking about their experience of God; the women in Bunyan's congregation were asking for the right to hold meetings alone, without men. The title-page of *A Case of Conscience Resolved* describes the founding problem of the text as '*Whether, where a Church of Christ is Situate, it is the Duty of the Women of that Congregation, Ordinarily, and by Appointment, to Separate themselves from their Brethren, and so to Assemble together, to perform some parts of Divine Worship, as Prayer, &c. without their Men?*'[14] As the text explains, Bunyan is 'meddling' in this 'Controversie', because female members of his congregation had been holding '*Womens meetings*', assemblies which Bunyan argues have no 'bottom in the Word'.[15] No details are given about the nature of these meetings or of the numbers or status of the women who attended them. The female members of the congregation are described initially as readily acquiescing in Bunyan's assertion that the practice should cease: 'So subject to the *Word* were our Women, and so willing to let go what by *that* could not be proved a duty for them to be found in the Practise of.'[16] In the preface, 'The Epistle Dedicatory to those Godly Women concerned in the following Treatise', Bunyan is anxious to stress the spiritual worth and '*wise and quiet temper*' of the 'Honoured Sisters' of his congregation.[17] He is equally determined, it would seem, to deny any suggestion of female agency in this affair. In the initial address to the women concerned Bunyan states that:

> *I dare not make your selves the Authors of your own miscarriage in this. I do therefore rather impute it to your Leaders; who whether of a fond respect to some seeming abilities they think is in you for this, or from a perswasion that you have been better then themselves in other things or whether from a preposterous zeal, they have put you upon a work so much too heavy for you: I shall not at this time concern my self to inquire into. But this is certaine, at least 'tis so in my apprehension, that in this matter you are tempted by them to take too much upon you.*[18]

The '*Leaders*' mentioned above are not defined as male or female, but Bunyan swiftly moves in the preface to identify Mr K. as prime mover in the events which have led up to Bunyan's writing of this treatise. Despite his conviction of the women's wisdom and quiet temper, Bunyan anticipates a hostile response from some: '*I am like enough to run the*

Gantlet *among you, and to partake most smartly of the scourge of the Tongues of some, and to be soundly Brow-beaten for it by others.'*[19] But it is Mr K. who is identified as *'our Author, who will finde himself immediately concerned, for that I have blamed him for what he hath irregularly done both with the Word, to you, and me'.*[20] It is, in fact, the latter's written intervention in the affair which has occasioned Bunyan's own public intervention: *'indeed, I had not spoke a Word to this question in this manner, had not Mr. K. sent his Paper broad, and amongst us, for the encouraging this practise with us, in Opposition to our peace'.*[21]

An opposition is established here between Mr K., as the outsider intervening in the affairs of an otherwise 'quiet' community of believers, and Bunyan, who writes only for his sisters' *'Honour and good order'.*[22] The opinions of women involved in the argument can thus be exiled from the text. Female reactions to the text are reduced in advance to a 'Gantlet' of scourging tongues which, like the voices of the women in the local debate preceding the publication of this treatise, is markedly different from the voices of the other Bedford women whose effect on Bunyan was represented in *Grace Abounding*. Bunyan's insistence that women cannot be *'Authors'* of their own actions is accompanied by a number of statements which appear to deny the legitimacy of the female voice, as his argument against women's separate meetings gradually develops into an argument against women having any voice in public affairs. In his explanation of how he received word of Mr K.'s challenge Bunyan explicitly questions the veracity of a letter presented to him by local women, eventually believing it to be real only because 'I had heard something of this before'.[23] A fierce debate was clearly raging locally, as elsewhere, on this issue, for, despite the emphasis on a community of quiet, godly women who wanted nothing more than to be relieved of the 'duty' of separate meetings, the letter and Mr K.'s treatise are presented to Bunyan 'two years after' he had apparently resolved the matter to everyone's satisfaction.[24]

Offering a summary of Mr K.'s arguments, Bunyan accuses him of *'Boldness* in *Fathering'* his mis-understanding upon the Authority of the Word of God'.[25] Mr K. is thus both an outsider, seeking to interfere in the business of the congregation, and a rival father figure who has both exceeded his position by imposing his own meanings on the Word of God and failed in his duty to maintain 'his Women' in their ordained position. Bunyan's own familiar and familial relationship with his congregation is stressed by reference to a previous discussion of the question of women's meetings, 'when I handled it among my Brethren'. The repetition of phrases such as 'our question' and 'among us' suggests a consensus which effaces gendered difference within the congregation, locating Mr K. and 'his Women' as the other against which Bunyan's 'Brethren', male and female, are to be defined.[26]

Mr K.'s religious affiliations are not presented in the text, nor is his full name given. In his introduction Underwood suggests that Mr K. is probably the London-based Baptist William Kiffin, with whom Bunyan had conducted arguments in print before.[27] The relationship between the two men would appear to have been extremely hostile, as Christopher Hill's descriptions of their clashes on matters of personal and social standing, education and class, as well as doctrinal matters, suggest.[28] Yet in this text Mr K. stands as the main object of address in a move which effectively allows Bunyan to make a series of general pronouncements about women, whilst implying that such concerns are properly decided by a man and his God. Whatever their differences, both men, according to Bunyan's argument, are held in a special relationship to God which is not available to women.

Identity and difference operate as key concepts in the text, as Bunyan attempts to fix male and female positions in relation to God's truth by reference to the Word. The 'Epistle Dedicatory' opens with a reassurance to women that *'the Lord doth put no difference betwixt* Male *and* Female, as to the communications of his Saving Graces'.[29] Many women, moreover, have been made *'eminent for piety'*, even exceeding men in spiritual devotion, for *'The love of Women in Spirituals (as well as in Naturals) oft times out-goes that of men'*.[30] This initial statement of parity as recipients of divine grace echoes that offered in a number of texts on the position of women, including *Womens Speaking Justified*, Margaret Fell's pamphlet of 1667.

Fell opens her defence with an assertion that in the creation of men and women God 'joyns them together in his own Image, and makes no such distinctions and differences as men do; for though they be weak, he is strong; and as he said to the Apostle, His Grace is Sufficient'.[31] Both Fell and Bunyan proceed from this first assertion of original parity to an analysis of scriptural writings on the role and position of women as they may be applied to seventeenth-century Christian practice. Whilst a great deal of the scriptural material is common to both analyses, it is mobilised in very different ways. Fell charges 'You dark Priests, that are so mad against Womens Speaking' and 'you blind priests that speak against Womens Speaking' to 'hearken to', to 'read' and 'see' the voices of women in biblical times, and to recognise 'the Spirit of Truth, and the Power of the Lord Jesus Christ' as communicable to and through the female voice.[32] Fell argues that the church exists in a new age, that 1,200 years of 'darkness', the 'Night of Apostasy', is drawing to an end and that those who deny women an equal share in an active participation in this new era of 'the joy of morning' would thereby 'limit the

Power and Spirit of the Lord Jesus'.[33] The rhetoric of enlightenment firmly locates the opposition of ministers such as Bunyan within an age of 'Darkness' which is both historically defined as the years of papacy but which is also seen to operate in the post-Reformation nonconformist and dissenting churches. An opposition is developed between the power of Christ operating through men and women and an Antichristian determination to limit the operation of that power manifest in certain male voices which act as agents of darkness and ignorance in an age of spiritual enlightenment.

Fell's text not only reinscribes female voices and positions whose scriptural authority she argues has been denied by centuries of misreading, but it also acts as a performative text, standing as the latest manifestation of divine truth communicated through the female voice. Fell was an active member of the Quaker movement, and her career may be read as paradigmatic of the changing involvement of some dissenting women in church affairs. As Felicity Nussbaum's introduction to the Augustan Reprint Society edition of *Womens Speaking Justified* relates, her role changed from that of the 'cohesive centre', the woman at home in Swarthmoor Hall 'caring for her large household' and maintaining written communication in letter form with the travelling preachers of the Quaker movement, to a role as traveller, visiting imprisoned members and attending meetings throughout Britain.[34] Her first departure from the domestic setting was to petition Charles II on behalf of George Fox, a mission which she accomplished successfully in 1660. Fell wrote and published a number of texts in defence of Quaker beliefs and positions, texts which were translated into Hebrew, Latin and Dutch as part of the Quaker drive to convert the Jews.[35] *Womens Speaking Justified* both expanded on and modified the earlier Quaker text on women's position in church affairs, *The Woman Learning in Silence*, published in 1656 by George Fox, whom she was to marry two years after the publication of her own text. Her involvement in the activities of the Quaker movement led to her imprisonment first in 1664 under sentence of praemunire, second in 1670, the result, as the introduction suggests, of 'her son's attempts to discredit her in order to get her estate', and again in 1683, the year of the Rye House conspiracy and of Bunyan's publication of *A Case of Conscience Resolved*.[36]

Sixteen years before Bunyan denied women the position of '*Authors*' of their actions, Fell had claimed a place in the public world of authorship, her texts, like those of Bunyan, exceeding the constraints imposed on the body and voice of their author by imprisonment. Both writers were condemned for speech which was unauthorised and for challenging, explicitly or implicitly, the authority of existing social and political institutions and discourses which withheld authority from them. Bunyan never addresses Fell's text directly, as he addresses points raised by Mr K., yet his text as it develops a position antithetical to that established in hers may be seen to respond to the very thing which it cannot acknowledge as worthy of recognition.

The publication of *A Case of Conscience Resolved* in the year of the imprisonment of the female author of *Womens Speaking Justified* is not without significance. Richard L. Greaves has offered an analysis of Bunyan's response to the renewed persecution of dissenters which followed the discovery of the Rye House conspiracy.[37] Greaves examines the development of an 'ethic of suffering' in Bunyan's work at this time which accompanied and accommodated his condemnation of those involved in the conspiracy, his attempts to dissociate himself from those arrested and executed and his repeated assertions of personal loyalty to the monarch and of the duty of Christians to 'Let not talk against governors, against powers, against men in authority be admitted'.[38] Greaves analyses in some detail Bunyan's response to political events as outlined in *Seasonable Counsel: or, Advice to Sufferers*, the text published in 1684 from which the above quotation is taken. *A Case of Conscience Resolved* is referred to only in passing as having been published in October.

It is possible, however, to read this text as an important example of Bunyan's attempts to negotiate a spiritually and politically legitimate position which would sustain his authority as writer and preacher by a process of excluding those disruptive elements which might prevent the establishment of such a position. As his statement 'I do not believe [women] should Minister to God in Prayer before the whole Church, for then I should be a Ranter or a Quaker' reveals, Bunyan insists on his doctrinal difference from groups associated with antinomianism and the related threat to the social order, whilst simultaneously adopting a conservative stance towards a possibly more disruptive force, namely female agency.[39] Although his work has been extremely important in revealing the complexities of seventeenth-century religious and political relations, Greaves's implicit relegation of *A Case of Conscience Resolved* to the position of also-published may, in turn, be read as an example of the continued marginalisation of the question of women by traditional critics of Bunyan's writings. In his contribution to *John Bunyan: Conventicle and Parnassus*, Greaves offers a summary of Bunyan's changing relationship to nonconformity and, in a section entitled 'Political crisis, evangelical concerns, and the nonconformist community', gives a half-page account of the publishing of *A Case of Conscience Resolved*.[40] The account locates the occasion of its publication in the activities of 'London Nonconformists' and offers a range of possible identities for Mr K.[41] Significantly, the paragraph on this text is followed by another which commences 'The most striking change that marks this period of Bunyan's life concerns his political outlook' and describes this in terms of his attitude to the monarchy and to 'matters of state'.[42] Questions of women's position in church affairs, as addressed in *A Case of Conscience Resolved*, are thus implicitly differentiated from 'political' matters. The representation of the text as a response to 'London Nonconformists' and the provision of a list of possible male opponents mirrors Bunyan's own presentation of the text, whilst the implicit denial of the political dimension of the argument effectively colludes in the explicit refusal made by Bunyan's text of a public position from which women might be allowed to speak.

A reading which adopts a wider definition of the political may, however, find that there is in the Bunyan text an implied recognition of the threat to existing power relations posed by women in the church, both to local structures and to an entire metaphysical framework. This is a recognition which demands that the question of women be offered as a minor, local dispute which can be handled by two men sorting out their differences, yet which involves Bunyan ultimately in the exposition of an apparently universal and transcendent denunciation of woman, described by Christopher Hill as 'a remarkably explicit assertion of male ascendancy'.[43] Although Bunyan never acknowledges or responds to the contributions to this debate made by women such as Margaret Fell, his text may be read as a response to the threat such women posed. In its very denial of a political position for women it attempts to fix the meaning of 'woman' in relation to God and to the structure of the Church. State authorities deemed it politically expedient to remove Margaret Fell from the sphere of public activity, as they had once removed John Bunyan, unlicensed preacher; John Bunyan, official minister of a nonconformist sect and self-proclaimed writer of God's Truth, deemed it politically and spiritually incumbent upon him to remove women as an entire category from the discursive space of public religious practice.

Whereas Fell's text deals throughout with the single question of women's capacity to communicate God's truth, Bunyan's text starts as an attempt to prove that women have no 'duty' to establish or attend separate meetings and progresses through a series of scriptural interpretations to a final assertion that women can have no legitimate place in the public affairs of the Church. Not only are separate meetings unlawful, but the female voice in mixed assemblies is not to compete with the male: 'They should also not be the mouth of the Assembly, but in heart, desires, grones, and Tears, they should go along with the Men.'[44] Women are 'an Ornament in the Church of God', but must bear the 'badge of [their] inferiority, since the cause thereof, arose at first from your selves.

'Twas the *Woman* that at first the *Serpent* made use of, and by whom he then overthrew the World'.[45] An original act of transgression against the divinely ordained patriarchal order is thus seen to condemn women to a life of perpetual acknowledgement of inferiority:

> Wherefore the *Woman*, to the Worlds end, must wear tokens of her *Underlingship* in all Matters of Worship. To say nothing of *that* which she cannot shake off, to wit, her pains and sorrows in Childbearing (which God has *riveted* to her Nature) there is her *Silence*, and *shame*, and a *covering for her face*, in token of it, which she ought to be exercised with, when ever the Church comes together to Worship.[46]

Women are to 'abide' in this 'subjection' and are offered a description of the one legitimate position ordained for them within church affairs. This is, perhaps not surprisingly, the 'Closet':

> Be as often in your Closets as you will; the oftener there, the better. This is your Duty, this is your Priviledge: This place is Sanctified to you for service by the Holy Word of God. Here you may be, and not make Ordinances enterfere, and not presume upon the Power of your Superiors, and not thrust out your Brethren, nor put them behinde your backs in Worship.[47]

The necessity of women staying in this ordained place or space is offered as a matter of the utmost importance, for '[w]hen Women keep their places, and Men manage their Worshipping God as they should, we shall have better days for the Church of God, in the World'.[48] Women who claim a voice in public worship are presented as claiming a power to which they are not entitled, a power which has been granted only to 'the principal Men of the church'.[49] Congregations are defined as Christ's 'Body *Politick*', modelled 'by the skill that his Ministers have in his Word, for the bearing up of his name, and the preserving of his Glory in the World against *Antichrist*'.[50] The patriarchal position earlier identified by Fell as Antichristian is here offered as the worldly 'Foundation' of 'the True Mystical Body of Christ'.[51] Its 'Laws, and Statutes' and 'Government' are divinely ordained and demand the exclusion of women from positions of executive power or spiritual authority:

> Now where there is *Order*, and *Government* by Laws and Statutes: There must, of necessity, be also a distinction of *Sex*, *Degrees* and *Age*: Yea, *Offices*, and *Officers* must also be *there*, for our furtherance, and Joy of Faith. *From which Government and Rule, our Ordinary Women are excluded by Paul*; nor should it, since it is done by the Wisdom of God, be any offence unto them.[52]

The reference to 'our Ordinary Women' alludes to the distinction drawn between the 'prophetess' Miriam, who had been cited by Mr K. in his argument, and those 'Ordinary Women' who Mr K. would tempt to 'a

Work that he has a superstitious affection for'.[53] Bunyan repeatedly establishes differences between the women offered as examples by Mr K. and the women who might follow those examples. The example of Esther is disallowed by a revealing opposition drawn between her position and that of seventeenth-century women. Esther *'the Queen'* was, it is asserted, 'a Woman in Bondage', unable to worship with any but the female members of her household.[54] Her 'Womans Meeting' is thus removed to a private, domestic domain in which *'Esther* did Pray with her Maids in her Closet, because Shee could not come out to her Brethren'.[55] The example of 'a Woman in Bondage' is not to be offered as 'a Law to Women at Liberty', even if their liberty is only to be described later as 'subjection'.[56] The free women of the seventeenth century are offered the 'Priviledge' of returning to the 'Closet' which signified the bondage of Esther.

The paradoxical nature of liberty within Calvinist metaphysics is here thrown into relief as it is further complicated by questions of the relative liberty of gendered subjects. Women are offered a vision of freedom from the ordained limits of their sex only in the dissolution of gender distinctions which will accompany the day of salvation:

> Wherefore my beloved sisters, this inferiority of yours will last but a little while: When the day of Gods Salvation is come, to wit, when our Lord shall descend from Heaven, with a shout, with the voice of the Archangel, and the trump of God, these distinctions of Sexes shall be laid a side, and every pot shall be filled to the Brim. For with a *notwithstanding* you shall be saved, and be gathered up to that state of Felicity; if you continue in Faith, and Charity, and Holiness, with sobriety.[57]

Even this final promise of the dissolution of worldly differences in the absolute being of God carries an assertion of the patriarchal nature of the hierarchy of divinely ordained being: women will be saved *'notwithstanding'* their sexual difference. The trace of hierarchically defined difference in this offer of an eventual release from ordained inferiority is a necessary component of a discursive strategy which demands the association of maleness with order and divinity and femaleness with disorder or unruliness and transgressive humanity.

Throughout the text, references to prohibitions on female behaviour are accompanied by assertions of the special allowances granted to men. Both sets of rules are offered as divinely ordained and inscribed in the Word. Thus, whilst women are to cover their faces in acts of worship as a recognition of shame, 'The Men are admitted in such Worship, to stand with open Face before God (a token of much admitance to liberty and boldness with God) a thing denied to the Women.'[58] Although such distinctions are presented as absolute, certain passages of the text indicate that the meanings of man and woman in the Bible were being contested at this time. Just as Bunyan, Mr K. and, earlier, Fell, offered different interpretations of the significance of individual women in Biblical examples, so the range of meanings of the signifiers 'man' and 'woman' is open to conflicting interpretation.

Bunyan posits an objection to his assertion that men should manage all acts of worship: '*But the Woman is included in the Man, for the same Word signifies both*'.[59] This formulation of the female as a component of the male may be retrospectively identified with patriarchal strategies to deny women a distinctive discursive position. It has subsequently been mobilised, for example, in defence of sexist pronoun use. Yet here it is clearly presented as an argument employed by those who challenged those patriarchal structures which would allow them no position of difference from which to speak. Bunyan's response to the objection thus posited reveals an intense anxiety about the threat posed by separate meetings of women, which might well be seen to represent autonomous female subjectivity. The passage tellingly contrasts the inclusion of 'Woman' in the term 'Man' with the threat of exclusion posed to male worshippers by female refusal of male supremacy:

> 1. *Answer*. If the Woman is included here, let her not exclude the Man. But the Man is Excluded: The Man is Excluded by this Womans Meeting from Worship; from Worship, though he be the Head in Worship over the Woman, and by Gods Ordinance appointed to manage it, and this is an Excluding of the worst Complexion, 1 *Cor. 11.3*
> 2. Though the Woman is included, when the Man sometimes is named, yet the Man is not Excluded, when himself as Chief is named. But to cut him off from being the Chief in all Assemblies for Worship, is to Exclude him, and that when he for that in Chief is named.
> 3. The Woman is included when the Man is named, yet but in her place, and if she Worships in Assemblies, her part is to hold her Tongue, to learn in silence; and if she speaks, she must do it, I mean as to Worship, in her Heart to God.[60]

Women's actions in meeting separately have clearly threatened male structures of authority within the Church and, by extension, the order of the Church. At a time when such churches were struggling to maintain a place within an increasingly hostile political climate and when ministers such as Bunyan were anxiously disavowing any connections with revolutionary or anti-monarchical movements, the association of the female voice with unruliness and the exclusion of such disruptive voices from threatened nonconformist discourse is an attractive strategy. It is a strategy for which a clear precedent had been set during the later Commonwealth and Protectorate.

The unruly female voices of the 1680s may have invoked memories of the disruptive voices and texts of female prophets during the 1640s and 1650s. As Christine Berg and Philippa Berry's essay, '"Spiritual Whoredom": an essay on female prophets in the seventeenth century', suggests, the contents and styles of female prophetic utterances during this period posed a threat to social, religious, sexual and political orders. Women such as Mary Cary, Eleanor Davies and Anna Trapnel intervened in political and religious debates in what Berg and Berry term an 'irruption of female speech into the once tabooed domain of public activity'.[61] Female prophets both published texts and made oracular speeches in public places, such as Whitehall and Parliament. Although the shifting attitudes of state and church authorities towards individual prophets may indicate that their activity was licensed or prohibited according to its political usefulness, the major threat which female prophetic utterance posed to the dominant social/sexual order may be seen to have overridden questions of political expediency. Berg and Berry argue that female prophesying during this period may be read as a 'non-rationalist discursive mode', which they liken to Luce Irigaray's 'language of the feminine' and Julia Kristeva's 'semiotic'.[62] They locate the threat of female prophecy in this non-rationalist discourse: 'By the sustaining of a multiplicity of various levels of speech and meaning, as well as by relinquishing the "I" as the subjective centre of speech, the extremist forms of prophetic discourse constitute an extremely dangerous challenge to conventional modes of expression and control within seventeenth century patriarchal society.'[63]

The threat of this potent ir-rationality is seen to have been compounded by some of the claims by individual prophets:

> The verbal transmission of the *logos* appears to have been threatening enough – the possibility of a physical logos being produced, in the shape of a new Messiah, induced even greater traumas. A number of women in this period proclaimed at different times that they were pregnant with the Christ, announcements which usually prompted rapid precautionary measures by the State. Probably the best known of these, a woman called Mary Adams, was immediately thrown into prison upon making the announcement. It was then proclaimed in a public statement (which suggests that popular interest in the matter had run high) that she had given birth to a monster and committed suicide. What really happened is anybody's guess, but the incident was certainly symptomatic of a deep anxiety about the possession of meaning.[64]

Berg and Berry argue that 'rough treatment' of female prophets increased as the revolution 'sought to become more stable'.[65] They also argue that the period of 'revolutionary activity on both the physical and verbal planes, a period characterised not only by Civil War but also by a fierce debate over the possession of meaning, of the logos', came to an end by 1660.[66] The depiction of Eve in Milton's *Paradise Lost* is presented as part of a troubled analysis of the failure of revolutionary activity, but one which ultimately cannot 'admit women to possession of the logos, and so to a specific relation with God'.[67] This is a persuasive analysis of female prophetic activity and the evidence that such activity had largely stopped by 1660 seems conclusive. I wish to argue, however, that traces of this earlier unruly female speech and writing can be detected in texts of the later seventeenth-century, texts by both men and women.

Fell's writings bear little stylistic resemblance to those of Eleanor Davies or Anna Trapnel; her career bears much resemblance to that of Bunyan. Yet Fell's claim to a subject position from which to speak and write in the discourse of dissenting Christianity provokes a reaction from state and church authorities which not only mirrors Bunyan's treatment by the same authorities, but echoes the attempted suppression of the intrusive, threatening difference of the female prophets 20 years earlier. As a claimant to a position of authority whose legitimacy is denied by the State and challenged by rival claimants, Bunyan appears to invoke the conventional association of the female voice with unruliness in order to shore up his own fragile authority. The stress on order in Bunyan's writings and the identification of disorder (social, political, religious and sexual) with certain groups may, in this context, be read as part of a strategy of exclusion. Exclusion, however, necessarily suggests the possibility of resistance. An authoritative male writer may deny female subjects the right to possession of meaning, but in so doing he exposes the imaginary status of his own control over meaning.

## II  Contra-dictions

*A Case of Conscience Resolved* may be read as an interdictory text, which attempts to prohibit certain forms of female behaviour. Its interdictions are, however, undermined by a number of contradictions both within the text and in the interrelationship of this text and others. The confident assertion of male authority and authorship and the attempted exclusion of the female voice may be read as producing figures of resistance. These are female speakers and writers who claim, like Margaret Fell, a different position of authority and whose challenges to the patriarchal order act as powerful contra-dictions to Bunyan's exclusive framework. These figures are both 'real' and fictional; they reside in the texts themselves, in the margins of the texts, in church records and conversion narratives. Their textual voices, positions and activities connect with the unruly female prophets of the pre-Restoration period and with the diversity of feminist readers and writers of the late twentieth century.

Bunyan's denial of the legitimacy of the female voice in public affairs may be examined in relation to a series of other statements on appropriate female behaviour and inappropriate female speech. In *Christian Behaviour* (see Bunyan, *Misc. Works, Vol. III*), published 20 years earlier than *A Case of Conscience Resolved* and four years before Fell's *Womens Speaking Justified*, he offers a succinct formulation of the place and duties of women within the domestic space which he was later to define as the only one available to them. A treatise 'Teaching *Husbands, Wives, Parents, Children, Masters, Servants, &c*, how to walk so as to please *God*', *Christian Behaviour* addresses the subject of '*The Duty of Wives*' in terms which echo many of the conduct manuals of the period. The wife must look upon her husband as 'her head and lord', she 'ought in every thing to be in subjection to him, and to do all she doth, as having her warrant, license and authority from him'.[68] Afforded a position analogous to that of the Church which must acknowledge the absolute authority of Christ, the woman must beware of an '*idle, talking* or *brangling tongue*', of 'a wandring and a gossoping spirit', '*immodest apparel*' or '*wanton gate*'.[69] Whilst Bunyan adds a caveat that he does not 'intend women should be their husbands slaves', the ordained 'subjection' of women under their husbands is offered as absolute.[70] Even the wife who has a '*froward, peevish and teasty*' unbeliever or '*a sot, a fool*' as husband must 'take heed of desiring to usurp authority over him'.[71] The association of woman with the Church, with the human and fallible, and the husband with Christ, divine and infallible may be read as derived from an established tradition of Scriptural oppositions which privilege the male as divine and the divine as male over woman as worldly. Patriarchal and Christian imperatives thus reinforce one another in the development of the model family in which 'wives should be about their own husbands business at home'.[72]

Whilst *Christian Behaviour* operates by reference to the same basic patriarchal hierarchical oppositions as *A Case of Conscience Resolved*, its concentration on desirable Christian behaviour within familial and domestic relationships signals a different textual or discursive strategy in the text of the early 1660s from that of the 1680s. Bunyan's publication of a guide to 'works' is, at least in part, a necessary counterbalance to the emphasis in his writings on the operations of Grace as the key to salvation. In the prefatory Epistle, Bunyan remarks on the lack of a '*particular Discourse*' on 'Good Works', a lack which has led to a situation in which he finds '*every one too much left at uncertainties (as from them) of their several Works under their particular Relations, which I think is one reason of that disorder in Families and Places, where God's People live, to their shame, and the dishonour of their God'.*[73]

The early 1660s were, like the early 1680s, a period in which radical or revolutionary plots, or rumours of them, were rife. The Venner rising of Fifth Monarchists in 1661 was repudiated by Bunyan as the Rye House Plot was to be in 1683.[74] That a text on the need for a clear framework of good, Christian conduct should be produced at such a time seems significant. In *Grace Abounding* Bunyan had dissociated himself from his early involvement with members of the Ranter movement, a group whose antinomianism was widely perceived to imply a license to unbridled individual freedoms which would undermine the fabric of the political and social order. *Christian Behaviour* identifies a *'disorder in Families and Places'* which might be attributed by some sections of society to the activities and teaching of those who, like Bunyan, advocated the supremacy of Grace and the individual conscience in matters of religion.[75] This text thus operates as a corrective to Bunyan's writings on grace which might be otherwise misappropriated by antinomian sectaries as well as establishing his own position as different from theirs.

No reference is made in this text to public behaviour. Women are addressed only as wives and parents and their duties defined only in terms of familial and domestic relations. This is in marked contrast to *A Case of Conscience Resolved*, in which Bunyan may be read as anxiously trying to restore women to their legitimate domestic place in response to their social and textual disruptiveness. Whilst it might be too simplistic to attribute the difference between the two texts to the effects on Bunyan of increasing female activity in public religious affairs during the period, his writings and operations upon his texts during the 1680s reveal an intriguing concern with women and their representation which is in marked contrast to the ways in which such subjects are addressed in writings before this point.

Up to 1679 Bunyan's writings show little concern for issues of gendered subjectivity within the discourse of salvation. A survey of the treatises and 'literary' works of this period reveals few references to women at all, except for conventional associations of women with carnality by reference to scriptural quotations on Eve and the harlot. In *Grace Abounding* Bunyan refers to a wife who is defined only as someone 'whose Father was counted godly' and her contribution to Bunyan's life is described as bringing with her a dowry of devout books left to her by her father and as talking of her father's piety.[76] The wife depicted here, who exists only as a channel for material and spiritual goods from father to husband, stands in marked contrast to Bunyan's second wife who appears in the relation of his imprisonment which remained un-published until 1765.[77] The difference does not lie in any individual contrast of character or behaviour. Both wives have only a shadowy existence as individual characters; neither is named by Bunyan and the name of the first is still unknown. The difference lies rather in the role ascribed to the second wife, a role which Bunyan argues in *A Case of Conscience Resolved* should never be allotted to a woman.

Bunyan argues that 'if those most fond of the Womens Meetings for Prayer, were to petition the King for their lives, they would not set Women to be their Advocates to him'.[78] Yet in the account of Bunyan's imprisonment and trial it is related that Bunyan's wife petitioned the judges at the Midsummer Assizes of 1661 for her husband's release. Her actions and words are circumscribed by assurances that it is Bunyan who is acting 'by' her and that her feelings in anticipation of such unaccustomed public endeavour are appropriately 'feminine'. She thus approaches the judges' chamber 'with a bashed face, and a trembling heart', both characteristics recommended to women in the act of wor-ship in *A Case of Conscience Resolved*.[79] Her address to the judges, however, betrays no such hesitancy or anxiety. Her speech, as reported, is direct and accusatory as she challenges the judges to release her husband on the grounds of wrongful imprisonment, offering a succinct analysis of his problem as 'he is a Tinker, and a poor man; therefore he is despised, and cannot have justice'.[80] Whilst the text cannot be treated as a verbatim account of the woman's encounter with public authority, it is presented as a factual account which represents a woman doing precisely what, according to Bunyan's later argument, she should not and could not do.

*Grace Abounding* was the first of Bunyan's texts which made explicit, and offered a narrative justification of, his claim to an authoritative position from which to exercise pastoral power, a claim which had resulted in his persecution and imprisonment by political authorities. In this context the decision not to publish an account of his wife's inter-vention in the matter may well be read as symptomatic of a response to the existence of rigorous state censorship which would undoubtedly regard the substance of such a text as politically unacceptable. It is possible, however, to argue that this representation of a 'real' woman taking a vocal part in a political struggle over religious issues was also incompatible with the representation of women which Bunyan was gradually developing as a means of containing the conflicting demands of consolidating his own authoritative position and of establishing a safe discursive position for an increasingly active, vocal female congre-gation and readership. Bunyan's second wife is unnamed in his writings. His contemporary biographer names her Elizabeth, but the absence of any texts in her name has restricted her position within traditional criticism of seventeenth-century writings to that of a shadowy figure in her husband's supposedly extra-textual life.[81] As a figure of contradiction within a text, she may occupy a more powerful position, empowering interrogations of exclusion and resistance within texts bearing more author-itative names.

One section concerning women was added to *Grace Abounding* during Bunyan's lifetime. In 1680 Bunyan added a number of passages to the text, including an extensive refutation of charges of womanising, 'that I had my *Misses*, my *Whores*, my *Bastards*, yea, *two wives at once*, and the like'.[82] The passage moves from a refutation of such charges to an assertion of his difficulty in maintaining even polite relations with women:

> Those know, and can also bear me witness, with whom I have been most intimately concerned, that it is a rare thing to see me carry it pleasant towards a Woman; the common Salutation of a woman I abhor, 'tis odious to me in whosoever I see it. Their Company alone, I cannot away with.[83]

The section continues in this vein as Bunyan calls on 'men' and 'angels' to prove his guilt if they can before God. The section is traditionally interpreted as an indirect response to the 'Agnes Beaumont affair', in which Bunyan was implicated when a female member of his congregation was accused of patricide, after incurring her father's wrath by riding with Bunyan to a church meeting against his will.[84] It was, according to her narrative of her 'persecution', against Bunyan's will also, but accusations were made that the couple were engaged in an adulterous relationship.

Beaumont's account of the events, which happened in 1674, is a typical narrative of the persecution and eventual triumph of the Christian individual, but it is also a remarkable description of the dilemma of a devout daughter who attempts to negotiate a position of dutiful obedience to two opposing fathers, her own father and her pastoral father, Bunyan.[85] Her mother is dead, her father refuses to allow her to attend a meeting at which Bunyan is to preach – she has work to do, looking after her father. To obey her father would be to deny her duty to her divine father, God, figured to her in Bunyan.

After much debate her father agrees that she may attend the meeting. As a young woman, she cannot travel alone. Her brother, a parish officer, who appears to have been sympathetic to the nonconformist cause but not a member of the Bedford congregation, attempts to provide her with transport, first with a friend who fails to arrive and then with Bunyan himself, who called at her brother's house unexpectedly on the way to the meeting. Bunyan is described as reluctant to help the woman, anticipating her father's anger, but as eventually giving in to her brother's entreaties. Beaumont recounts that her father, on hearing that she has travelled with Bunyan, 'fell into a pastion' and intended to pull her 'off of horse backe' if he caught up with them.[86] She acknowledges a sense of pleasure and pride which she felt on riding with 'such A man as he was', but recalls that 'my pride had a fall' when a local priest sees Bunyan and Beaumont together and later 'did scandalise us after a base maner, and did raise a very wicked report of us, which was altogether false, bleesed be god'.[87] It is this report which seems to connect with the refutations of womanising in *Grace Abounding* and with the later description of her father's mistrust of Bunyan's use of his pastoral authority.

Left alone after the meeting, at which she received 'new manifestations' of divine 'love' which she suggests early in the text always preceded some trial or misfortune, she returns home to find herself locked out by her father and threatened with disinheritance unless she promises not to attend a meeting again. The conflicting demands upon her of the rival fathers cannot be reconciled. Her choice is between two sacrifices – of social position, a place in society, or of salvation, a place in heaven. Beaumont's description of her attempt to negotiate her conflicting duties to God and father emphasises both the force and 'reality' of her spiritual and mental struggle and the terrifying consequences of disobedience to either father.

Her physical exclusion from her father's house is seen as mirroring the exclusion from heaven should she fail to obey her divine father's commands. The description of her father's repeated questions and of his holding 'the key out to mee' similarly locates her situation within a tradition of scriptural trials, whilst emphasising the particularity of the dilemma of an excluded woman. She is offered protection by her brother, which she reluctantly accepts, yet his attempts to intervene with their father on her behalf are rebuffed by her on the grounds that the father 'was more provoked with what he said then he was with mee'.[88] Whilst herself challenging paternal authority when it conflicts with her duty to God, Beaumont resists association with her brother's threat to her father's authority, which might not be read as similarly motivated or justified, and refuses to be relocated within her brother's household. It is clear that, whilst the consequences of exclusion from her father's house were terrifying on several levels, Beaumont refused to evade them by appealing to an alternative figure of male protection.

The struggle is presented as that of father and daughter, and emphasis is repeatedly placed on the closeness of that relationship and its complex network of relations of power and desire. It is implied towards the end of the text that Beaumont had been allotted a larger part of her father's property in his will. The father is thus seen to afford his daughter a degree of material independence after his death, which contrasts sharply with his response to her actions during his lifetime. John Beaumont is presented as an irascible and, at times, physically threatening character, but he is not demonised or presented as ungodly. His behaviour towards his daughter cannot be interpreted as stemming from any individual malice, but is offered as the result of the conflicting pressures brought to bear upon him in the collision of different models of authority.

Beaumont tries to gain entry to the house by various means, after spending a night of torment in the barn, but eventually, despite her resolve to 'begg my bread from doore to doore', she succumbs to her father's demand and promises not to attend any more meetings during his lifetime.[89] Beaumont describes her behaviour at this point as 'peeter like' and having been admitted to her father's house is assailed by Scriptural texts which reinforce her conviction that by not forsaking her father she has forsaken Christ who will, in turn, deny her before God the father. Her 'terrour and gillt and rendings of Contience' are barely assuaged by her 'poore father' who was then 'very loveing to mee, And bid me gitt him some Supper'.[90] On the following night her father tells of his anxiety about his daughter's behaviour when first converted in terms which echo other writings on female prophets: Beaumont, it appears, did not eat, drink or sleep, and was assumed by her father to be 'distracted'.[91] The father acknowledges that her conversion had, however, led him to 'Crye to the Lord in Secret' and to 'goe to meetings', but that an 'evill minded man in the towne would set him against the meetings'.[92] Another day passes and while the daughter is still in 'a sorrowfull frame', her father 'did eate as good A dinner as ever I saw him eate'; after supper and 'A pipe of Tobacco' her father retires to a bed which his daughter has warmed with 'Coales'. As she is 'Covering of him' the words 'runn through' her mind: 'The End is Come, The End is Come, the time drayeth neere'.[93] She is later awoken by her father who complains of 'A paine at my heart'; there follows a detailed account of what appears to be a fatal coronary, as the father finally collapses after attempting to 'have A stoole'.[94] Beaumont tries to lift him and in her description of this she refers to the subsequent interpretation by others of a dream mentioned earlier in the text, in which she had tried and failed to lift a fallen apple tree in her father's garden, as 'signifying' this scene. As Vera J. Camden has suggested, this prophetic dream may bear a trace of wish-fulfillment, acting as a vehicle for the daughter's desire which cannot be reconciled with the law of the father.[95] Her recollection of this dream, and her acceptance of the interpretation of it as prophetic, also acts as a counterbalance to her apparent guilt that her father's collapse was occasioned by her neglect of her daughterly duties.

Finally she runs to her brother's house for help, through 'deepe' snow and wearing 'noe Stockins'.[96] When she returns with her brother their father dies and funeral arrangements are made the next day. Before the funeral can take place, Beaumont is accused of murdering her father on Bunyan's counsel, with 'stuffe' given to her by Bunyan. Her accuser is the aptly named Mr ffeery, a rejected suitor. An inquest is held to determine whether there is sufficient evidence to try Agnes Beaumont for petty treason, for which the penalty would be burning at the stake. No evidence can be found and the daughter survives her ordeal not only to attain a secure social position, eventually marrying two husbands in later life, the second called Stor(e)y, but to write her own. In so doing she begins to chart a different space – a space of writing.

In her writing, Agnes Beaumont is presented as a female character whose actions are seen to threaten the precarious balance of patriarchal power relations within which Bunyan's position of authority and her position of subjection are constructed. Claiming the position of writer, she presents a text which both exposes the tensions and contradictions within such power relations and stands as a contra-diction, a woman's text which tests the limits of textual and discursive strategies of exclusion. By the end of the text both fathers have been effectively silenced; it is the daughter's, the woman's turn.

The text generally conforms to the model of nonconformist spiritual narrative and is offered as evidence of the double action of God upon his subject: subjecting her to 'tryalls and temptations' whilst granting her 'his teaching and comfortable presence'.[97] On the first page God is thus presented as having 'often given me cause to say it was good for me that I have been afflicted'.[98] But the narrative invites conflicting interpretations of the cause of her character's suffering. Although divine judgement is offered as paramount and human interpretation offered as flawed, the text both includes alternative readings of events and their significance, as in the dream of the apple tree, and invites the reader to make judgements about her situation on the basis of her textual evidence, as the coroner does at the inquest. As Agnes Beaumont, the character, requested that her father's body be 'opened' to reveal the cause of death, so Agnes Beaumont, the writer, presents a version of her self which the reader is invited to examine. The narrative ends with an account of Beaumont's triumphant self-display in the market as she deliberately shows herself in public to those who had spread rumours that 'now I had Confest that I had poysoned my father, and yt I was quite distracted'.[99] The misreading of her condition, by those who confuse spiritual abjection or ecstasy with clinical distraction or abnormality, including her father and her neighbours, is countered by the presentation of textual evidence which both contradicts that reading and has contradictory effects. At the end of the text God the father ostensibly remains in place as source and guarantee of truth and meaning. The implicit connection between divinity and patriarchy has, however, been interrogated and Beaumont's text may be read as a contra-diction within a discursive framework which its author could not evade.

Beaumont's text was not published until 1760. The popularity of Beaumont's text in the eighteenth century may be partly because of its anticipation of fictional narrative models, but the text has also domesticated the spiritual. This may not in itself be seen as necessarily conservative in effect: texts such as Bunyan's *Grace Abounding* have been criticised by Felicity Nussbaum and others for stripping away the historical and material specificity of the stories they tell, allowing readers to view them as accounts of a universal spiritual condition which is separated from its political context.[100] Beaumont's text, with its combination of domestic detail and spiritual project, is certainly anchored within a world which is to be read not only for signs of divine meaning but for signs of personal and social struggle. The spiritual may have been domesticated but the domestic is revealed as thoroughly political.

The text was certainly employed to provide a good example for an eighteenth-century readership who would expect spiritual piety to be accompanied by a fair degree of social propriety. It was first printed in a collection of the writings of exemplary women, mostly the daughters of clergymen. Beaumont's concentration on the domestic details of her story and on the reality of her spiritual and material sufferings pushes the rumours about Bunyan, and the dangerous sexual instability and excess they connote, to the margins of the text, although paradoxically until recently reference to her own text has only been found in footnotes to Bunyan's writings. In an interesting addendum to one of the two manuscript versions of her narrative, reference is made to later rumours that on the journey to meeting with Bunyan, she had received a proposal of marriage which would have necessitated the murder of her father who would not have consented to such a match and that they had in fact married. The writer, supposedly but not certainly, Beaumont, refutes these rumours on the grounds that Bunyan was already married, but states that she 'could not but tell this news to several myself, and it did serve to divert me sometimes'.[101] Whether this is a genuine authorial addition or not, it signals the participation of this text in an ongoing process of constructing narratives to explain the relations between men and women within nonconformist communities which were struggling to cope with often incompatible drives towards salvation and respectability.

In editions and criticism of Bunyan's writings, Beaumont's narrative has been recuperated as a marginal note. In a move which perhaps suggests the recognition in her narrative of a trace of earlier, syntactically and culturally unruly female writing, the editor of one modern edition of her text, confronted with what he termed 'a reckless prodigality of commas', has corrected her 'hopeless' punctuation.[102] The insertion of a hyphen between contra and diction in this section may also be defined as an example of 'hopeless' punctuation, but as a reader of Agnes Beaumont's text and writer of this text, that is a definition which I would hope to contra-dict.

If the passage added to *Grace Abounding* does constitute Bunyan's reaction to the accusations levelled against him in this affair, the protestations of abhorrence towards women may be read not only as an extraordinary display of callousness towards a woman in whose troubles he had played an active, if spiritually and morally irreproachable, part, but also a certain anxiety about the disruptive potential of women in the interrelationships of male figures of authority which dominate Bunyan's formulation of the entry of the spiritual into the social or political domain. Agnes Beaumont's is one of the first names to be entered in the church records of the Bedford congregation in Bunyan's own hand in 1672, the year after he had been elected as minister.[103] The congregation, like many other dissenting religious groups, was composed of a majority of women, but these women, although addressed in *A Case of Conscience Resolved* as 'Sisters', were subsumed under the general title of 'brethren' and subject to the pastoral authority of male elders.

A group of entries in the Bedford Church Book in 1673, the year after Agnes Beaumont was admitted to the congregation, indicate Bunyan's direct involvement in the expulsion from the Church of a female member accused of 'railing'. The entries are in Bunyan's handwriting, recording that 'an accusation was brought against our sister Witt, otherwise Worrin, for railing', that at a congregation meeting 'it was also concluded that the sister to be dealt with should first be heard (because she pretends she can make her defence) at the next Church meeting' and ultimately the decision of that meeting is recorded:

> was cast out of the church the wife of Bro. Witt, for railling and other wicked practices. Concluded that som days be sett appart for humiliation with fasting and prayer to god because of som disorders amongst som in the Congregation specially for that som have runn into debt more than they can satisfie to the great dishoner of god and scandall of religion.[104]

Sister Witt, once known as Sister Worrin, who dared to raise her voice not only to rail but to present her own defence, is first denied autonomous status as a member of the congregation, being referred to now as 'wife of Bro. Witt', and then expelled from the congregation. Here textual strategies of exclusion, the subsuming of the woman under her husband's name and the omission of her defence, mirror the physical exclusion of the 'railing' woman from the congregation. The silencing of Sister Witt is, however, only partial, as her disruptive voice connects with that of other female figures which surround the figure of John Bunyan, figures which raise questions about the stability and status of his authoritative position.

Bunyan's position as minister was, it seems, already a fragile one before the accusation made against him of complicity in Beaumont's 'unnatural' crime, a crime whose structure bears much resemblance to the narratives of female crimes against the natural order such as that of Alice Arden which, as Catherine Belsey has argued, formed part of a contest for the meaning of marriage in a time of change.[105] Beaumont's supposed crime is not against her husband, but against her father. Her decision to reject the absolutist authority of her material father in preference for, and deference to, God as the ultimate patriarch is presented as a choice to adopt the figure of Bunyan as a mediation of divine and worldly authority. Her action threatens to explode the delicate framework of negotiations between divinely ordained and discursively produced meanings by which Bunyan's position is maintained. The meaning of pastoral relations, apparently purged of physical or sexual implications in a Christian discourse which privileges spiritual relations to God over material relations with family members, husbands and wives can, it seems, be all too easily misinterpreted. The relationship between a minister and a female member of his congregation may, when it threatens the existing order of social relations by encouraging that woman to neglect her filial duties, be interpreted as a sexual relationship in which the minister seduces her away from her father's control.

This implied definition of the minister as seducer is neatly inverted in one strand of Bunyan's writings on women which locate them as the seducers, relying on a conventional figuration of Eve as the first transgressor who seduced her husband into sin.[106] The vehemence of Bunyan's rebuttal of charges of womanising in Grace Abounding and the insistence that contact with women of any kind is abhorrent to him, can thus be read not as an example of rabid personal misogyny but as a means of defending an embattled position of authority by relocating the threat to social and spiritual harmony, identifying it not within relations of difference but within a different group whose transgressive and inferior status is enshrined in the Word.

The section in which Bunyan effects this transfer was published three years before A Case of Conscience Resolved. The phrase 'Their Com-

pany alone, I cannot away with' which stood as the culmination of
Bunyan's denunciation of women in the earlier text has a different
resonance when read in the context of the claims to a voice in church
affairs implicit in the separate meetings which occasioned the publication of the later text. In the later text Bunyan does indeed reject the
concept of '[t]heir Company alone', of women arranging and controlling their own acts of worship, but whilst he attempts to deny the
female voice a position within the public utterance of God's truth, he
cannot evade the effects of women's increasing vociferousness in nonconformist Christianity. As a minister he might succeed in expelling
from his congregation railing women such as Sister Witt, but, as an
evangelical author whose attempts to stir up the consciences of individual sinners as a prerequisite of salvation demanded an individual
address, Bunyan was forced to address issues of gendered difference in
the representation of women demanded by the technique of individual
address. *A Case of Conscience Resolved* ends with a double-edged
conclusion, which both asserts the author's position as a judge and
suggests that the issue has yet to be resolved: 'I have done, after I have
said, that there are some other things, concerning Women, touching
which, when I have an Opportunity, I may also give my Judgment. But
at present, I intreat that these lines be taken in good part, for I seek
Edification, not Contention.'[107]

An examination of the 25 other treatises and sermons, published
after *A Case of Conscience Resolved*, reveals no such engagement with
questions of women's involvement in religious affairs, nor with issues of
gender. Within the framework of his pastoral ministry, Bunyan continued to defend his position of authority against various challenges, from
rival ministers, disruptive church members and outside agencies, and to
publish treatises which attempted to differentiate between his position,
theologically and politically, and those which threatened his authority.
However, the drive to enlist reading subjects within a discourse of
salvation, evident in the texts which adopt the 'fictional' model of *The
Pilgrim's Progress, Part One*, both necessitates an engagement with
issues of cultural difference, including gendered difference, and exposes
the author to a different set of challenges to his author-itative position,
challenges which may be read as effects of writing. Although *The Holy
War*, an allegory of the battle between good and evil for, and within, the
human soul, affords no active roles for women, all the 'literary' texts
from 1680 on, which have a social setting, may be read as engaging in
the problematic questions of relationships between gendered subjects
and between human subjects and their divine author. In doing so, the
texts necessarily problematise their own definitions of the meanings
ascribed to women and raise the possibility of different readings by

different reading subjects. Just as Elizabeth Bunyan's confident confrontation with the appeal judges, suppressed during Bunyan's lifetime, returned after the death of the author to stand as a challenge to his prohibition on such actions, so the female characters of Bunyan's later works may be read as disrupting to varying degrees the discursive framework in which they are contained.

# CHAPTER FOUR

# The limits of authority: Bunyan's other readers

## I  Framing the author

On Tuesday 19 November 1991 Terry Waite, released from 1,763 days of captivity in Beirut, addressed journalists at RAF Lyneham in Wiltshire. After thanking a variety of different organisations for their support during his years as a hostage of the Islamic Hizbollah, he told a story about an occurrence during his captivity:

> I'll tell you a small story which I told in Damascus. I was kept in total and complete isolation for four years. I saw no one and spoke to no one apart from a cursory word with my guards when they brought me food.
>
> And one day out of the blue a guard came with a postcard. It was a postcard showing a stained glass window from Bedford showing John Bunyan in jail.
>
> And I looked at that card and I thought, 'My word Bunyan you're a lucky fellow. You've got a window out of which you can look, see the sky and here am I in a dark room. You've got pen and ink, you can write but here am I, I've got nothing and you've got your own clothes and a table and a chair.'[1]

The postcard which Terry Waite had received was reproduced on the front pages of many newspapers the next day, described on one tabloid front page as 'the image that helped save him'.[2] *The Independent* printed the text of Waite's speech at RAF Lyneham in full with an abridged version of the section on the postcard in enlarged type as a header and a quarter-page reproduction of the postcard.

Waite's anecdotal association of his situation with that of Bunyan as Christian prisoner/author clearly offered the British media a narrative and an image which could be seen to appeal to different readerships. The association of Terry Waite, Special Envoy of the Archbishop of Canterbury and Western hostage of Islamic fundamentalists, with John Bunyan, a Christian whose writings appeared to allow him to transcend his status as a prisoner, invites the reader to make a number of comparisons. A connection has been made between two Christian Englishmen, across the boundaries of time and culture. Waite, isolated in an alien culture and deprived of social interaction, apart from 'a cursory word with [his] guards', has received a communication from his home culture which reinforces his link not only with that culture in the late twentieth century but with a Christian tradition of suffering located in a distant, yet familiar, past. Waite himself suggests that he viewed Bunyan's position as a prisoner as less restrictive than his own. Although his tone in the delivery of the speech and the use of the familiar address to Bunyan in the speech and transcript seek to avoid any concomitant self-aggrandisement, it is clear that the sequence of comparisons between Bunyan's apparently 'soft' prison regime and the strictures of Waite's captivity enables Waite both to emphasise his own sufferings and to claim a position in a line of Christian prisoners of note.

The postcard had been sent to Waite by a stranger, who is not named in his address, and bore the following message: 'We remember, we shall not forget. We shall continue to pray for you and to work for all people who are detained around the world.'[3] Waite connects this message with the work of agencies such as Amnesty International whose work his speech endorses, together with that of the BBC World Service. The move which links Amnesty International with the World Service is significant. In the context of an acknowledgement of indebtedness to two different organisations whose activities lessened the sense of isolation of the Western hostages, this double vote of thanks seems understandable. Amnesty International promotes itself as a non-partisan, international organisation which campaigns for prisoners of conscience and condemns the persecution of political prisoners by regimes in East and West. The fact that Waite was taken hostage whilst attempting to secure the release of other hostages by negotiating with a number of Islamic groups, may be seen to identify him with the aims and values of Amnesty International in a double sense. As a hostage, he is presented as the object of its campaigning activities, whilst his own campaign is seen to mirror that of the organisation.

The BBC World Service connects English speakers or listeners in non-English-speaking cultures with the source and origin of English and Englishness. In Waite's address emphasis is placed on the work of the religious department, thus reinforcing the connection between Englishness and Christian spirituality. The World Service does not exist only, however, to provide a home from home along the air waves. Waite's speech ends with a condemnation of hostage-taking which, as *The Independent* coverage states, caused the Union Jacks waved by the crowd to drop, 'as Mr Waite must have wanted': 'It is wrong to hold people in such a way. It is self-defeating and those who do it fall well below civilised standards of behaviour, no matter who they are, no matter what nationality or what organisation they belong to.'[4]

The political dimension of Waite's captivity is here both effaced and revealed. The political and religious aims of the Hizbollah are seen as no excuse for their 'uncivilised' behaviour and Waite's own intervention in the political affairs of another culture as a representative of a Western Christian organisation is not mentioned. The Islamic captors are denied the rationale of political strategy and the Christian captive is presented as a passive victim of their actions. In the days following Waite's release, the initial euphoria surrounding the return of the most famous of the hostages (Waite was the only hostage who had been a well-known, politically active figure before his capture) was accompanied by a growing disquiet about his activities in the Lebanon. Suggestions were made that Waite had been co-operating with the CIA in their efforts to secure the release of hostages, that he had met Colonel Oliver North, the discredited US 'Arms for Hostages' dealer, and that, wittingly or unwittingly, he had been engaged in activity whose political dimensions appeared to tally with accusations made by Hizbollah at the time of his capture. Whilst these accusations have not been substantiated, and Waite has consistently presented himself as, in this particular context, an unknowing subject, their existence casts a new light on Waite's Lyneham address and on his use of the image and figure of Bunyan in that address.

Whereas the Union Jack flags waved by onlookers at RAF Lyneham may have signalled Waite's national and political position in a manner which threatened to disrupt the apparently transcultural and non-political framework of his message, the figure of Bunyan may have offered a more subtle emblem of the triumph over oppression. In the implied connection between Bunyan and Waite, the spirit of one individual human being, physically locked up in seventeenth-century England, is seen to transcend the constraints on, and of, the body, space and time, to communicate with that of Waite. This spiritual connection of individual human subjects, across the barriers of time and space, mirrors that assumed by traditional literary criticism in which texts act as conduits for the transmission of thought from the mind of the author to that of the reader. In the case of Bunyan and Waite, the author, Bunyan, is presented as addressing the condition of the reader, Waite, not by means of a written text, but by means of a pictorial representation on a postcard. The image on the postcard purports to represent the author and operates as a link in a double chain of communication, between addressor and addressee, the anonymous sender and Waite, the recipient, and between the represented author, Bunyan, and the reader, Waite. The imaginary nature of the transparency of representation is, ironically, signalled by the fact that the representation of Bunyan reproduced on the postcard is literally transparent. The postcard shows a stained-glass window in the Bunyan Meeting Free Church in Bedford but, just as the materiality of writing necessarily abolishes the possibility of direct communication between minds, so the materiality of the card itself makes the transparent image opaque.

As a text, the postcard invites different readings. The image of Bunyan on the postcard is, of course, a representation of a representation. The postcard re-presents a twentieth-century representation of a scene from the seventeenth century. The stained-glass window depicted on the postcard was commissioned in 1978 and bears the inscription, 'In commemoration of the tercentenary of the publication of The Pilgrim's Progress on the 18th February 1678'. The commemoration of the publication of a text apparently takes the form here of a depiction of its author. The figure of Bunyan is depicted in the foreground of the window, at a table, quill in hand, gazing into the middle distance. On the table are quills, ink, paper and a candle, the material means of writing. Behind him is a barred window or grill, through which the viewer can see what appears to be another window which frames a small cluster of buildings in the foreground and a stylized building surmounted by a shining star, above a wall with a gateway, at the apex of a pathway which leads from the figure of Bunyan. The tops of both of these inner windows are masked by a band of symbols and words which forms the inner frame of the stained-glass window. This frame presents a version of the first sentence of The Pilgrim's Progress, which surrounds the image of the imprisoned author, whose features closely resemble those of seventeenth-century portraits of Bunyan.

The use of perspective thus draws the eye of the viewer from the figure of Bunyan, through the two inner windows, to the shining star, whose rays shine back towards the figure in the foreground, apparently providing the illumination for the author, literally as well as metaphorically, as the candle is not burning, and for the viewer in front of the window. If the stained-glass window were to be viewed *in situ*, the illumination would literally come from behind the image, as sunlight would occupy the place of the shining star. The figure of the author and the viewer are thus held together in a path of light from star to eye, in a process of double illumination. The light falls upon the author, deep in thought, as if awaiting illumination, and illuminates the scene of writing for the viewer, allowing the writing figure to be seen clearly, poised forever just at the moment of putting quill to paper. The writing implements are slightly shadowed, the quill is poised just above the paper, but no words are visible on the paper. In this scene of writing, writing is always about to, but can never, begin. It has, of course, as ever, already begun.

The writing of The Pilgrim's Progress literally frames the image of its writer here, with the opening words of the text forming a scroll around the scene of the prison cell: 'As I walked through the wilderness of this world, I lighted on a certain place, where there was a den; and I laid me down in that place to sleep: and as I slept I dreamed a dream.' These are not, however, the opening words printed in the first edition, or in subsequent scholarly editions. The standard text reads 'where was a den', not, as here, 'where there was a den'. The insertion of the word 'there' brings the quotation into line with modern English sentence construction and thus effaces the textual difference of the original, and the historical difference it suggests. In this way the 'meaning' of the text is made clear to the modern reader/viewer of the window, by means of a textual addition. The text which surrounds the image of the author is not, then, written by that author. This text must have an author or authors, but he, she or they are absent. This text is a twentieth-century construct, produced for a twentieth-century reader. What then is the status of the author reproduced in this window-text, framed as he is by this supplementary text, this simulated 'quotation'?

The written text, although standing as the ostensible occasion for this celebratory text, is placed at the margin, at the edge of the gaze of the viewer. A viewer who recognises the significance of the marginal, as any reader of Bunyan's extensive marginalia, must do, may, however, question this apparent marginalisation of writing. The eye that travels to the frame of the window and returns to the central image may read differently. The framing text may operate as an explaining gloss, reinforcing the pictorial representation of the figure of Bunyan, but it also alters the significance of various aspects of that representation. The stylized edifice surmounted by the shining light may be read as the Celestial City, Christian's final destination in The Pilgrim's Progress, and the path which leads from the figure of Bunyan to that point may be read as the path to salvation in the text. In this reading, might not the author too be read as an effect of the text?

The window reproduced on the postcard is one of five in the sanctuary of the Bedford church. The other four windows all depict scenes from The Pilgrim's Progress. Although the first, installed in 1927, presents Christian as a stylized figure in armour, the rest portray the text's protagonist as closely resembling the conventional image of Bunyan. The life and death of writer and character are conflated, culminating in the most recent window, a representation of Christian crossing the River of Death to the Celestial City, which commemorates Bunyan's death. This collection of window-texts situates author and character within a specific context. They are literally fixed in the material location of the church and held in place in a double frame of reference in which figures from text and church history are superimposed upon each other.[5] The figure of the author which dominates this window and is presented as the focus of the viewer's gaze is a character in a text, assembled, like the chair he sits on, from fragments of glass. This author is an illusion, a trick of the light. Like the holographic image of Shakespeare employed as a symbol of authenticity and security device on credit cards, however, this illusory figure has material effects.

The image of the inspired and inspiring author, presented in the postcard-text, could be employed by Terry Waite to underpin his narrative of Christian suffering and forbearance. The version of John Bunyan presented on the postcard is apparently very much like the version of Terry Waite presented in Waite's account of his experiences. Bunyan sits in a prison cell, the recipient of divine inspiration, poised to make his own contribution to the illumination of the world, spiritually and artistically; Waite sat in a prison cell, receiving comfort from anonymous well-wishers and the World Service, and awaiting his moment to call for 'justice and peace' for captors and captives alike. The conjunction of the opening words of *The Pilgrim's Progress* with the image of the inspired author invokes the conventional interpretation of the dreamer in the den as Bunyan the prisoner. The confinement of the figure of Bunyan is signalled only by the two windows, and the barred effect these create. No reference, visual or verbal, is made to the political dimensions of the author's activities or imprisonment. His imprisonment is signalled as symbolic, serving, perhaps, to signal the capacity of the human spirit to transcend material constraints on the body.

It is, however, the material conditions represented in the postcard which Waite, as a prisoner, initially focuses on as being different from his own. The process of identification between the imprisoned reader and the imprisoned author thus involves a recognition not only of similarity, but of difference. The postcard sent as a message of support, described by the BBC as a message which 'inspired' Waite and 'kept his hope alive', served ironically to emphasise the greater strictures of his own situation.[6] In Waite's narrative of his receipt of the postcard, he addresses the figure of Bunyan directly, as if present. Temporal and spatial distances are collapsed, but the difference between the speaking Waite and the 'listening' Bunyan is the subject of the communication: 'my word Bunyan you're a lucky fellow'. Waite's reading of the text, and the subsequent rereadings of his reading in the British media, thus testify both to the powerful effects of identification in reading, but also to the intrusion of difference even in an apparently single reading by an individual subject.

## II  Bunyan's Progress

In his preface to the collected works of Bunyan, published in 1853, George Offor presents an image of Bunyan as the great Christian author who transcended the constraints of imprisonment and persecution, by means of the written word, to reach an international audience and to attain a pre-eminent position in British literature's hall of fame:

> Limited in preaching to the few who were within the sound of his voice, and knowing that poisonous errors had extended throughout the kingdom, he sought the all-powerful aid of the press, and published several searching treatises before his imprisonment. Soon after this, he was called to suffer persecution as a Christian confessor, and then his voice was limited to the walls of his prison, excepting when by the singular favour of his jailers, he was permitted to make stolen visits to his fellow Christians. From the den in this jail issued works which have embalmed his memory in the richest fragrance in the churches of Christ, not only in his native land, but nearly all the kingdoms of the world.[7]

Here, as in the window, prison cell and 'den' are conflated, and the spirit of the author is assumed to be transmitted to other cultures by his writings as it would be again by the postcard to Terry Waite. If Bunyan's 'memory' is seen to be 'embalmed' in the 'richest fragrance' of Christian churches of 'nearly all the kingdoms of the world', his 'name' is clearly identified as British: 'Bunyan's name is now as much identified with British literature as that of Milton or of Shakespeare.'[8] Although Queen Victoria's possession of copies of Bunyan's writings is cited as proof of Bunyan's status as a great British author, it is the inroads made by his texts into other nations and cultures which are seen to guarantee his status as 'the prose poet of all time':

> Well may it be said of him:– Simple, enchanting man! what does not the world owe to thee and to the great Being who could produce such as thee? Teacher alike of the infant and the aged; who canst direct the first thought and remove the last doubt of man; property alike of the peasant and the prince; welcomed by the ignorant and honoured by the wise; thou hast translated Christianity into a new language, and that a universal one! Thou art the prose poet of all time![9]

Bunyan's 'translation' of Christianity into a 'universal' language did, however, itself require translation in order to reach the 'multitudes' in 'other lands and other languages' who, according to Offor, 'feel the sanctifying and happy effects of reading these works, and imbibing their peaceful spirit'.[10] As Offor notes of The Pilgrim's Progress, 'The Caffarian and Hottentot, the enlightened Greek and Hindoo, the remnant of the

Hebrew race, the savage Malay and the voluptuous Chinese – all have the wondrous narrative in their own language.'[11]

Bunyan's 'universal', 'wondrous' text is presented by Offor as a gift to diverse races, characterised in different ways, as 'enlightened', 'savage' or 'voluptuous' recipients of divine truth translated into their own languages. Bunyan's original literary and spiritual gift, his 'native genius', which enabled him to transcend the constraints of his own social position and persecution, is seen in 'beautiful and striking passages' of his writings, which 'scintillate and sparkle like well-set diamonds'.[12] These textual gems, reflecting their author's singular brilliance, are, in turn, part of a process of spiritual and cultural enlightenment. Different readers, in different cultures, have been, and are to be, exposed to the spiritual enlightenment afforded by contact with the voice of Christian truth, made available in translations of Bunyan's texts. The analogy between Bunyan's 'striking passages' and 'well-set diamonds' has a particular relevance in this context. Whilst these passages are described as 'none borrowed', but flowing 'from his native genius', diamonds were not native to Britain in either the seventeenth or nineteenth centuries.[13] Diamonds were *mined* in other countries and their acquisition formed part of the commercial impetus of British imperialism. The imagery of 'precious stones; recalls that employed in the original preface to *The Pilgrim's Progress* in which Bunyan likens the truth within his fable to gold and pearl and emphasises the power to illuminate of 'Truths golden Beams'.[14] A textual link is thus formed between the author and his critic, yet in the changed context of the nineteenth century, the imagery of diamonds may have a different resonance. It is, perhaps, appropriate that in order to describe the native genius of this great British author, whose texts are presented as offering enlightenment to the ignorant, the savage and the voluptuous, Offor employs an analogy which exposes a different aspect of British interaction with other cultures.

The reference to diamonds, rather than to the 'golden beams' of divine truth of Bunyan's preface, is unsettling in a second sense. Diamonds, which are multifaceted, do not simply reflect but refract light, producing a plurality of rays which masks the source of the light. Similarly, perhaps, writing denies the possibility of access to its origin in any stable or singular form. The texts presented to different national groups, 'in their own language', stand at a double remove from their imaginary point of origin, whatever form that origin may take: individual subject, divinely inspired author, great Briton, or God himself. These are different texts in which the true meaning of the 'wondrous narrative' is open to question. The quintessential Britishness, or, more properly, Englishness of this version of the author can be seen as a product of the combined missionary and imperial endeavours of nineteenth-century Britain. The cultural difference and diversity of the contexts in which Bunyan's most famous text was being circulated and read serves to reinforce both its, and his, reputation as essentially English.

In 1928, the critic Augustine Birrell described Bunyan as 'a plain Englishman to the core, and as good an Imperialist as it is possible for any Christian man to be' and The Pilgrim's Progress as a 'link of Empire'.[15] This assertion of the involvement of the figure of the author and of his most famous text in British imperialism is supported by evidence of the publication of The Pilgrim's Progress throughout the nineteenth and early twentieth centuries. An examination of editions of the text, listed in Books in Print and The National Union Catalog, reveals a massive increase in the variety of languages into which it was translated, and therefore of cultures in which it was employed, from the early nineteenth century onwards. The survey which follows is only a guide to the types of editions published during certain periods. It does not attempt to list all the different editions published in each language or dialect, nor does it distinguish between editions of either part of The Pilgrim's Progress and of both volumes printed together. Many of the nineteenth- and twentieth-century translations were published in a number of successive editions, but it is beyond the scope of this study to produce an exhaustive record of all extant material. I have therefore decided to list the various languages and dialects into which some or all of The Pilgrim's Progress was translated in each period, together, where possible, with the first recorded publication date.

Records of seventeenth-century editions list translations into Dutch, French, German and Welsh. In the eighteenth-century editions are listed in Danish, Dutch, French, German, Spanish, Swedish, and Welsh, together with a dual-language version in English and Tamil, published in 1793. Between 1800 and 1850, the following editions were published: Chuana (1848), Esthonian (1842), Modern Greek (1824), Irish, Rarotongan (1846), Tahitian (1847), English and Tamil (1826), Czech (1815), Gaelic (1815), Hawaiian (1842), Arabic (1834), Hebrew (1844), Samoan (1846). Between 1850 and 1900 editions were published in the following languages or dialects: Aneityumese (1880), Benga (1886), Bulgarian (1866), Chuana (1894), Cree (1886), Czech (1864), Dakota (1857), Dual(l)a (1885), Dutch, Dyak (1879), Efik (1868), Esthonian (1859), Fanti (1886), Fijian (1867), Finnish (1880), French, Gaelic, Greek, Hungarian (1867), Icelandic (1865), Italian, Khasi (1870), Manganga (1894), Maori (1854), Marathi (1853), Norwegian (1892), Nyunja (1894), Portuguese (1862), Rarotongan (1892), Romanian (1890), Serbo-Croat (1879), Sgau Karen (1863), Spanish, Swedish, Tongan (1884), Urdu (1853), Xosa (1889), Yoruba (1866). The following translations are listed for the period 1900 to 1956: Bambatana (1950), Basa (1933), Bulu (1917), Cheyenne (1904), Chuana (1901), Congo (1901), Dyuer (1926), Efik (1907), Eskimo (1901), Esperanto (1907?), Ewe (1955), Finnish (19??), Friesian (1953), Ganda (1927), Ibo (1932), Kafir/Banhu (1929), Kele (19??), Luo (1926), Malay (1905), Manx (1901), Mbundu of Benguella (1904), Motu (1951), Nyunja (1902), Portuguese and Umbundu (1945), Samoan (1924), Sgau Karen (1922), Slovakian (1922), Tabele (1902), Teso (1956), Thonga (1916), Turkish (1905), Twi (1949), Ukranian (1910), Xosa (1902).[16]

Many of the editions published in the nineteenth and twentieth centuries were produced by mission presses and Christian publishers, such as the Society for Promoting Christian Knowledge, the Religious Tract Society and the London Missionary Society. The date of the publication of editions of *The Pilgrim's Progress* in particular languages can in many cases be seen to fall within a period of economic or cultural imperialist activity by English-speaking nations within specific regions. The publication of numerous editions in a variety of African languages in the mid-nineteenth to early twentieth centuries by British missionary presses parallels British imperial expansion in that region, whilst the translation of the text into Cree, Dakota and Cheyenne by American publishers coincides with the United States government's attempts to control and Westernise the various Native American nations.[17] These texts can thus be seen as functioning within imperialist and colonialist frameworks, as material to be employed to enlist and control non-Western, non-Christian subjects. They are produced to promote certain values, succinctly defined by the missionary and explorer, David Livingstone, as 'Christianity, Commerce, and Civilisation'.[18]

Livingstone's letters to members of his family, including his father-in-law, Robert Moffat, a fellow missionary, reveal much about missionary conversion techniques and about the role of translated texts in the conversion process. Livingstone worked as a missionary in Africa from 1840 to 1856, acting as a missionary teacher, connected to the London Missionary Society, and pursuing his own scientific and geographical interests. Whilst it is as an explorer, as the man who 'discovered' the Victoria Falls, that Livingstone is chiefly renowned in the popular history of British colonial expansion, his 'mission' was primarily evangelical. The letters offer a wealth of material for a study of the interrelationship between religious and economic imperial drives in general, apparently supporting the notion of a crusade to civilise and save non-Western, non-Christian subjects, whilst acknowledging, sometimes with astonishing directness, the economic need for British expansion into other regions. A response to his parents' proposed emigration from Scotland to America in 1850 makes explicit the interweaving of spiritual, economic and imperialist drives in colonialist discourse:

> You are fulfilling the prophecy which in a few years hence will probably be realised much more plainly. Many shall run to & fro, & knowledge shall be increased. Emigration must take place from England sooner or later by millions. The subject will probably be the question of the day. If the immense capital which can scarcely find means of investment once takes the turn of promoting emigration, the world will teem with the Anglo-Saxon race. Capitalists are not likely to find a more certain return for the prodious [sic] sums of money they now sink in railways than in the emigration schemes now being formed. If He in whose hand are the silver & the gold only turns the tide that way, the enlightenment of the world will not be the work of missionaries; nor is it so very distant as a poor fellow like myself, enveloped in the thick darkness of heathenism and seeing so little progress made, is sometimes despondingly to think.[19]

Here Christian and economic grounds for imperialist expansion and colonialist settlement are almost seamlessly united. Capital investment in emigration schemes will be profitable to the investor and contribute to a process of global enlightenment in the name of God, or, rather, 'He in whose hand are the silver & gold'. 'Immense capital' and divine authority seem to be interchangeable underwriters of this imperialist venture, in which profit takes many forms, material and spiritual. Edward Said has argued that profit alone could not sustain the Western imperialist project:

> In the expansion of the great Western empires, profit and hope of profit were obviously tremendously important, as the attractions of spices, sugar, slaves, rubber, cotton, opium, tin, gold, and silver over centuries amply testify. So also was inertia, the investment in already-going enterprises, tradition, and the market or institutional forces that kept the enterprise going. But there is more than that to imperialism and colonialism. There was a commitment to them over and above profit, a commitment in constant circulation and recirculation, which, on the one hand, allowed decent men and women to accept the notion that distant territories and their native peoples *should* be subjugated, and, on the other, replenished metropolitan energies so that these decent people could think of the *imperium* as a protracted, almost metaphysical obligation to rule subordinate, inferior, or less advanced peoples.[20]

In Livingstone's letter, written at the beginning of large-scale imperialist expansion into Africa in the nineteenth century, one type of metaphysical obligation is already explicit. The capitalist venture is also a Christian crusade, a crusade for souls. Capital investment in such projects may result in a double profit through the process of conversion.

The note of despair at the end of Livingstone's letter appears to connect with a story of initial success and eventual failure in one specific conversion attempt which other letters reveal in episodic form. Livingstone spent the first eight and a half years of his mission in Africa in southern Bechuanaland [now Botswana] and was able to claim only one convert to Christianity, albeit a notable one. Sechele was chief of the main section of the BaKwana from 1831 to 1892 and is the subject of much of Livingstone's correspondence, as a primary object of his missionary endeavours. The narrative of Sechele's conversion to Christianity is a narrative of 'enlightenment'. Sechele first learns to read his own language, using spelling guides produced by the mission press. He starts in 1845 by acquiring 'a perfect knowledge of the alphabet in two days', progresses to 'reading or rather spelling words of two syllables' and, by 1847, is described as 'a sensible man' who 'reads pretty well, is fond of his Testament, and has an intense desire for everything connected with civilisation'.[21] Sechele was however not as yet converted and a letter to Robert Moffat in September 1847 suggests that his reluctance stems from the discrepancy between BaKwana social customs and those inscribed in Christian teaching. Sechele was a polygamist and could not be baptised until he disposed of what Livingstone terms his 'superfluous wives'.[22] Letters between 1847 and 1848 suggest that Sechele's 'education' was now one of Livingstone's priorities and that lessons in reading his own language were to be combined with an introduction to the English language.

On 19 January 1849 Livingstone wrote to his sister, Janet, with good news. Sechele had applied for baptism and had been received into the church. The triumph for Livingstone is, it seems, also a testament to his father-in-law's endeavours as a translator: 'The Pilgrim's Progress has been translated, & is much admired by the converts. Some parts of the Pilgrim's experience and his are exactly alike, and makes him extol the wisdom of Johane Bunyana.'[23] The edition referred to is Robert Moffat's translation into Sitchuana or Chuana, entitled *Loeto loa Mokareseti ...* or 'Journey of a Christian ... ', published by the Mission Press at Kuruman in 1848. Livingstone later corresponds with Moffat about this translation, commending his success in 'expressing the meaning', but suggesting some revisions to specific words which Moffat has chosen in Kuruman dialect and which therefore have a different meaning, or no detectable meaning at all, in the Sequain region in which Livingstone operates.[24] The translated text is thus perceived as a valuable aid in the conversion process, as Sechele's apparent identification with the Pilgrim's experience suggests. The fact, however, that some parts of the translation are incomprehensible sounds a warning note, as regional linguistic differences, overlooked by the British translator, change or render nonsensical the intended meaning of individual elements of the text and of its overall message of salvation and civilisation.

Sechele's decision to convert, and his subsequent rejection of his 'superfluous wives', is described as arousing 'much excitement & opposition', in part because these women were the 'daughters of influential people'.[25] Livingstone presents Sechele as battling against the 'opposition' and 'hatred to the gospel' of his people, who 'curse Sechele very bitterly'.[26] He stresses their civility towards him, yet acknowledges that 'some woman or other wished the lion which bit me here were to finish me'.[27] The attempt to present Sechele as an embattled, newly converted soul, resisting the pressure to betray his faith by submitting to social or cultural forces, echoes both Christian's rejection of social and familial ties in *The Pilgrim's Progress*, and Livingstone's presentation of himself as a lone Christian 'in the thick darkness of heathenism'.[28] White missionary and black convert are, for a moment, united in a narrative which can only efface their difference from one another by defining both against ignorant, heathen others, who are presented as nameless natives. It is, however, a brief moment and the transcendence of cultural difference it implies is imaginary.

Four months after Livingstone announced Sechele's conversion, his renunciation of polygamy, and the part played in this by *The Pilgrim's Progress*, he informed Robert Moffat of Sechele's confession that he had continued to have sexual relations with one of the 'superfluous wives', who had become pregnant. Livingstone, implicitly acknowledging, albeit belatedly, the force of cultural construction, attributes this lapse to Sechele's being 'so accustomed to their customs, it was like his ordinary food'.[29] Despite protestations of contrition, Sechele is suspended from communion and finally expelled from the fellowship in May 1849.[30] In the same letter where Livingstone reports this event, he announces his conviction that 'if another station were in existence on which to spend a part of the year, it might tend to the furtherance of the gospel', and makes his suggestions for revisions to Moffat's translation of *The Pilgrim's Progress*.[31] It is tempting to connect this section of the letter with the failure to enlist Sechele successfully within the parallel discourses of Christianity and civilisation; blame for this failure cannot be attached to the Holy Spirit, but errors in translation can be seen as obstructing the transmission of divine truth or authorial wisdom. Soon after writing this letter, Livingstone left Bechuanaland, denouncing the BaKwana as 'truly *slow* of heart to believe'.[32] His return visits to the BaKwana were brief and infrequent. His remaining years in Africa were spent in missions to other regions in the north-west and in making the journeys across the continent for which he was hailed on his return to England, in 1856, as the greatest of African 'explorers'. Sechele continued to rule the BaKwani until his death in 1892 and the few references to him in Livingstone's correspondence suggest that he never returned to the Christian fold.[33]

Bunyan's 'wondrous narrative' and 'universal language', to employ Offor's terms, clearly had limitations as a means of enlisting at least one colonial subject. *The Pilgrim's Progress* may be translated into a different language, its author may be translated into 'Johane Bunyana', but the translator has no more control over the meanings construed by the nineteenth-century colonial reader, than Bunyan has over the readings by seventeenth-century Western readers.

Other stories have been written about the Pilgrim's unstable progress into different cultures as an evangelical text, the most momentous of which is told by Christopher Hill:

> In the 1850s and early 1860s the Taiping rebels came very near to conquering the whole of China; nearer than any other nineteenth-century rebellion. They drew in hundreds of millions of people. The Taiping were a radical Christian sect, who strongly emphasised hymn-singing, and made the Ten Commandments their basic disciplinary code. Their leader, Hong Xiuquan, called his capital (Nanjing) the New Jerusalem. His two favourite books were the Bible and *The Pilgrim's Progress*. If the Taiping had won, Bunyan's allegory might have become China's earlier little red book.[34]

The Taiping rebellion was crushed in 1864, as a result, at least in part, of the intervention by England and France. Initially reluctant to oppose a Christian movement, the Western powers gradually perceived the threat to their economic interests posed by an increasingly anti-imperialist revolutionary group. To protect existing trade agreements, they supplied arms and expertise to the ruling dynasty. In an ironic twist to the already complex involvement of Bunyan's text in this crisis of imperialism, it seems that the leaders of both sides in the conflict may have been reading the same book. Hill has already recorded Hong Xiuquan's reading preferences. A glance at the journal of General Charles George Gordon, who led the British force against the Taiping rebels, before his more famous, and fatal, involvements in Africa, reveals that he too was a keen Bunyan reader. As Thomas Pakenham suggests in *The Scramble for Africa*, by 1876 Gordon was writing in the style, and using the characters, of *The Pilgrim's Progress* to discuss his own involvement in the tortuous North African campaign.[35]

As Hill notes, 'readers transform what they read' and mission press publishers were clearly unable to guarantee that readers would interpret the text in a way which supported Western cultural or economic interests.[36] The conventional conjunction of Christian and imperialist techniques of enlistment was evidently, and inevitably, unstable. Every attempt was made, however, to present the text in ways which would appeal to readers on the basis of their own cultural difference, whilst promoting Western values, as the example of a later edition in a Chinese dialect shows.

The 1870 translation of *The Pilgrim's Progress* into Canton vernacular by the Reverend G. Piercy of the Wesleyan Mission, was published 'with Chinese illustrations'[37] and in the 1880 *Intas va Natga u Kristian, par apan an pece Upene*, an abridged version of the original text was accompanied by a First Catechism and Hymn Book, but also a list of ordinal numbers and chart of sunset and sunrise times at Aneityum.[38] The attempts to transpose a Western Christian narrative of salvation to a non-Western, non-Christian setting clearly involved the addressing of targeted reader-subjects in terms with which they were familiar. If Christian is to stand as Everyman, his white, Western features must be overlaid with the printer's ink appropriate to each different culture. The inclusion of additional material, such as the chart of local sunset and sunrise times, suggests the plurality of techniques employed in the attempts to convert different cultures to the Western, Christian way, with narrative material offered alongside more obviously useful information, so enabling the missionary to assume the position of a doubly-knowing subject. Similarly, the inclusion of overtly pedagogical material would seem to indicate the ultimate intention to introduce the subjects interpellated by the translated narrative into the Western framework of knowledge veiled in the fiction.

In addition to the systematic production of versions of *The Pilgrim's Progress* for other cultures, this period also saw the adaptation of the text for specific groups within the domestic 'market'. Large format, illustrated editions, editions *'de luxe'* were produced for the chapel and the Christian home; phonetic and braille editions were produced to reach a newly active readership; most significantly perhaps, a wide range of editions specifically adapted for children were made available, including two different versions entitled, *The Pilgrim's Progress, in Words of one Syllable*.[39] Although the variety of types or groups of readers targeted during this period can be seen as the greatest at any point in the history of the publication of Bunyan's writings, there is evidence that at least some of these groups had already been targeted in earlier centuries.

From the late seventeenth century on, *The Pilgrim's Progress* had been published and circulated by a variety of religious and evangelical presses. Within a few years of its publication, numerous adaptations, pirate editions and 'copycat' texts had been published throughout Europe and the text continued to be a popular, if not universally critically approved, component of religious publishing strategies in the eighteenth century.[40] The most significant eighteenth-century edition was an abridged, and amended, version produced by John Wesley in 1743. This text, like Wesley's version of *The Holy War*, included in his 50-volume collection of religious writings, *A Christian Library*, was altered in order to modify Bunyan's Calvinist and predestinarian theology and to bring it into line with the more optimistic Methodist doctrine of perfection.[41] The publication and dissemination of Bunyan's writings, albeit in modified form, within Methodism, the most influential popular movement of religious dissent in the eighteenth century, kept the texts in circulation during a period when the author's reputation as a writer was threatened by the emphasis on refinement and good taste in mainstream literary and philosophical circles. Scathing, or patronising, criticism by Edmund Burke and David Hume, among others, which focused on the 'inferiority' of Bunyan's style, effectively located his writing as the poor relation of the refined, classical tradition.[42] *The Pilgrim's Progress*'s readership up to this point had extended beyond the limits of organised dissenting movements. As a reference in 1800 to *The Pilgrim's Progress* as 'companion of our childhood, till the refinements of modern education banished him from our nurseries' testifies the text had already been categorised, and subsequently challenged, as reading for children.[43]

The contrast between the text's, and Bunyan's, reputation in high and popular cultural contexts was dramatically lessened in the early and mid-nineteenth century as Romanticism's privileging of a rediscovered, or reconstructed, popular tradition of culture and experience created a climate in which text and author could be celebrated for the very features which embarrassed or disgusted an earlier literary élite. In addition to receiving the attention of Coleridge, who founded the Conventicle/Parnassus opposition which has influenced traditional literary critical work on Bunyan to the present day, the writer and his works were established as respectable, even eminent, literary objects or subjects through the production of a biography by the Poet Laureate, Robert Southey, in 1830.[44] The endorsement of author and text by famous figures throughout the nineteenth century undoubtedly enhanced its status as a suitable vehicle for the dissemination of a range of religious and cultural ideas, while its allegorical form allowed editors and publishers to sidestep some of the aspects of Bunyan's theology which were no longer compatible with contemporary religious and cultural frameworks.[45]

By the end of the nineteenth century *The Pilgrim's Progress* had been addressed to a far wider range of readers, at home and abroad, than those cited in the preface to *Part Two*. An examination of the effects of these attempts to enlist specific groups within the domestic market might well reveal different readings which parallel those of the colonial subjects in Africa and Asia, as the popularity of the text within radical political movements such as Chartism suggest.[46] It is my intention now, however, to examine the development of some of the techniques of enlistment in the seventeenth century.

## III   Prefaces to reading

Whilst the techniques and texts employed and circulated in the nineteenth century must be read within the specific historical and cultural conditions of the period, they bear a striking resemblance to aspects of Bunyan's own techniques of addressing his readers. There is little evidence in Bunyan's writings of any engagement with cultural difference in terms of race. Blackness and heathenism are consistently presented as inseparable; no subject position is made available for non-white readers. Readers are acknowledged to possess different national identities, but only within a European and North American context. In one respect, however, Bunyan's attempts to enlist different subjects may be seen to exceed those of the later translators and adaptors of his material. There is little evidence, for example, in the later period of any attempt to enlist women as a specific group, whereas at least two of the original texts, *The Pilgrim's Progress, Part Two* and *A Book for Boys and Girls*, clearly include an address to women as a separate readership. Gender is clearly, if problematically, acknowledged to be an important factor in the construction and positioning of reading subjects.

If Bunyan's writings can be read as a continuation of an oral ministry of the Word, as redemptive texts which are offered as supplements to the Logos, then the questions of which readers are addressed, the method of address and the positions made available to those readers in relation to the individual texts and to the discourse of salvation as a whole are clearly of paramount importance. N. H. Keeble, in *The Literary Culture of Nonconformity in Later Seventeenth-Century England*, places considerable emphasis on the explicitly purposive nature of texts such as Bunyan's:

> Nonconformist writing presupposed a reader. Its composition was not a private pursuit for personal ends (however personal its immediate occasion and inspiration may have been), but a public service, and, furthermore, a service whose full performance demanded not only diligence in writing but an equal diligence in transmitting the text to potential readers and in persuading them to acquire it, read it and act upon it. Nonconformist texts were very rarely thought of as having intrinsic merit; their virtue resided in their potential to transform lives.[47]

Whilst it is possible to argue that all writing presupposes a reader, be it only the writer, the continual stress in Bunyan's writings on their re-demptive status would seem to support Keeble's argument. The major-ity of treatises and tracts on theological matters are specifically addressed to the elect, either to Bunyan's own Bedford congregation or to the wider church of believers. However, even the first published work, *Some Gospel-truths Opened*, which is described on the title-page as 'Published for the good of Gods chosen ones', includes an address in the preface by John Burton to those who are merely 'covered over with an outside profession'.[48] The believing reader presupposed by the text is, it seems, already defined in contrast to another potential reader whose salvation cannot be guaranteed by correct interpretation of this text, ultimate salvation being dependent on the saving grace available only through the offices of the Holy Spirit.

*Grace Abounding*, published ten years after Bunyan's first writings, is similarly addressed to 'THOSE WHOM GOD HATH COUNTED HIM WORTHY TO BEGET TO FAITH, BY HIS MINISTRY IN THE WORD'.[49] The preface makes explicit the pastoral relationship between writer and readers, the latter addressed as 'Children' and 'My dear children' for whose spiritual welfare Bunyan's soul has 'fatherly care'. The text is offered as 'a drop of that honey, that I have taken out of the carcase of a lion (Judges xiv. 5–9). I have eaten thereof myself also, and am much refreshed thereby.'[50]

The relationship between author and readers as an attempted con-tinuation of that of minister and congregation is reinforced by reference to others who do not comprehend his message. Following the passage above, whose scriptural metaphor is often read as a veiled reference to Bunyan's conflict with the authorities, there is a short sentence which establishes a contrasting body of readers: '*The Philistians understand me not.*'[51]

Keeble's research into nonconformist prison writing has led to the assertion that letters and other texts operated to reaffirm the relation-ships between communities of believers, a practice which was extended by the nonconformist printing and publishing industry. He argues that the accompanying pressures of censorship and suppression of dissenting material necessitated the development of self-censorship and coded ref-erence to contentious matters, a point also made by Christopher Hill.[52] The term '*Philistians*' may be read as a reference to Bunyan's persecu-tors, whose failure to understand him, or his text, is but an extension of a greater failure to interpret the Word of God correctly.

Bunyan's intended readership here is, it seems, one which is defined by its relationship to another text. Bunyan's readers, it is assumed, already occupy a privileged position as attentive readers of the Word, competent to understand the scriptural metaphors and allusions which form the basis of the address. Yet just as knowledge of the Word, through diligent study of the Scriptures, is no guarantee of salvation without the operation of the Spirit in the individual soul, so the attempt of the human writer who seeks to reinforce the message of the Scriptures must, it seems, mirror the dual process of the operation of the Word. In the description of his struggle to discover his position within the discourse of salvation which forms the basis of this text, Bunyan refers to an early experience in which, having failed to receive assurance of salvation because he could not be counted as a member of the Israelites, 'the peculiar People of God', he listens to a sermon and finds himself 'thinking and believing that he made that Sermon on purpose to show me my evil-doing'.[53] Although the guilt induced by this experience does not last and Bunyan returns to 'sports and gaming', the effects of this perceived personal address do, as 'a voice did suddenly dart from Heaven into my Soul' in the middle of a 'game at Cat' to reinforce the impression of God's displeasure.[54] This passage reveals both the potential and the limitations of the technique of individual address.

No human ministry can operate as a substitute for divine grace, yet the awakening of the individual conscience as a prerequisite of salvation may, it seems, be prompted by human intervention. This potential, whatever its limitations, may be interpreted as one of the justifications for a significant difference between those texts addressed solely to an existing community of believers, or those which engaged in disputes with other theologians, and the body of texts which largely comprise what is traditionally held to be Bunyan's 'literary' work, namely both parts of *The Pilgrim's Progress, The Life and Death of Mr Badman, The Holy War* and the poetry, particularly *A Book for Boys and Girls*. The traditional distinction between the Bunyan of Conventicle and Parnassus, which assumes an opposition between theological and aesthetic impulses at work in Bunyan's writings, locates the differences between texts in a founding tension in the consciousness of the author. A more productive distinction may be made between texts on the basis of the readers addressed.

An analysis of the prefaces to the texts listed above reveals the extent to which these writings were directed at a readership greater in number than that of the treatises, yet one in which the subject positions offered are defined with increasing specificity. The preface to *The Pilgrim's Progress*, first published in 1678, may be read as an extensive justification of the allegorical mode in which it is written, by reference to scriptural precedent. As in the prefaces to earlier texts, the redemptive purpose is offered as paramount:

*This Book will make a Travailer of thee,*
*If by its Counsel thou wilt ruled be;*
*It will direct thee to the Holy Land,*
*If thou wilt its Directions understand:*
*Yea, it will make the sloathful, active be;*
*The Blind also, delightful things to see.*[55]

The explicit claim that this text will have a decisive effect on the reader, '*will make a Travailer of thee*', operates by an individual address which offers a range of potential positions for the reader together with suggested reasons why the text will appeal to, and benefit, such readers. Potential readers are not here defined in terms of gender, class or age, but rather in terms of their spiritual and mental states, such as the '*sloathful*' and '*the Blind*', addressed in the quotation above. The '*forgetful*' and '*Helpless*' will benefit from '*my fancies*' which will '*stick like Burs*', the '*listless*' will be affected by the '*Novelty*' of the '*Dialect*' in which the text is written.[56] This section is followed by a series of questions which mobilise yet contain the apparent paradoxes inherent in the status of the text as '*Truth within a Fable*' by appealing to the reader's desire for pleasure, diversion and '*picking-meat*', together with his or her desire for instruction and revelation.[57] The preface culminates in an appeal to the reader's supposed desire for a dual experience of escape from the self and self-knowledge which the text will offer:

*Wouldest thou loose thy self, and catch no harm*
*And find thy self again without a charm?*
*Would'st read thy self, and read thou know'st not what*
*And yet know whether thou art blest or not,*
*By reading the same lines? O then come hither,*
*And lay my Book, thy Head and Heart together.*[58]

Individual pleasure and spiritual instruction are thus constructed as legitimate aspects of the reading experience. Whilst scriptural precedent is cited in order to legitimate the choice of an allegorical method, it is the effects of the text on an individual subject which are offered as the ultimate 'profit' of the book. The reader is enlisted as an essential component of the active progress of the text which can only be complete when '*my Book, thy Head and Heart*' are combined in the process of attentive reading.

The popularity of *The Pilgrim's Progress* in the seventeenth century, if assessed in terms of the number of editions published, seems to have been considerable. Keeble estimates that the 22 editions printed in the seventeenth century would have represented over 30,000 copies, priced largely in the middle-range of 1s. or 1s. 6d.[59] Although such a figure exceeds that of other nonconformist texts, it can be located, as it is by Keeble, within a burgeoning market for nonconformist texts in which sales of a great variety of texts far outstripped any on what he terms 'the conformist side'. It is clearly difficult to ascertain the type of readership which this text attracted, but the preface to *The Pilgrim's Progress, Part Two* includes a defence of the first part which stresses the universal popularity of the text by reference to a list of disparate types of readers, who have been enlisted as subjects within the discourse of salvation.

First, the text's popularity in a range of different countries is proclaimed:

> My Pilgrims Book has travel'd Sea and Land,
> Yet could I never come to understand,
> That it was slighted, or turn'd out of Door
> By any Kingdom, were they Rich or Poor.[60]

France, Flanders, Holland, the Highlands, Ireland and New England are cited as areas in which the text is *'esteem'd a Friend, a Brother'*, counted *'worth more than Gold'*.[61] Reception of the text *'nearer home'* is described as equally favourable within very different cultural groups from *'Brave Galants'* and *'Young Ladys, and young Gentle-women'* to the *'very Children that do walk the street'*.[62]

Whereas the preface to the first part did not specify its projected readership in terms of gender, age, class or race, here these differences are carefully itemised yet held together in a description of a universal appreciation of a text whose 'profit' to individual readers is deemed to outweigh those differences. The text's universal message and *'pretty riddles in such wholsome strains'* have succeeded in converting or enlisting even those who initially resisted it:

> Yea, some who did not love him at the first,
> But cal'd him Fool, and Noddy, say they must
> Now they have seen & heard *him, him* commend,
> And to those whom they love, they do him send.[63]

The project of the first text, here referred to as male-gendered in a conflation of the pilgrim as character, Christian, and as text, is to be advanced by the second. The preface is addressed to the text itself, or rather herself, for here the new protagonist is Christiana, Christian's wife, and, as in references to the earlier text, the identity of the female addressee slips between character and text. The production of this text, defined as female in contrast with the original, male text, cannot be read as an acknowledgement of sexual difference in an obviously positive or radical sense. *'Sweet* Christiana' is always defined in terms of her relation to her husband and four sons, to her male protector, Great-Heart. Just as Christiana embarks on her pilgrimage later than her husband, so this 'female' text follows the lead of the male. It is, in effect, another supplement in the endless supplementation of Bunyan's writings, which seek to re-present an ultimately patriarchal truth. Its existence as a supplement serves, however, to unsettle the apparently secure position of the text it supplements.

It is significant that it is in the preface to this supplementary text that the range of cultural differences which threaten to obtrude in the process of communicating a transcendent and universal truth are acknowledged. Whilst the overall argument is that all subjects, whatever their differences, may be enlisted as 'pilgrims', engaged in the quest which leads eventually to the effacing of all difference in the absolute indifference of God, the method by which those subjects are to be enlisted is precisely by appealing to those differences. The description of the different subjects enlisted by the first text is followed by a passage in which this new text is urged to continue the process of enlistment by making a direct appeal to different groups. Thus the character of Mercy, Christiana's neighbour, is to be of particular importance to young women: '*Yea, let young Damsels learn of her to prize / The World which is to come, in any wise.*' Similarly, the character of '*old* Honest' may '*with some gray Head ... prevail*'.[64]

Here the perception of material signs of identity and difference is to be mobilised in order to enlist subjects within a discourse in which any potentially disruptive meanings of those differences must be effaced. It may be necessary to acknowledge the different position which women occupy culturally in order effectively to address them as potential readers and pilgrims, but the female position remains ultimately defined as secondary. Women are objects of address, and apparently, given the predominance of female subjects addressed in this preface, an important and distinctive target group for enlistment, yet the voice of the addressor must remain male.

But the struggle to redefine meanings and positions inevitably informs the most seemingly univocal of texts. Just as in France and Flanders, where *The Pilgrim's Progress* was apparently received as friend and brother, a struggle was being waged over political and religious issues, so in England women were demanding a more active role in the promulgation of a doctrine which assigned to them only a position of passivity. *The Pilgrim's Progress, Part Two* was published two years after Bunyan published his response to such demands from women in his own congregation. These material struggles to define the meanings of political and religious concepts, and to claim different subject positions within a particular society, clearly inform the text which, despite its own dissenting claims, attempts to efface them.

In *The Pilgrim's Progress, Part One* Christian stops his ears to block out the voices of Christiana and her children which might deter him from his progress from a corrupt material world to a perfect, spiritual existence. The second volume attempts to integrate these insistent, potentially disruptive, voices within the narrative of progress, by acknowledging the specificity of cultural differences only to collapse them ultimately in a supposedly transcendent and universal discourse which sustains a rigid hierarchy of gender positions. The preface which has attempted to enlist a range of female subjects, ends with a confident assertion of the text's value not to a female reader but to a male purchaser:

> Now may this little Book a blessing be,
> To those that love this little Book and me,
> And may its buyer have no cause to say,
> His Money is but lost or thrown away.[65]

In *Fictions of the Feminine: Puritan Doctrine and the Representation of Women*, Margaret Olofson Thickstun develops a powerful argument about conflicting imperatives within Puritanism and their effects on the representation of women within a particular tradition of writing. Thickstun suggests that in writings by, amongst others, Spenser, Milton and Bunyan, a pattern emerges in which 'male protagonists displace females from the positive roles women traditionally inhabited and come to personify virtues women conventionally represented'.[66] This pattern, she argues, derives from a Pauline 'metaphorical understanding of gender relations', specifically the assertion of an analogous relationship between man/woman and head/body or spirit/flesh, which is seen to offer a 'logic' by which male believers can resolve the feelings of spiritual insecurity and self-contempt which lie at the heart of the individual struggle for salvation.[67]

In her chapter on Bunyan, 'From Christiana to Steadfast: Subsuming the Feminine in *The Pilgrim's Progress*', Thickstun presents a significant revision of the traditional analysis of the main difference between the first and second parts of the text. The conventionally accepted reading locates the difference in the contrast between the solitary quest of the individual believer, represented in *Part One*, and the depiction of the struggles of a community of believers in *Part Two*.[68] Thickstun accepts, but modifies, this analysis. In her reading, Christiana is, like Christian, a 'representative' believer, whose spiritual journey conforms to the pattern established in *Part One*, but unlike Christian, she cannot be afforded universal significance. She is 'a representative *female* believer', whose gender is seen to determine her actions and whose relationship to God is significantly different from that of her male predecessor on the journey. Whereas Christian's relationship to God had been defined as that of a subject to a king, Christiana's, in accordance with Pauline analogies, is offered as that of bride to bridegroom. Christian's male virtue of loyalty and sin of treason are replaced, in the case of Christiana, by marital chastity and sexual misconduct. Christiana, it is argued, articulates this relationship in her conflation of 'her union with God with her reunion with Christian, for her husband, as the head of their spiritual body, acts as God's representative to her'.[69]

Thickstun's analysis of textual differences between the two parts of *The Pilgrim's Progress* establishes the contrasting frameworks of Christian and Christiana's progresses, as 'domestic' scenes and images which act as the locations of Christiana's journey, replace the public, martial events and images of her husband's. In a move which mirrors and exceeds the change of scenes from public to private, the nature and location of the burden of sin carried by the female characters is depicted as significantly different from that carried by the male. Whereas Christian's burden was an external one, literally carried by the character and removed at the appropriate time, Christiana's and Mercy's burdens of sin are located within the body: 'their sin, being their sexuality and not a simple "burden", is within'.[70] The ultimate effacement of the female protagonist is seen to be performed by the eventual subsuming of female virtue within a masculine figure, as Stand-fast, 'the male perfection of the feminine', usurps Christiana's role as the perfect Bride of Christ.[71]

Thickstun's reading is both careful and provocative. It stands as a warning against simplistic assumptions that female protagonists betoken a feminist text. In the main body of the text and in the preface female difference is initially acknowledged in, for Bunyan, an unusually positive manner, but is ultimately subsumed within a narrative of male supremacy. Nevertheless, there are, I would argue, ways in which the text may operate as a more problematic and unsettling intervention in the struggle to establish the meanings of gender relations. Conceptually it may attempt to reinforce the Pauline view of female insufficiency presented in Bunyan's writings, and the linear narrative may present Christiana's progress as a return to her husband, but this return itself is a departure.

It is relatively easy to characterise the representation of women in *The Pilgrim's Progress, Part One, The Life and Death of Mr Badman* and *The Holy War* as mirroring Scriptural and conventional categorisation of women into figures of virtue or vice. The representation of women in the later text is rather more complex. In the texts which were published before *A Case of Conscience Resolved* and *The Pilgrims Progress, Part Two*, female characters are generally presented as wives, mothers, daughters or harlots, functioning as adjuncts to male characters or as personifications of specific qualities.

In *The Pilgrim's Progress, Part One*, Christian's wife is presented, like Bunyan's own wives, without a name, and described, with her children, as part of his family group of relations. The 'relations' misinterpret Christian's desire for salvation as distraction and refuse to be enlisted by his 'talking to them'. They try to 'drive away his distemper by harsh and surly carriages to him' and are eventually abandoned, as Christian runs away:

> Now he had not run far from his own door, but his Wife and Children perceiving it, began to cry after him to return: but the Man put his fingers in his Ears, and ran on crying, Life, Life, Eternal Life: so he looked not behind him, but fled towards the middle of the Plain.[72]

Tempted by Mr Worldly-Wiseman to reunite with his wife and children in the village of Morality, under the protection of Legality, Christian is saved from error by Evangelist, who exposes Mr Worldly-Wiseman as 'an alien' and Legality as 'the Son of the Bond woman which now is, and is in bondage with her children'.[73] Christian must abandon his wife and family as worldly distractions and accept as his only human guide a man, depicted in the House of the Interpreter, who 'can beget Children, Travel in birth with Children, and Nurse them himself when they are born'.[74] The image is of the ideal pastor, who is represented as subsuming female reproductive and nurturing capacities within a spiritual model of support and guidance. The Gospel is, in turn, represented by a 'Damsel', who sprinkles water on a dusty room to signify the 'sweet and precious influences' of the Gospel on the heart and soul.[75] This damsel is, however, like the 'virgins of the place' at the House Beautiful, Discretion, Prudence, Piety and Charity, operating under an ultimately male authority. Presented as analogous to the Church, these female characters both present an idealised image of female virtue, and virtuous conduct, and, in their successive discourses with Christian, enable the male protagonist to explain, and justify, his rejection of wife and children. The final dismissal of Christian's wife and children as '*implacable to good*' and his absolution from any blame for their destruction is voiced by the female character, Charity.[76] The women feed and arm Christian, show him 'the Pedigree of the Lord of the Hill', their invisible, but absolute, master, and send him on his way with 'a loaf of Bread, a bottle of Wine, and a cluster of Raisins'.[77]

The remaining female characters in *The Pilgrim's Progress, Part One* are, without exception, figures of vice or sin. Wanton, the female incarnation of the sins of the flesh, whose '*Net*' and 'flattering tongue', promising 'all carnal and fleshly content', fails to ensnare Christian's fellow pilgrim, Faithful, who shuts his eyes in order to avoid being 'bewitched with her looks'.[78] Rejected, Wanton rails at the departing man who, clearly subject to carnal desire, then rejects after some hesitation Adam the First's offer of marriage to his daughters, The Lust of the Flesh, The Lust of the Eyes and The Pride of Life. It is the character of Faithful who later, in a debate with Christian about false signs of Grace, employs the following images of two female figures:

> Josephs *Mistris cried out with a loud voice, as if she had been very holy; but she would willingly, notwithstanding that, have committed uncleanness with him. Some cry out against sin even as the Mother cries out against her Child in her lap, when she calleth it slut, and naughty Girl, and then falls to hugging and kissing it.*[79]

The reference to Joseph's mistress or Potiphar's wife, earlier identified as a version of Wanton by Christian, is more conventional, and less provocative, than the second analogy between mother and child and sinner and sin. Sin, it appears in Faithful's analogy, is female. Faithful also applies to Talkative '*The Proverb*' which '*is said of a Whore*; to wit, *That she is a shame to all Women; so you are a shame to all Professors*'.[80] Christian, as a married man, is never directly confronted by the temptations of carnal desire and does not have recourse to such references. Three characters, Lady Faining, whose virtue is only a matter of breeding, Diffidence, the wife of Giant Despair, and Lot's wife, present only in her traditional pillar-of-salt form, complete the catalogue of female characters in *The Pilgrim's Progress, Part One*.

*The Life and Death of Mr Badman*, published two years later, presents two female characters who, while they appear more substantial than the overtly allegorical figures of the earlier text, function, at least partly, as virtue and vice figures with a twist. This is a narrative of reprobation which parallels the earlier narrative of salvation, but is presented as a true case history of an individual sinner, related in a dialogue between two men, rather than as an allegory, framed as an author's dream. The interweaving of the spiritual and social in this text, described by Bunyan as a response to the fact that 'England *shakes and totters already, by reason of the burden that Mr.* Badman *and his Friends have wickedly laid upon it*', results in a delineation of individual characters which resembles that of later techniques in realist fiction.[81] The inclusion of anecdotal material on 'real' characters, whose experiences support the theological and doctrinal points made by the two speakers, Wiseman and Attentive, and of details of Badman's life, domestic, commercial and social, contribute to the text's apparent presentation of concrete social observation and to the illusion that the characters delineated in it are rounded figures, rather than types. An examination of the two main female characters may suggest that this is not the case.

Badman, like Bunyan, has two wives, the first a 'poor honest Maid', a 'Godly' orphan with 'a good portion' who should have 'looked better to herself' but was seduced by Badman's feigned honesty and godliness,[82] the second 'a very Whore' who 'was as good as he, at all his vile and ranting tricks'.[83] The first marriage is an example of the dangers of the union of believers with unbelievers, warned against in *Christian Behaviour*. Wives who are 'in great slavery by reason of their ungodly husbands' are to be 'pittied and prayed for, so they should be so much the more watchful and circumspect in all their wayes'.[84] The wife of an ungodly man should attempt, with discretion, to convince her husband of the error of his ways with 'sound and grave sayings of the Scriptures', but must be patient, 'faithful to him in all the things of this life' and 'take heed of desiring to usurp authority over him'.[85] The godly wife is always 'under the power and authority' even of the ungodly husband.[86]

The story of Badman's first wife, related in the dialogue of Wiseman and Attentive, is an explicit catalogue of the sufferings of the godly woman whose conduct as a wife is exemplary, but whose misfortunes are attributed to her mistaken reliance on 'her own poor, raw, womanish Judgment'.[87] Repeatedly referred to as a 'poor woman', the first wife is, nevertheless, allowed to disobey her husband, without reproof by Attentive and Wiseman, when, after failing to persuade her husband with 'fair words and entreaties', she resolves to attend a sermon. Her justification of her disobedience to her husband's authority recalls Christian's dialogue with Charity and is legitimated by reference to its scriptural origin:

> At last she said she would go, and rendred this reason for it; I have an Husband, but also a God; my God has commanded me; and that upon pain of damnation, to be a continual Worshipper of him, and that in the way of his own Appointments: I have an Husband, but also a Soul, and my Soul ought to be more unto me, than all the world besides. This soul of mine I will look after, care for, and (if I can) provide it an Heaven for its habitation. You are commanded to love me, as you love your own body, and so do I love you; but I tell you true, I preferr my Soul before all the world, and its Salvation I will seek.[88]

The theological justification of the wife's disobedience to her husband as obedience to a higher, divine authority, is reinforced by reference to material evidence of her husband's reprobate status, as he threatens to 'turn informer' and 'weary out those that she loved, from meeting together to Worship God; or make them pay dearly for their so doing'.[89]

Badman's second wife is depicted as a mirror opposite of his first. The first was godly and chaste, the second is 'a whore of her body':

> The first woman loved to keep things together, but this last would whirl them about as well as he: The first would be silent when he

chid, and would take it patiently when he abused her, but this would give him word for word, blow for blow, curse for curse; so that now Mr. Badman had met with his match. [90]

The second wife is not merely presented as the opposite of the first, but as God's judgement on Badman: 'God had a mind to make him see the baseness of his own life, in the wickedness of his wives [sic].'[91] The two wives stand as exemplary figures of virtue and vice, both for Badman and the reader. Female professors are not addressed in the preface to this text, which is addressed to a singular 'Courteous Reader', but are the subject of an exchange between Wiseman and Attentive about the sin of pride in appearance. Wiseman rails against proud women 'with their Bulls-foretops, with their naked shoulders, and Paps hanging out like a Cows bag', against women 'painting their faces' and making a 'spangling shew of fine cloaths'.[92] He concludes that 'what it was, that of old was called the Attire of an Harlot: certainly it could not be more bewitching and tempting than are the garments of many professors this day'.[93] Attentive agrees and expresses a wish that *all the proud Dames in* England *that profess, were within the reach and sound of your words*'.[94] Wiseman's response is that if the female professors had failed to heed '*Moses* and the *Prophets*' they would not respond to 'such a dull sounding Rams-horn' as he.[95]

Although these references to proud women may be interpreted as a critique of the affluent, the vehemence of this denunciation of the bewitching vice of some female professors echoes Bunyan's proclaimed abhorrence of female company in *Grace Abounding*. It may also be connected with the type of accusations of improper sexual conduct which were made against Bunyan and which are described in this text as slanders raised by Badman himself: 'He would also raise slanders of his wives friends, himself affirming that their doctrine tended to lasciviousness, and that in their assemblies they acted and did unbeseeming men and women, that they committed uncleanness, *etc.*'[96] As in *Grace Abounding*, accusations of sexual transgression within nonconformist religious groups which might undermine Bunyan's authority as a minister are accompanied by a denunciation of women as seductive figures who entice male believers into sin. Both texts exemplify what N. H. Keeble suggests is the major feature of Bunyan's use of the feminine: 'The figurative usefulness of the feminine to Bunyan's texts is thus frequently to supply images of temptation, and in this guise it exerts a baleful fascination and enjoys a malignant power.'[97] Published three years before *A Case of Conscience Resolved*, *The Life and Death of Mr Badman* initially divides women into the godly and ungodly and then suggests that a large number of the apparently godly are, in fact, ungodly.

In *The Holy War*, published one year before *A Case of Conscience Resolved*, women are barely represented at all. In this allegorical narrative of the struggle of the human soul, the only female characters are relatives, presented simply to establish the lineage or familial framework of male characters. The representation of women in *The Pilgrim's Progress, Part Two*, published two years later, cannot be read as constituting a radical departure from, or revision of, the Pauline framework of female inferiority promoted by the earlier texts. The initial depiction of female agency and the apparent endorsement of Christiana's rejection of conventional views of female insufficiency are swiftly followed by a narrative incident in which the women's inability to progress without male guidance is presented in a literally forceful manner. Having embarked on their journey without adult male assistance, Christiana and Mercy are subjected to attempted rape. They escape only by crying out for help and are rescued by the Reliever who comments on their folly in travelling alone: '*I marvelled much when you was entertained at the Gate above, being ye knew that ye were but weak Women, that you petitioned not the Lord there for a Conductor: Then might you have avoided these Troubles, and Dangers: For he would have granted you one.*'[98] Both women acknowledge their folly and, after a further series of lessons, specifically designed for women, in the House of the Interpreter, are granted Great-heart as a guide for the remainder of the journey, on which they are accompanied by the infirm and the inadequate.[99] The brief moment of limited female independence is thus ended in a frightening reminder of the physical perils which women's boldness may not only expose them to but may actually cause. On one level *The Pilgrim's Progress, Part Two* may operate as a fictional supplement to Bunyan's denunciation of women's attempts to play a more active role in religious affairs in *A Case of Conscience Resolved*. The lesson to female readers seems clear: women, like men, must undergo the privations and perils of the road to salvation, but cannot hope to do so as independent subjects without male assistance. Their 'Company alone' can never be enough. The lesson may be clear but is it the only one which might be learnt from this text? Could the text be read differently?

## IV    But, for, her, she, did, doe, all, his, way, you, may, say, nay

The key to the possibility of different readings of the position of women, and of other subjects, from that ostensibly offered in Bunyan's texts may lie, paradoxically, in the attempts in the texts to enforce correct reading. Female readers in the seventeenth century, African and Asian readers in the nineteenth, are encouraged to recognise themselves within a text and to accept its meanings and values as their own. But this process of identification, of self-recognition in the text, is also a process of interpretation. Difference, as the condition of meaning in the written text, may intrude in the transmission of the meaning of the text, allowing interpretations which defy or exceed the constraints on meaning of a specific text, and suggesting the possibility of subject positions other than those offered.

Bunyan's writings, as I have suggested in earlier chapters, reveal an intense anxiety about the possibility of misreading, of the construing of aberrant meanings from a text which is produced in deference to the absolute truth and meaning of God. Throughout Bunyan's writings the reader is repeatedly advised to beware the pitfalls of careless reading and misinterpretation. The metaphoric qualities of language may, it seems, be exploited to great effect when harnessed to a theory of representation which offers all material, readable signs as revelations of an anterior truth, as the defence of allegorical method in the preface to *The Pilgrim's Progress, Part One* argues. Yet numerous warnings of the dangers of misinterpretation suggest that undue emphasis on the surface of signification could result in a dangerous breakdown in the transmission of the true meaning of the text.

In an afterword or 'Conclusion' to *The Pilgrim's Progress, Part One* Bunyan explicitly warns the reader against paying undue attention to the surface:

> *Take heed also, that thou be not extream,*
> *In playing with the* out-side *of my Dream:*
> *Nor let my figure, or similitude,*
> *Put thee into a laughter or a feud;*
> *Leave this for* Boys *and* Fools; *but as for thee,*
> *Do thou the substance of my matter see.*[100]

In the preface to *The Holy War*, published in 1682, Bunyan draws the reader's attention to a key weapon in his battle against misinterpretation, the marginal notes which accompany all the allegorical texts: '*Nor do thou go to work without my Key,/(In mysteries men soon do lose their way)*.'[101] The margin of the text is thus invoked to set the limits of its possible signification, to act as an authoritative gloss on a narrative in which the absolute singularity of meaning might otherwise be lost. But, as Valentine Cunningham argues in his summary of what he terms the 'post-modernist argument' about the 'deconstructive logics' of such textual material, the marginal gloss may also gloze:

> Glosses, like allegories – which are extended, fictionalized glosses indulged in the margins so to say of some anterior or precedent text, story, historical situation, moral case – undermine the idea of

textual monodicity, the authorising status of texts as original, authoritative, final, necessary and self-sufficient source and guarantor of meaning. Glosses, like allegories, undermine logocentricity.[102]

The supplementary status of marginal notation is seen to create practical
problems for the reader, who must decide which part of the text to read
first, the main body of the text or the margin. Gloss turns to gloze, as the
imaginary originality and authority of the text is undermined by this
process of textual and hermeneutic accumulation. In Cunningham's reading, Bunyan, like other seventeenth-century Christian writers, attempts to
'wrest back margins and marginalia from the glozing hands of Satan, By-
ends, and Giant Despair'[103] presenting the margin not as glozing, but as
'glazing, the installation of windows giving on to the text and providing
helpful views into it'.[104] As Cunningham notes, the marginal gloss is
described in the preface to *The Holy War* as '*the window*', which is, in
turn, glossed in the margin as 'The margent'.[105] Windows, however, may
not always offer a clear view of what lies behind them. They may, like the
window on Terry Waite's postcard, interpose a different text, a different
meaning or set of meanings, between the reader and the assumed and
imaginary source of those meanings. Bunyan's insistence that his supplementary marginal texts serve to illuminate his main texts, just as his
writings as a whole, in supplementing the Word, serve to enlighten the
reader, may be read as an attempt to police interpretation. The reader is
guided to significant material in the main text and offered a reading of its
significance in the margin. But, as Cunningham argues, this 'propaganda
for margins [ … ] cannot entirely rebut the presumption that the kind of
reading and rereading going on is not just simply secondary and
juxtapositive but is also alternative, divisive reading'.[106]

The battle of words about, and on behalf of, the Word, resulted in a
double-edged emphasis on written signification as the location of truth
but also as an area of contestation, defined in these texts as misinterpretation. The possibility of such misinterpretation, of alternative readings
is clearly perceived as a real threat to the authority of the Word, yet it is
a possibility which any written ministry may be seen to invite. In order
to enlist subjects within the discourse of salvation it was necessary to
address reading subjects, to teach existing subjects to read correctly and
to extend the range of potential subjects by, literally, teaching them to
read. In this context, the nonconformist tradition of educational re-
form, the development of new disciplines and methods of experimental
knowledge which mirrored the concerns and concepts of Puritan theology, may be read as a vital component in the drive to enlist new
subjects within the discourse of salvation.[107]

Bunyan's disclaimers of conventional education as having any formative influence in his spiritual development may in part serve to empha-

sise the direct intervention of divine Grace in the process of salvation, but they also reflect a common nonconformist distinction between classical, university-based education and the Word in which the latter alone may stand as a true object in the pursuit of the ultimate knowledge of God and of one's own relation to God. Opponents frequently accused Bunyan of inability correctly to interpret scripture because of his ignorance of the original Hebrew.[108] Bunyan's response, like that of the majority of nonconformists, was to propose a different scheme of knowledge, a scheme in which classical languages and texts were to be supplanted as the material of knowledge by the Bible in the vernacular and by such aspects of human learning which would reflect divine wisdom.

Whilst Bunyan's commitment to a different framework of knowledge is less explicit than that of a writer such as Richard Baxter, whose statement, 'Preachers may be silenced or banished, when Books may be at hand', is taken by Keeble as the most succinct expression of the nonconformist literary culture, at least one of Bunyan's texts shows quite clearly the link between the promotion of literacy and the enlistment of subjects.[109]

A Book for Boys and Girls, a collection of poems which draw 'Comparisons' between empirically perceived objects and events and theological truths, was published in 1686. Perhaps more than any other Bunyan text, this prefigures, both in the material it contains and in its overall strategies, the popular reworkings of the nineteenth century. The preface to this text opens with an explicit description of the intended readers and of Bunyan's project:

> The Title-page will show, if there thou look,
> Who are the proper Subjects of this Book.
> They'r Boys and Girls of all Sorts and Degrees,
> From those of Age, to Children on the Knees.
> Thus comprehensive am I in my Notions;
> They tempt me to it by their childish Motions.
> We now have Boys with Beards, and Girls that be
> Big as old Women, wanting Gravity.[110]

A twofold readership is thus projected. Adult men and women who have failed to receive the message of salvation addressed to them before when ministers 'Dealt with them, counting them, not Boys but Men' will here be enlisted and saved by a text in which Bunyan will 'like a Fool stand fing'ring of their Toys; / And all to shew them, they are Girls and Boys'.[111] Metaphors of enticement and catching the readers are combined with a defence of employing mundane material to reveal divine truths. One section, in particular, echoes the language of Puritan and nonconformist educational aims and methods:

*And if some better handle can a Fly,*
*Then some a Text, why should we them deny*
*Their making Proof, or good Experiment,*
*Of smallest things great mischiefs to prevent?*[112]

The men and women who have resisted enlistment up to this point, the *'artificial Babes'*, are to be encouraged to read the work of God in the examples offered by the created world *'Which he put in their hand, that to obtain / Which is both present, and Eternal Gain'*.[113] The world is thus to be read as a collection of signs of divine wisdom which echos the form of the world identified by Foucault in his analysis of the sixteenth-century episteme, yet the place of language, of reading and writing suggests a partial shift towards the modifications to that episteme which he locates in the seventeenth century. In the seventeenth century, Foucault argues, language 'has withdrawn from the midst of beings themselves and has entered a period of transparency and neutrality'.[114] Whereas in the earlier period signs were viewed as pre-existing, and not dependent on knowledge of them as a condition of existence, in the seventeenth century, he suggests, signs are constituted by the act of knowing, defined into existence through analysis of their relations. In *A Book for Boys and Girls* objects from 'Piss-ants' to candles are shining signs whose significance is pre-ordained and to be discovered by attentive perception. The address to the second group of potential readers, however, suggests a different basis for a different form of knowledge in which reading in a literal sense becomes the precondition of all wisdom. Bunyan announces his intention to teach children 'their A,B,C' for *'All needs must there begin, that wou'd be wise'*.[115]

What follows is 'An help to Chil-dren to learn to read English' which consists of the alphabet in six different type styles, lists of vowels and 'Con-so-nants' and 'dou-ble Let-ters', a brief guide to spelling and a chart 'To learn Chil-dren to spell a-right their names'.[116] In the latter section the names are divided in terms of gender, apparently endorsing a binary opposition which, in Bunyan's writings, usually positions woman in the inferior or secondary position. Here the boys' names are on the left, the girls' on the right. If I read across the page in the conventional Western manner, the first name is always that of a boy. My construction as a Western reader guides the way in which I read literally and informs the way I make sense of textual material. There is, however, even in a text like this which seeks to stabilise reading and writing practices, a suggestion that readings and meanings could be different. A chart of numbers in 'Figures' and 'Numeral Letters' completes this section which Bunyan deems 'enough for little Children to prepare themselves for Psalter, or Bible'.[117] Whilst this last statement harnesses learning to read to a specifically redemptive process, the method employed to teach the construction of words in the preceding section suggests an organisational linguistic principle which has little direct relationship to divine authority.

Words in the section are printed with breaks to mark each syllable, a guide to spelling states that 'e-ve-ry word or syl-la-ble (tho ne-ver so small) must have one vow-el or more right-ly placed in it', and a list of non-words is offered: 'sl, gld, strnght, spll, drll, fll'.[118] The suggestion that words exist on the basis of meeting internal, systematic or structural criteria is not tempered by any reference to divinely-ordained meaning, indeed to meaning at all. In this context the final sentence, or group of words, may be of crucial importance. The spelling guide ends with 'Words con-sis-ting of three Letters, But, for, her, she, did, doe, all, his, way, you, may, say, nay'.[119] Each word in this sequence meets the outlined criteria for being a word, each is divided from the other by a comma which holds the words apart yet does not end the sequence. It would seem possible, however, from my position at least, to read this sequence of words as 'meaning' something, not as having any intrinsic meaning released by correct interpretation, but as a sequence of signifiers which appear to address me. I may connect it with the female subjects of the seventeenth century who did not 'doe, all, his, way', with Margaret Fell, Elizabeth Bunyan and Agnes Beaumont. I may read it as a potentially subversive gloss on *The Pilgrim's Progress, Part Two* and its supplementary relation to its male 'original'.

If it is possible for these words, defined in the text only as separate signifiers, to be interpreted from a feminist subject position which is not that specified in the text's address, what are the implications for the interaction of the nineteenth-century reworkings of Bunyan's writings and the different subjects whose enlistment within colonial discourses of Christianity and civilisation prompted their production?

In a prefatory address to 'The English Kaffir reader', which accompanied his 1866 translation of *The Pilgrim's Progress* into the Kaffir language, *Uhambo Lo Mhambi, owesuka kweli liwe, waye esinga kwelo lizayo*, the Reverend Tiyo Soga explained the reason for the addition of an appendix to his text:

> At the end of the Book, he has appended a small list of theological terms used in it. These, it is suggested, Kaffir scholars should consider, with the view of fixing their signification. A few of them have here been variously translated, from the fact that the translator has not yet quite determined in his own mind how to adjust their shade of meaning.[120]

Soga, the colonial writing subject who presents himself, always in the third person, as the pupil of William Govan, 'One of the long-tried, unwearying, constant friends and benefactors of the Native Races of South Africa', locates the failure to fix the meaning of these terms in his own mind. His appeal to English readers of Kaffir suggests that they are assumed to have greater control over their 'native' language than Soga, that he is appealing to them as being nearer the source of the meanings of Christian theology than he. Within the context of an explicitly evangelical, and covertly imperialist, drive to enlist different reading subjects within the discourses of Christianity and 'Western civilisation', this desire, this need, to fix the meaning of key words or concepts testifies both to the paramount importance of language as the means and material of enlistment and, implicitly, to its dangerous instability. The African pupil-writer urges English teacher-readers to fix the meanings of both English and Kaffir words, to find the exact and stable correspondence between words in two different languages which he has been unable to establish. Soga's apparent lack of mastery over meaning and his appeal to English readers to fix meaning, reinforce his concrete historical and cultural positioning as a colonial subject who must defer to the knowing subjects whose command of their 'native' language is assumed to give them more control over meaning. There is no evidence that Soga ever received a reply from his English readers and the goal of fixing signification was not, and could not be, attained. The meanings of words can never, of course, be fixed, even by the most knowing, the most authoritative, of subjects.

The similarities between the techniques of enlistment employed by Bunyan, operating in the seventeenth century, and by the imperialist writers, translators and compilers in the nineteenth, may testify, paradoxically, to the power of difference. The didactic imperative which demands that subjects be taught to read, to read and recognise their true position within a discourse, be it of salvation or civilisation, necessarily involves exposing those subjects to the differentiating, deferring effects of language. In effect, the subject may contest the proffered meaning of his or her subject position within that discourse and reject the basis of the authority or authorities in whose name that subjection is demanded.

Letters, on a page, or in the post, on a postcard or in a spelling guide, are addressed to specific readers, actual or implied. They may, however, as the troubled 'correspondence' between Terry Waite and John Bunyan and my reading of it show, fall into the wrong hands, even when they apparently reach their proper destination. Whilst interfering with the mail may be prohibited in this culture at this historical moment, the deferring, disseminating effects of writing will continue to cause interference in the transmission of messages. Until authority – divine, political or cultural – can express itself without language it will always be open to question.

# Conclusion: Bunyan @ large

It is impossible to conclude, or close, the study of the writing of an author; new encounters between texts and readers will continue to challenge the accepted meanings of 'John Bunyan' and his work. I want, however, to end this study of the writing of John Bunyan with a brief examination of the status of the name and the texts as they circulate in the final years of the twentieth century.

In 1996, apart from the scholarly editions published by Clarendon Press, and paperback scholarly editions of *The Pilgrim's Progress*, *Grace Abounding*, and *The Life and Death of Mr Badman*, Bunyan's writings are published primarily by Christian presses, the majority based in the USA. The publications include cheap editions of many of the treatises as well as modern-English, large-print and children's editions of *The Pilgrim's Progress*.[1] As products of an evangelical drive to enlist readers, these texts have much in common with the nineteenth- and early twentieth-century editions of *The Pilgrim's Progress*, but print is no longer the only medium for written communication. In the years following the tercentenary of the death of Bunyan there has been a significant, and according to some views potentially revolutionary, technological development in communication. The writing of John Bunyan, both in the sense of name and of texts, can now be read on the Internet. It is clearly to early to make any reliable judgements about the effects of the Internet as a system both of communication and of the circulation of information on our understanding of authority or authorship, but it may be useful to discover how the name and texts of Bunyan figure in this context.

A search for the name 'John Bunyan' in September 1996 revealed that the majority of sites in which the name is found are religious. Apart from citations in academic reference sources such as library collections and on-line course materials, the search led primarily to sites produced by a variety of Christian organisations and individuals, based in the USA. The search revealed very few sites in the United Kingdom: apart from citations in the résumés of academics working on Bunyan, references were found in promotional material, such as the Bedfordshire Tourist Board's site, which features Bunyan under 'Famous Bedford People'. Here, illustrated text on Bunyan's career and on the history of the Bunyan Meeting are combined with maps of the region and a brief feature on Terry Waite who is depicted in front of the window which featured on the postcard. In his country of origin Bunyan seems to figure either as an object of academic study or as a tourist attraction, as a part of a heritage industry.

In sites originating in the USA, Bunyan is deployed as a far more active figure in an ongoing evangelical project. In these sites Bunyan features as an exemplary figure in a history which is deemed to have culminated in the contemporary religious culture or movement promoted by the group who have produced the site which they call 'home' and as an author of texts which are promoted as having a predominantly religious rather than literary significance. Some of these organisations and individuals offer merchandise featuring Bunyan and/or his writings. These include a video of a BBC drama-documentary of Bunyan, described as an 'authentic sample of 17th-century Puritan preaching', a video of a drama based on Bunyan's life and *The Pilgrim's Progress* produced by the New Life Community Church, framed engravings of Bunyan and other famous Christian figures, and CD-Roms which offer samples of famous preacher's sermons. Their main service, however, is to offer digitised and translated versions of Bunyan's writings, which can either be read on screen or downloaded to the reader's computer and printed out, and accounts of the impact of reading Bunyan on contemporary Christian readers' lives. Bunyan's own account of his conversion and call to ministry in *Grace Abounding* is thus supplemented by later narratives in which the reader, like Terry Waite, recognises his or her own experience in the text of the seventeenth-century writer. These narratives emphasise the continuity of the story of individual Christians' encounters with divine truth but this continuity may itself be read as the product of a narrative constructed by specific religious groups within a cultural and historical context which both resembles and differs from that of Bunyan's England.

The Christian groups who use the Internet might be regarded as, in some senses at least, modern equivalents of the sectaries of the seventeenth century, ranging in doctrinal and political position from mainstream, such as the Baptist and United Reformed Churches, to extreme, but all offering members and 'users' a potential home (page) in a hostile world. Like the Palace Beautiful in *The Pilgrim's Progress* the groups' Internet sites offer the individual believer an interactive experience in a community which offers spiritual support. Finding the right site, or community, is, however, not an easy process. *Grace Abounding* presented a narrative of Bunyan's flirtation with the antinomian ideas of the Ranters and his texts in general testify to his need to differentiate his model of Christianity from that of rival groups such as the Quakers. In the age of the Internet, Christian groups reveal the same anxiety to differentiate their message and theological and cultural identity from that of alternative Christian movements as well as from the secular world.

As an extension of an apparently ecumenical ministry, some organisations provide guides to Christian sites on the Internet which, in the words of one, the 'Christian Resource Network', are 'dedicated to bringing tools and resources to the Christian body'. These guides lead the browser from one site to 'related' sites in a less haphazard way than the commercial search engines which operate by identifying a name, or combination of letters, within a text or site. In my search, commercial search tools led me not only to the home pages of Christian groups and to academic resources, but also to a citation in a list of famous people who 'received a scientific diagnosis of mental illness' in the 'Famous Manic-Depressives' site, and to a quotation from *The Pilgrim's Progress* in a site devoted to heavy metal rock music. The Christian guides filter out such sites, pointing the user/reader to the locations of appropriate or edifying material, in a manner which is reminiscent of the hand in the margin of Bunyan's texts, guiding the eye of the reader to significant passages in the main body of the work. Just as Bunyan's attempted promotion of divine truth through written ministry necessitated the development of strategies to control or limit misinterpretation, so contemporary efforts to communicate a contemporary Christian 'truth' through the Internet require the supplementary device of the guide to keep readers on the right path. But, as in seventeenth-century England and in the contexts of nineteenth-century evangelism and imperialism, attempts to keep the reader on the right path are not always successful. The Internet, as a text, offers many links or byways which can lead the reader in unexpected directions.

My search also led to an apparently conventional Christian page in the 'Patriot Knowledge Base' which offers access to Bunyan's writings. Like the other evangelical sites, this appears to offer the Christian reader or the casual browser an opportunity to read edifying material, connecting the experience of Bunyan in seventeenth-century England with that of the individual wherever he or she may be. It is possible that the reader may follow the signs to Bunyan's writings and then leave the site. But if he or she chooses instead to return to the home page, the difference between this site and other Christian sites is revealed. In addition to making available texts such as *Grace Abounding* the site offers material of an explicitly political nature including invective against a wide range of liberal political and cultural movements and ideas, from the United Nations and the gun control lobby to abortion. My search also led to a quotation from *The Pilgrim's Progress* in an electronic call for help from a young man trying to 'escape' from the Los Angeles branch of the Church of Christ, an organisation which recruits members to act as God's élite in the battle against Satan.

As they figure in these sites, Bunyan and his writings might be read as circulating in interlocking and competing discursive formations which resemble those of the seventeenth century but which are formed by and respond to a different social and cultural context. This is a context in which the story of Bunyan's struggles with the oppressive authority of the State may be deployed on behalf of an extreme version of Christian political individualism which might be read as a development from Puritan and nonconformist ideas, but which is inflected by a particularly vehement response to perceived constraints on individual freedoms within the USA. It is also a context in which Bunyan's writing may be mobilised against a religious organisation which is perceived as exerting too much control over an individual's life, an organisation which resembles a seventeenth-century sectary in many of its doctrinal and disciplinary features but which in the late twentieth century is read as a sect. In both examples what seems to be at stake is the status of the human subject, defined against the authority of a collective, in the form of state or church, which is seen to threaten individual autonomy. In the early modern period predestinarian theology foregrounded the fraught and paradoxical relationship between free will and determinism in a theocentric model of human existence, creating the conditions for the development of an authoritative yet anxious individual subject, at once bound and free; in the Western post-modern condition, in which theocentric frameworks are no longer dominant, the fragile authority of the individual subject is asserted in the face of different, social and economic determinisms.

As I argued at the start of this study, one of the effects of the writing of John Bunyan was the production of the author as source of meaning which challenged the absolute authority of God but was itself revealed as a textual construct. Whatever difficulties were encountered in subsequent attempts to categorise Bunyan as an author in the post-Romantic sense, the rise of the figure of the individual, of which the author is one of the most authoritative manifestations, has been apparently inexorable. The extent of cultural investment in the ontological, and ethical, primacy of the individual is revealed in contemporary reactions to technological developments in communication and the production of knowledge, or meaning. Much has been written recently about the impact of the Internet on the ways in which knowledge is circulated, apparently bypassing or crossing traditional boundaries, both geographical and disciplinary. Positive interpretations of the possibilities of this technological development emphasise the opportunities offered for individuals to communicate without the restrictions or encumbrances of classification by race, class or gender which 'actual' rather than 'virtual' presence involves. Negative readings stress the atomising and isolating effects of this model of communication as the individual substitutes electronic discourse for involvement in collective action. The former envisages an inter-, or supra-, national community of individuals who have exceeded the constraints of the body, who participate in a conversation which exceeds the limits of traditional divisions of knowledge. The latter fears a world of users lulled into a dream of involvement while the illusion of shared community and free access to knowledge obscures the commercial and political interests of those who ultimately control the means of communication, the cable networks. Both Utopian and apocalyptic responses can be read as driven by a desire to sustain and develop the autonomy, independence and power of the individual. There are obvious similarities between the hopes and fears for this new technology of communication and those attached to Puritan and nonconformist attempts to harness the power of print in order to overcome the enforced isolation of believers and to communicate to a wider readership than that allowed by earlier techniques. In the seventeenth century, print allowed Bunyan to exceed the constraints on the body of imprisonment and enforced separation from the community in order to communicate with readers who might never see him; in the late twentieth century the Internet allows individual users to escape, virtually if not materially, from the constraints imposed by their social and cultural position, communicating their ideas without encountering the immediate barriers of censorship and regulation which are already in place within print technology. Bunyan employed the authority of print to struggle against the social and political formations which denied him the authority to preach; similarly marginalised or disenfranchised subjects today may exploit the new possibilities of electronic communication. In both cases the ability to make use of technology depends on having basic financial means or support and on occupying a subject position from which it is possible to communicate.

Seventeenth-century nonconformity contributed to the extension and diversification of the range of subjects who could speak or write with authority, however fragile, but, as Bunyan's reaction to women's desire for separate prayer meetings suggests, there were limits to, and hierarchies within, this range. The inclusive and expansive ideal of the Internet can be read as similarly restricted. Today Agnes Beaumont's narrative might be communicated immediately across the world rather than depending, as was the case in the seventeenth century, on the development of an appropriate publishing context, but the difference is a matter of speed rather than of access. Beaumont could write her story; other women in Bunyan's congregation almost certainly could not have done so. In the seventeenth century and on the Internet literacy is the basic requirement for communication. In *A Book for Boys and Girls* Bunyan's spelling guide revealed both the regulatory and destabilising features of writing. On the Internet, as in printed texts, there are conventions, rules and protocols which establish what can be communicated. Because

English is the dominant language of the Internet, if not of all sites, the global reach of the new technology may, for example, be read as a continuation of English, or more probably North American, cultural hegemony. But as the unexpected results of the use of Bunyan's writings within evangelical and imperialist drives to enlist subjects in Africa and China testify, the assertion of any authority entails the production of possible positions of resistance.

The space offered by the new technology is neither entirely free nor absolutely regulated by some anterior commercial or political force. It is, like that afforded by print technology, a space created by existing discursive institutions and practices. As such it is informed by current understandings of subjectivity and authority but also provides a context for continuing debate about their meanings. If texts may be read as sites of contestation, in and with which struggles and debates over meaning are conducted, then the sites of the Internet may be read as texts of contestation. In this context as in those of the seventeenth and nineteenth centuries the writing of John Bunyan will continue to be deployed both on behalf of oppressive or restrictive knowledges and as material for their resistance.

# Notes

## Introduction: Traces of Authority

1. See Bibliography for list of Bunyan's writings.
2. A list of works 'incorrectly ascribed to Bunyan' is published by the Borough of Bedford Public Library in the *Catalogue of the John Bunyan Library (Frank Mott Harrison Collection)* (Bedford: Borough of Bedford Public Library, 1938), pp. 24–5. There are discussions on Bunyan's signature in John Brown, *John Bunyan: His Life, Times, and Work* (London and Glasgow: Hulbert Publishing, 1928), pp. 122–3, and Richard L. Greaves, 'A John Bunyan signature', *Baptist Quarterly*, 25 (1974), p. 379.
3. Christopher Hill, *The English Bible and the Seventeenth-Century Revolution* (Harmondsworth: Allen Lane, 1993), p. 52.

## Chapter 1: The Name(s) of the Author

1. These included N. H. Keeble (ed.), *John Bunyan: Conventicle and Parnassus* (Oxford: Clarendon Press, 1988), Anne Laurence, W. R. Owens and Stuart Sim (eds) *John Bunyan and his England 1628–88* (London and Ronceverte: Hambledon Press, 1990), and Robert G. Collmer (ed.), *Bunyan in our Time* (Kent, Ohio and London: Kent State University Press, 1989).
2. Keeble, *John Bunyan*, p. v.
3. Valentine Cunningham, 'Glossing and glozing: Bunyan and allegory', in Keeble, *John Bunyan*, pp. 217–40; Isabel Rivers, 'Grace, holiness, and the pursuit of happiness: Bunyan and Restoration Latitudinarianism', in Keeble, *John Bunyan*, pp. 45–69.
4. Keeble, *John Bunyan*, p. v.
5. This phrase is from a manuscript fragment with notes on *The Pilgrim's Progress* reproduced in George Whalley (ed.), *The Collected Work of Samuel Taylor Coleridge: Marginalia I* (London: Routledge and Kegan Paul, 1980), p. 801.
6. Keeble, *John Bunyan*, p. v.
7. Ibid.
8. Ibid.
9. James F. Forrest and Richard L. Greaves, *John Bunyan: A Reference Guide* (Boston: G. K. Hall, 1982), pp. 203–26.
10. Ibid., pp. 205, 212.
11. For a useful analysis of the history of the develoment of the discipline see Chris Baldick, *The Social Mission of English Criticism 1848–1932* (Oxford: Clarendon Press, 1983).
12. Walter Raleigh, *The English Novel: Being a Short Sketch of Its History from the Earliest Times to the Appearance of Waverly* (London: John Murray, 1894), pp. 114–18; Arthur T. Quiller-Couch (ed.), *John Bunyan: Selections* (Oxford: Clarendon Press, 1908).

13. 'Is Bunyan Read To-Day?', *Daily Graphic* (London, 6 November 1909), cited in Forrest and Greaves, *John Bunyan*, p. 163.

14. Alfred Noyes, 'Bunyan – a revaluation', *Bookman*, 75 (October, 1928a), pp. 13–17.

15. See Forrest and Greaves *John Bunyan* for details of the contributions to the debate; Alfred Noyes, 'Rejoinder', *Bookman*, 75 (November, 1928b), pp. 104–6.

16. James Simson, 'Was John Bunyan a gipsy?', *Notes and Queries*, 5 (April 1858), p. 318.

17. The most obvious example of this apparently paradoxical adherence to the notion of the importance of the author is one strand of Marxist work on Bunyan. For a useful critical survey of the history of Marxist approaches to Bunyan see David Herreshoff, 'Marxist perspectives on Bunyan', in Robert G. Collmer (ed.) *Bunyan in Our Time*, pp. 161–85. The influence of individualism is evident in the publishing history of one of the most recent, and widely respected, Marxist studies of Bunyan. Christopher Hill's *A Turbulent, Seditious, and Factious People: John Bunyan and his Church* (Oxford: Oxford University Press, 1988), is published in the United States under the title, *A Tinker and a Poor Man: John Bunyan and His Church, 1628–1688* (New York: W. W. Norton, 1990). This shift in emphasis from a collective to an individual subject (the subtitle does not appear on the book's spine) is intriguing, especially in the light of recent comment by Hill on North American evangelical Protestantism. In an appendix to *The English Bible and the Seventeenth-Century Revolution*, pp. 447–51, Hill suggests parallels between twentieth-century Catholic liberation theology in Latin America and seventeenth-century radical religion in England, and argues that the former has benefited from Marxist ideas. This combination of Christian and Marxist frameworks in action is contrasted with the influx into South America of North American-financed evangelical missionaries promoting the 'liberal protestant theology' of Western capitalism. The altered title of Hill's earlier text may retain the reference to the class position of its subject but the change in focus from collective to individual may present a more acceptable figure to some North American readers.

18. Roger Sharrock, 'General editor's preface', *The Miscellaneous Works of John Bunyan*, Vol. I, T. L. Underwood (ed.) (Oxford: Clarendon Press, 1980), p. viii.

19. Michel Foucault, 'What is an author?', in Bouchard, Donald F.(ed.), *Language, Counter Memory, Practice* (Oxford: Basil Blackwell), p. 123.

20. Bunyan, *Some Gospel-truths Opened, The Miscellaneous Works of John Bunyan*, Vol. I, (hereafter *Misc. Works*, Vol. I), p. 5.

21. Bunyan, *A Vindication of the book called Some Gospel-truths Opened*, *Misc. Works*, Vol. I, p. 121.

22. Bunyan, *A Few Sighs from Hell*, *Misc. Works*, Vol. I, p. 230.

23. Bunyan, *The Doctrine of the Law and Grace Unfolded*, *Misc. Works*, Vol. II, R. L. Greaves (ed.) (Oxford: Clarendon Press, 1976), p. 9.

24. Bunyan, *Profitable Meditations*, *Misc. Works*, Vol. VI, G. Midgley (ed.) (Oxford: Clarendon Press, 1980), p. 3.

25. There are examinations of Francis Smith's activities as a printer during this period, including his work with Bunyan, in N. H. Keeble, *The Literary Culture of Nonconformity in Later Seventeenth-Century Eng-*

*land* (Leicester: Leicester University Press, 1987), pp. 60, 97, 98, 113, 118, 121, 122, 305 and Hill, *A Turbulent, Seditious, and Factious People*, pp. 123, 238, 284–8. Both texts also offer useful information about Bunyan's other printers and about the context and activities of radical and dissenting publishing in this period.

26. Bunyan, *Christian Behaviour, Misc. Works, Vol. III*, J. S. McGee (ed.) (Oxford: Clarendon Press, 1986), p. ii.
27. Bunyan, *Grace Abounding to the Chief of Sinners* (Oxford: Clarendon Press, 1962), p. 1.
28. Ibid., p. 1.
29. Ibid., p. 2.
30. Ibid., p. xliv.
31. Lawrence A. Sasek, *The Literary Temper of the English Puritans* (Baton Rouge: Louisiana State University Press, 1961), p. 21.
32. Ibid., p. 24.
33. Ibid.
34. Henry Abelove, *The Evangelist of Desire: John Wesley and the Methodists* (Stanford: Stanford University Press, 1990).
35. For a useful survey and analysis of Christian evangelical use of the media, see Steve Bruce, *Pray TV: Televangelism in America* (London and New York: Routledge, 1990).
36. Bunyan, *Light for them that sit in Darkness, Misc. Works, Vol. VIII*, R. L. Greaves (ed.) (Oxford: Clarendon Press, 1979), p. 57.
37. Bunyan, *Come & Welcome, to Jesus Christ, Misc. Works, Vol. VIII*, p. 387.
38. Bunyan, *Light for them that sit in Darkness, Misc. Works, Vol. VIII*, p. 49.
39. Ibid.
40. Ibid., p. 50.
41. Ibid., p. 49.
42. Ibid., p. 50.
43. Ibid., pp. 51, 49, 50.
44. Ibid., p. 51.
45. Ibid.
46. Ibid.
47. Ibid.
48. Ibid.
49. Ibid., pp. 51, 49.
50. Ibid., p. 50.
51. Jacques Derrida, *Of Grammatology*, trans. Gayatri Chakravorty Spivak (Baltimore and London: Johns Hopkins University Press, 1976), p. 12.
52. Ibid., p. 15.
53. Ibid.
54. Ibid., p. 7.
55. Bunyan, *Light for them that sit in Darkness, Misc. Works, Vol. VIII*, p. 51.
56. Ibid.
57. Ibid., pp. 49, 50.
58. Bunyan, *Instruction for the Ignorant, Misc. Works, Vol. VIII*, p. 20.
59. Ibid.
60. Bunyan, *Light for them that sit in Darkness, Misc. Works Vol. VIII*, p. 49.

61. Bunyan, *Instruction for the Ignorant, Misc. Works Vol. VIII*, p. 21.
62. Sasek, *The Literary Temper of the English Puritans*, pp. 27–8.
63. George Offor, *The Works of John Bunyan, Vol. III* (Glasgow and Edinburgh: Blackie and Son, 1860), p. 764.
64. Ibid., p. 765.
65. Ibid., p. 766.
66. Other texts are thought to have been written and may have been published during this period, including *The Heavenly Foot-man* and *Saved by Grace*, but I have chosen to refer only to those of which editions published between 1666 and 1678 are extant and which offer evidence of the form of the author's name used in this specific period. These are: *A Defence of the Doctrine of Justification by Faith* (Francis Smith, 1672), *A Confession of My Faith and A Reason of My Practice in Worship* (Francis Smith, 1672), *Differences in Judgment about Water-baptism no Bar to Communion* (John Wilkins, 1672), *The Barren Fig-tree* (Jonathan Robinson, 1673), *Light for them that sit in Darkness* (Francis Smith, 1675), *Instruction for the Ignorant* (Francis Smith, 1675), *The Strait Gate* (Francis Smith, 1676), *Come, & Welcome, to Jesus Christ* (Benjamin Harris, 1678). Charles Doe records the publication of an edition of *Peaceable Principles and True* in 1674, but the only extant copy, in the collection of the American Baptist Historical Society in Rochester, New York, lacks the title-page, and therefore evidence of the form of the name of the author used.
67. Bunyan, *The Jerusalem Sinner Saved, or Good News for the Vilest of Men, Misc. Works Vol. XI*, R. L. Greaves (ed.) (Oxford: Clarendon Press, 1985), p. 2; *A Discourse of the Building, Nature, excellency and Government of the House of God, Misc. Works Vol. VI*, p. 273; *The Acceptable Sacrifice, Misc. Works Vol. XII*, W. R. Owens (ed.) (Oxford: Clarendon Press, 1994), p. 2.
68. Foucault, 'What is an author?', p. 148, cited in Kevin Dunn, *Pretexts of Authority: The Rhetoric of Authorship in the Renaissance Preface* (Stanford: Stanford University Press, 1994), p. 10.
69. Dunn, *Pretexts of Authority*, p. 10.
70. Ibid., pp. 10–11.
71. Quoted in Keeble, *The Literary Culture of Nonconformity*, p. 93.
72. Dunn, *Pretexts of Authority*, p. 15.
73. Bunyan, *The Pilgrim's Progress* (Oxford: Oxford University Press, 1960), p. 5.
74. Ibid., p. 1.
75. Ibid.
76. Ibid.
77. See Keeble, *The Literary Culture of Nonconformity*, pp. 177–86.
78. Bunyan, *Grace Abounding*, p. 39.
79. Bunyan, *The Pilgrim's Progress*, p. 1.
80. Bunyan, *The Holy War*, R. Sharrock and J. F. Forrest (eds) (Oxford: Clarendon Press, 1980) p. 251.
81. Ibid.
82. Ibid.
83. Ibid.
84. Ibid.
85. Ibid.

86. *The Greatness of the Soul* (1682), *A Case of Conscience Resolved* (1683), *A Holy Life* (1683), *Seasonable Counsel, or Advice to Sufferers* (1684), *A Caution to stir up to watch against Sin* (1684), *The Pilgrim's Progress, Part Two* (1684–85), *A Discourse upon the Pharisee and the Publican* (1685), *Questions about the Nature and Perpetuity of the Seventh-day Sabbath* (1685), *A Book for Boys and Girls* (1686), *The Advocateship of Jesus Christ* (1688), *The Jerusalem Sinner Saved, or Good News for the Vilest of Men* (1688), *A Discussion of the Building, Nature, Excellency, and Government of the House of God* (1688), *The Water of Life* (1688), *Solomon's Temple Spiritualized* (1688).
87. Keeble, *The Literary Culture of Nonconformity*, p. 134.

## Chapter 2: 'I being taken from you in presence': *Grace Abounding to the Chief of Sinners* and claims to authority

1. George Offor, *The Works of John Bunyan, Vol. I* (Glasgow and Edinburgh: Blackie and Son, 1860), p. lxix.
2. John Bunyan, *Grace Abounding*, p. 8.
3. John Brown, *John Bunyan: His Life, Times and Work* includes a section on different opinions about Bunyan's military service in which he notes that '[t]he side on which Bunyan was arrayed in the great civil conflict of the seventeenth century, Parliamentarian or Royalist, has long been a matter of dispute' (p. 37). Brown presents the conflicting views of Lord Macaulay, who held that Bunyan enlisted in the Parliamentary army, and John Froude, who argued that Bunyan would have supported the Royalist cause. Macaulay, on the one hand, is seen to base his judgement on the resemblance between Bunyan's military characters, such as Greatheart, Captain Boanerges and Captain Credence, and the 'military saints' in Fairfax's army. Froude, on the other hand, cites the facts of Bunyan's father being of the 'national religion' and the Royalist sympathies of John Gifford, Bunyan's minister at Bedford, as evidence that 'probability is on the side of his having been with the Royalists' (p. 37). Brown accepts the evidence that Bunyan's father may have displayed Royalist sympathies, noting that he 'had a son christened Charles on the 30th of May, 1645', but denies that Gifford's allegiances would have had any bearing on Bunyan's actions as 'these two men did not even know of each other's existence till years after the Civil Wars were over' (p. 37). Brown's own analysis takes the form of a survey of the political trends in Bedfordshire as a whole. The county was overwhelmingly Parliamentarian and Brown eventually concludes not only that Bunyan would have served in the Parliamentary army, but suggests the name of a possible commanding officer, Sir Samuel Luke of Cople Wood End. Brown also presents conflicting interpretations of the events apparently referred to by Bunyan in his account of a siege in *Grace Abounding*. Again, Brown refutes the evidence of earlier critics whilst appearing to rely on a degree of conjecture in his own analysis. In an *addendum* to the 1928 edition of Brown's text, the editor, Frank Mott Harrison, argues that Brown's 'conjectures were sound' and reproduces a Muster Roll of the Newport Pagnell Parliamentary garrison of 1647, which

includes the name 'John Bunion'. This textual evidence is seen by Harrison
to be conclusive (pp. 46–51). A more recent survey of the evidence
about Bunyan's military service is provided by Anne Laurence in her
essay, 'Bunyan and the Parliamentary army', in Laurence, Owens and
Sim (eds), *John Bunyan and his England 1628–88*, pp. 16–29. Laurence
examines the evidence that Bunyan may have served with the Royalist
forces and finds it unconvincing, yet notes that although the majority of
Bunyan scholars, such as Brown, William York Tindall, Roger Sharrock
and Christopher Hill, now agree that Bunyan's service was with the
Parliamentary army, a contribution to the *New York Review of Books*
(2 March 1989) suggested that he was a Royalist soldier. Although there
would now appear to be a general consensus that Bunyan served with
the Parliamentary army, the inconclusiveness of the evidence appears to
continually question the certainty of any conclusive judgement of Bunyan's
military career.

4. Andrew Brink, 'Bunyan's *Pilgrim's Progress* and the secular reader: a
psychological approach', *English Studies in Canada*, 1 (1975), pp. 386–
405. A far more persuasive and productive use of psychoanalytic theory
is to be found in Elspeth Graham's essay, 'Authority, resistance and loss:
gendered difference in the writings of John Bunyan and Hannah Allen',
in Laurence, Owens and Sim (eds), *John Bunyan and his England 1628–
88*, pp. 115–30. Graham employs the theories of Lacan and Freud in her
study of authority and resistance, desire and obedience, which focuses
on language and subjectivity.

5. Bunyan, *Grace Abounding*, Appendix B, p. 169.

6. Ibid.

7. Ibid., p. 175.

8. See especially prefaces to Bunyan's *The Holy War* and *The Pilgrim's
Progress, Part Two*.

9. Paul Delany, *British Autobiography in the Seventeenth Century* (London: Routledge and Kegan Paul, 1969), p. 1.

10. Ibid., p. 55.

11. Ibid., p. 19.

12. Ibid., p. 18.

13. Ibid., p. 33.

14. Ibid., p. 81.

15. Even Delany's guarded definition of the prophet Arise Evans as 'a visionary rather than an out-and-out madman', is based on his privileging
of the rational aspects of his writings: 'His style is usually clear, and his
opinions on matters unrelated to his obsessions are reasonable', ibid., p.
83.

16. Ibid., p. 174.

17. Nigel Smith, *Perfection Proclaimed: Language and Literature in English
Radical Religion 1640–1660* (Oxford: Clarendon Press, 1989), p. 18.

18. Ibid., p. 348.

19. Delany, *British Autobiography in the Seventeenth Century*, p. 88.

20. Delany employs William York Tindall's analysis of the conventional
structure of *Grace Abounding* from *John Bunyan: Mechanick Preacher*
(New York: Columbia University Press, 1934), see Delany, *British Autobiography in the Seventeenth Century*, p. 89.

21. Bunyan, *Grace Abounding*, pp. xxxi, xxxii.

22. Ibid., pp. xxxi–xxxii.

23. Ibid., p. xxxii.

24. Ibid., pp. xxxii, xxxiii.

25. Delany, *British Autobiography in the Seventeenth Century*, p. 81.

26. Jeremy Tambling, *Confession: Sexuality, Sin, the Subject* (Manchester and New York: Manchester University Press, 1990), p. 92.

27. Ibid.

28. Ibid., p. 93.

29. Ibid.

30. Ibid.

31. Ibid.

32. Ibid., p. 94.

33. Ibid.

34. Bunyan, *Grace Abounding*, pp. 67–8. Partially quoted in Tambling, *Confession*, pp. 94–5.

35. Tambling, *Confession*, p. 95.

36. Bunyan, *Grace Abounding*, p. 41, quoted in Tambling, *Confession*, p. 95.

37. Tambling, *Confession*, p. 95.

38. Ibid.

39. Ibid.

40. Ibid., pp. 95–6.

41. '*Remember, I say, the Word that first laid hold upon you; remember your terrors of conscience, and fear of death and hell: remember also your tears and prayers to God; yea, how you sighed under every hedge for mercy. Have you never a Hill* Mizar *to remember? Have you forgot the Close, the Milk- house, the Stable, the Barn, and the like, where* God *did visit your Soul?*' (Bunyan, *Grace Abounding*, p. 3).

42. Tambling, *Confession*, pp. 94, 91.

43. Peter J. Carlton, 'Bunyan: language, convention, authority', *English Literary History*, 51 (1984), pp. 17–32.

44. Ibid., p. 18.

45. Ibid., p. 20.

46. *The Holy War* would seem to typify this genre.

47. Carlton, 'Bunyan', p. 27.

48. John Stachniewski, *The Persecutory Imagination: English Puritanism and the Literature of Religious Despair* (Oxford: Clarendon Press, 1991), p. 85.

49. Ibid., pp. 158, 131.

50. Ibid., p. 129.

51. Bunyan, *Grace Abounding*, pp. 26–7, quoted in Stachniewski, *The Persecutory Imagination*, p. 149.

52. Felicity Nussbaum, '"By these words I was sustained": Bunyan's *Grace Abounding*', *English Literary History*, 49 (1982), pp. 18–34.

53. Ibid., p. 19.

54. Ibid.

55. Ibid.

56. Ibid., p. 20.

57. Ibid., p. 21.

58. Ibid., p. 29.

59. Bunyan, *Grace Abounding*, pp. 31, 30.

60. Felicity Nussbaum, *The Autobiographical Subject: Gender and Ideology in Eighteenth-Century England* (Baltimore and London: Johns Hopkins University Press, 1989), p. 66.
61. Bunyan, *Grace Abounding*, p. 1.
62. Ibid., p. xliv.
63. Ibid., p. 1.
64. Ibid., pp. 104–31.
65. Michel Foucault, 'Politics and reason', Lawrence D. Kritzman (ed.), *Politics, Philosophy, Culture: Interviews and Other Writings 1977–1984* (New York and London: Routledge, 1988), pp. 57–85.
66. Michel Foucault, 'The subject and power' in Hubert L. Dreyfus and Paul Rabinow, *Michel Foucault: Beyond Structuralism and Hermeneutics* (Brighton: Harvester, 1986), pp. 208–26.
67. Ibid., p. 214.
68. Bunyan, *Grace Abounding*, p. 3.
69. Roger Pooley, '*Grace Abounding* and the new sense of self', in Laurence, Owens and Sim, *John Bunyan and his England 1628–88*, pp. 105–14.
70. Ibid., p. 114.
71. Bunyan, *Grace Abounding*, p. 4.
72. Stachniewski, *The Persecutory Imagination*, p. 139.
73. Ibid., p. 141.
74. Ibid., p. 145.
75. Bunyan, *Of Antichrist and His Ruine, Misc. Works*, Vol. XIII, p. 440.
76. Ibid., p. 488.
77. Ibid., p. 489.
78. Ibid., p. 428. Christopher Hill's *Antichrist in Seventeenth-Century England* (London and New York: Verso, 1990) includes comment on *Of Antichrist and His Ruin*, pp. 31, 80, 118, 147–8, 162, and offers a useful survey of the diverse deployments of the figure of the Antichrist in seventeenth-century theological and political writings.
79. Ibid., p. 489.
80. Bunyan, *Grace Abounding*, p. 114.
81. Ibid., p. 117.
82. Stachniewski, *The Persecutory Imagination*, p. 149.
83. Bunyan, *Grace Abounding*, p. 119.
84. Ibid., p. 129.
85. Ibid., p. 2.
86. Ibid., p. 3.
87. Ibid., pp. 3–4.

## Chapter 3: Authority, exclusion and resistance: from interdiction to contra-dictions

1. T. L. Underwood, Introduction to *Misc. Works*, Vol. IV, T. L. Underwood (ed.) (Oxford: Clarendon Press, 1989), p. liv.
2. Bunyan, *Grace Abounding*, p. 87.
3. See T. L. Underwood, '"It pleased me much to contend": John Bunyan as controversialist', *Church History*, 57 (1988), pp. 456–69; Hill, *A Turbulent, Seditious, and Factious People*, pp. 130–35.

4. T. L. Underwood, Introduction to *Misc. Works, Vol. IV*, p. liv.
5. Bunyan, *Questions About the Nature and Perpetuity of the Seventh-Day Sabbath, Misc. Works, Vol. IV*, p. 389.
6. Bunyan, *The Pilgrim's Progress*, pp. 7, 5.
7. Ibid., p. 5.
8. *I. Timothy*. 6.3.
9. See Patricia Crawford, *Women and Religion in England 1500–1720* (London and New York: Routledge, 1993), Richard L. Greaves (ed.), *Triumph over Silence: Women in Protestant History* (Westport and London: Greenwood Press, 1985), and Jim Obelkevich, Lyndal Roper, Raphael Samuel (eds), *Disciplines of Faith: Studies in Religion, Politics and Patriarchy* (London and New York: Routledge and Kegan Paul, 1987).
10. Bunyan, *Grace Abounding*, p. 14.
11. Ibid., p. 15.
12. N. H. Keeble, '"Here is her Glory, even to be under him": the feminine in the thought and work of John Bunyan', in Laurence, Owens and Sim, *John Bunyan and His England*, p. 133.
13. See Crawford, *Women and Religion in England 1500–1720* and Christine Trevett, *Women and Quakerism in the 17th Century* (York: Sessions Book Trust, 1991).
14. Bunyan, *A Case of Conscience Resolved, Misc. Works, Vol. IV*, p. 292.
15. Ibid., p. 297.
16. Ibid.
17. Ibid., pp. 295–6.
18. Ibid.
19. Ibid., p. 296.
20. Ibid.
21. Ibid.
22. Ibid.
23. Ibid., p. 298.
24. Ibid., p. 297.
25. Ibid., p. 299.
26. Ibid., p. 300.
27. Underwood, Introduction to *Misc. Works, Vol. IV*, p. xliii.
28. Hill, *A Turbulent, Seditious and Factious People*, pp. 140–41, 295, 308.
29. Bunyan, *A Case of Conscience Resolved, Misc. Works, Vol. IV*, p. 295.
30. Ibid., p. 295.
31. Margaret Fell, *Womens Speaking Justified* (Los Angeles: Augustan Reprint Society, 1979), p. 3.
32. Ibid., pp. 18, 15.
33. Ibid., pp. 11–12.
34. Felicity Nussbaum, 'Introduction' to Margaret Fell's, *Womens Speaking Justified*, pp. iii–xiv.
35. Fell's texts include *Declaration and an Information* (1660), numerous tracts and the autobiographical *A Relation of Margaret Fell*, collected in *A Brief Collection of Remarkable Passages* (1710).
36. Nussbaum, Introduction, p. iv.
37. Richard L. Greaves, 'Amid the Holy War: Bunyan and the ethic of suffering', in Laurence, Owens and Sim (eds), *John Bunyan and his England 1628–88*, pp. 63–75.

38. Bunyan, *Seasonable Counsel*, quoted in Greaves, 'Amid the Holy War', p. 69.
39. Bunyan, *A Case of Conscience Resolved, Misc. Works, Vol. IV*, p. 305.
40. Richard L. Greaves, 'Conscience, liberty, and the spirit: Bunyan and nonconformity', in Keeble (ed.), *John Bunyan: Conventicle and Parnassus*, pp. 21–43.
41. These are listed as Benjamin Keach, William Kiffin, Daniel King and Hanserd Knollys.
42. Greaves, 'Conscience, liberty and the spirit', pp. 39–40.
43. Hill, *A Turbulent, Seditious and Factious People*, p. 299.
44. Bunyan, *A Case of Conscience Resolved, Misc. Works, Vol. IV*, p. 324.
45. Ibid., p. 325.
46. Ibid.
47. Ibid., p. 329.
48. Ibid.
49. Ibid., p. 309.
50. Ibid., pp. 322–3.
51. Ibid., p. 323.
52. Ibid.
53. Ibid., p. 311.
54. Ibid., pp. 312, 313.
55. Ibid., p. 313.
56. Ibid., pp. 313, 327.
57. Ibid., pp. 323–4.
58. Ibid., p. 328.
59. Ibid.
60. Ibid., pp. 328–9.
61. Christine Berg and Philippa Berry, '"Spiritual Whoredom": an essay on female prophets in the seventeenth century', in F. Barker, J. Bernstein, J. Coombes, P. Hulme, J. Stone and J. Stratton (eds), *1642: Literature and Power in the Seventeenth Century* (Colchester: University of Essex Press, 1981), p. 38.
62. Ibid., p. 39.
63. Ibid., pp. 39–40.
64. Ibid., pp. 50–51.
65. Ibid., p. 39.
66. Ibid., p. 51.
67. Ibid.
68. Bunyan, *Christian Behaviour, Misc. Works, Vol. III*, p. 32.
69. Ibid., p. 33.
70. Ibid., p. 34.
71. Ibid., pp. 34, 36.
72. Ibid., p. 33. The connection between the social, the pastoral and the spiritual is emphasised in *The Greatness of the Soul*, published in 1682, one year before *A Case of Conscience Resolved*. Here the Christian subject is advised to take care in the choice of both pastoral and worldly associates: 'And as thou shouldst for thy Souls sake chuse for thy self good Soul-Shepherds; so also for the same reason, you should chuse for your selves a good Wife, a good Husband, a good Master, a good Servant, for in all these things, *the soul is concerned*', *The Greatness of*

*the Soul, Misc. Works, Vol. IX*, R. L. Greaves (ed.) (Oxford: Clarendon Press, 1981), p. 229.

73. Bunyan, *Christian Behaviour, Misc. Works, Vol. III*, p. 10.
74. As Hill notes in *A Turbulent, Seditious and Factious People* (p. 107), Venner's Fifth Monarchist rising took place in London shortly after Bunyan's arrest and it was assumed by some that when he visited London it was to plot insurrection.
75. Bunyan, *Christian Behaviour*, p. 10.
76. Bunyan, *Grace Abounding*, p. 8.
77. Bunyan, *A Relation of the Imprisonment of Mr. John Bunyan*, published with *Grace Abounding*, pp. 102–31.
78. Bunyan, *A Case of Conscience Resolved, Misc. Works, Vol. IV*, p. 308.
79. Ibid., p. 326.
80. Bunyan, *A Relation of the Imprisonment of Mr. John Bunyan, Grace Abounding*, p. 128. Christopher Hill notes that the presentation of Elizabeth Bunyan's activity here runs counter to Bunyan's statements elsewhere on female inferiority and necessary subordination in *A Nation of Change and Novelty: Radical Politics in Seventeenth-Century England* (London and New York: Routledge, 1990), pp. 53–4.
81. Elizabeth Bunyan is named in 'A continuation of Mr. Bunyan's life', published with *Grace Abounding*, p. 175.
82. Bunyan, *Grace Abounding*, p. 93.
83. Ibid., p. 94.
84. The phrase, 'Agnes Beaumont affair', is employed by Roger Sharrock in his annotation of sections 306–17 of *Grace Abounding*, p. 155.
85. First published in 1760. The most recent edition is Vera Camden (ed.), *The Narrative of the Persecutions of Agnes Beaumont* (East Lansing: Colleagues Press, 1992). The only other twentieth-century edition of the full text is G. B. Harrison (ed.), *The Narrative of the Persecution of Agnes Beaumont in 1674* (London: Constable and Co., 1930). Extracts of the text are published, together with selections from the writings of Bunyan and entries from the Bedford Church Book, in Monica Furlong (ed.), *The Trial of John Bunyan and The Persecution of the Puritans* (London: Folio Society, 1978). References in this book are to the Harrison edition.
86. Harrison, *Persecution of Agnes Beaumont in 1674*, pp. 15–16.
87. Ibid., p. 17.
88. Ibid., p. 51.
89. Ibid., pp. 37, 38.
90. Ibid., pp. 42–3.
91. See Elaine Hobby, *Virtue of Necessity: English Women's Writing 1649–88* (London: Virago, 1988), pp. 27–8, 34, 46, 52. Elspeth Graham, Hilary Hinds, Elaine Hobby and Helen Wilcox (eds), *Her Own Life: Autobiographical Writings by Seventeenth-Century Englishwomen* (London and New York: Routledge, 1989) includes material on accusations of madness and on fasting and eating disorders among female prophets and writers. See also Diane Purkiss, 'Producing the voice, consuming the body: women prophets of the seventeenth century' in Isobel Grundy and Susan Wiseman (eds) *Women, Writing History 1640–1740* (London: B. T. Batsford, 1992), pp. 139–58.
92. Harrison, *Persecution of Agnes Beaumont in 1674*, p. 48.

93. Ibid., p. 63.
94. Ibid., pp. 54, 58.
95. Camden, *Persecutions of Agnes Beaumont*, p. 24.
96. Harrison, *Persecution of Agnes Beaumont in 1674*, p. 59.
97. Ibid., p. 3.
98. Ibid.
99. Ibid., p. 87.
100. See Felicity Nussbaum, *The Autobiographical Subject*, pp. 72–3.
101. Harrison, *Persecution of Agnes Beaumont in 1674*, p. 91.
102. Ibid., p. vi.
103. Extract of *The Church Book of Bunyan Meeting*, reproduced in Monica Furlong, *The Trial of John Bunyan*, p. 118.
104. Extracts from *The Church Book of Bunyan Meeting*, reproduced in Harrison, *Persecution of Agnes Beaumont in 1674*, pp. xi–xii.
105. Catherine Belsey, *The Subject of Tragedy: Identity and Difference in Renaissance Drama* (London and New York: Methuen, 1985), pp. 129–48.
106. See *Grace Abounding*, pp. 93–5. See also the depiction of a number of female characters in *The Pilgrim's Progress, Part One*: Wanton, who attempts to ensnare Faithful; Lot's wife, transformed into a pillar of salt as 'an example'; Diffidence, the wife of Giant Despair. In *The Pilgrim's Progress, Part Two* the 'positive' representations of female protagonists are accompanied by characterisations of female vice: Mrs Bats-eyes, Mrs Inconsiderate, Mrs Light-mind, and Mrs Know-nothing, Mrs Love-the-flesh, Mrs Filth join Madam Wanton as Christiana's mocking and sceptical neighbours; Madam Bubble, glossed as 'this vain world' and described by Great-Heart as 'a bold and impudent Slut; She will talk with any Man' (pp. 301, 302). See Chapter 4 in this volume for a further analysis of the representation of women in Bunyan's writings.
107. Bunyan, *A Case of Conscience Resolved, Misc. Works, Vol. IV*, p. 330.

## Chapter 4: The limits of authority: Bunyan's other readers

1. *The Independent*, 20 November 1991, p. 3.
2. *Today*, 20 November 1991, p. 1.
3. *The Independent*, 20 November 1991, p. 3.
4. Ibid.
5. In the 1950 window, commemorating the 300th anniversary of the founding of the Church, Bunyan appears as Christian for the first time, with John Gifford, the first minister of the Church, as Evangelist, and the names of all ministers of the Church from 1650 to 1950 forming the scroll at the edge. The windows are all reproduced in Alan Girket, *A Souvenir Guide to the John Bunyan Museum, Library and Bunyan Meeting Free Church* (Essex: Fidelity Colour, 1992).
6. Quotations are from the BBC Television news report of Waite's meeting with Joy Brodier, the Bedfordshire woman who sent the postcard. The report on 10 July 1992 showed Waite and Brodier standing in front of the stained-glass window in the Bunyan Meeting Free Church in Bedford. Waite confirmed that the card had been his 'only contact with the

outside world for five years' and the reporter stated that 'the hostage and the housewife are set to be best of friends'. This 'friendship', which commenced with a postcard from a stranger had been sealed by the gift of a pot of 'home-made jam'. In the aftermath of the events of 1991 a new version of the postcard has been printed by the Bunyan Meeting Free Church in Bedford. The image of the window is the same as on the original postcard, but now the reverse side bears the following inscription: 'Window commemorating the tercentenary of the publication of The Pilgrim's Progress. John Bunyan in Bedford jail. A card of this window was sent to Terry Waite when held as a hostage.'

7. George Offor (ed.), *The Works of John Bunyan, Vol. I*, p. vi.
8. Ibid.
9. Ibid., p. xxxiv.
10. Ibid., p. vi.
11. Ibid., p. lvii.
12. Ibid., p. vii.
13. Ibid.
14. Bunyan, *The Pilgrim's Progress*, p. 6.
15. Augustine Birrell, 'Links of empire – books (IX): *The Pilgrim's Progress*', *Empire Review*, 47 (February 1928), pp. 79–87, quoted in Richard L. Greaves, 'Bunyan through the centuries: some reflections', *English Studies*, 64 (1983), p. 119.
16. This list is compiled from a survey of entries in *Books in Print* (New York: R. R. Bowker, 1991) and *The National Union Catalog* (Washington: Library of Congress, 1983). Earlier editions of both publications, including supplements, were also checked. Additional material on editions of Bunyan's writings is available in Frank Mott Harrison's appendix to the tercentenary edition of John Brown, *John Bunyan: His Life, Times, and Work*, pp. 439–83 and the Borough of Bedford Library, *Catalogue of the John Bunyan Library (Frank Mott Harrison Collection)*, pp. 5–24.
17. See Peter N. Carroll and David W. Noble, *The Free and the Unfree: a New History of the United States* (Harmondsworth: Penguin, 1988), pp. 165–84.
18. Thomas Pakenham, *The Scramble for Africa* (London: Abacus, 1991), p. xxiv.
19. Letter to Mr and Mrs N. Livingstone and daughters (28 July 1850) in I. Schapera (ed.), *David Livingstone: Family Letters 1841–1856, Volume II* (London: Chatto and Windus, 1959), p. 93.
20. Edward W. Said, *Culture and Imperialism* (London: Chatto and Windus, 1993), pp. 9–10.
21. Schapera, *David Livingstone, Vol. I*, pp. 143, 157, 191.
22. Ibid., p. 249.
23. Schapera, *David Livingstone, Vol. II*, p. 19.
24. Ibid., pp. 46–7.
25. Schapera, *David Livingstone, Vol. I*, p. 249.
26. Ibid., p. 255.
27. Ibid.
28. Schapera, *David Livingstone, Vol. II*, p. 93.
29. Ibid., p. 30.
30. Schapera, *David Livingstone, Vol. II*, pp. 29–30, 43.

31. Ibid., pp. 43, 46–7.
32. Schapera, *David Livingstone, Vol. I*, p. 15.
33. See Schapera, *David Livingstone, Vol. II*, p. 267.
34. Hill, *A Turbulent, Seditious, and Factious People*, p. 375. Hill's main source is R. G. Wagner, *Re-enacting the Heavenly Vision: the Role of Religion in the Taiping Rebellion* (Berkeley: Institute of East Asian Studies, University of California, 1982).
35. Pakenham, *The Scramble for Africa*, p. 82.
36. Hill, *A Turbulent, Seditious, and Factious People*, p. 376.
37. See entry in John Brown, *John Bunyan: His Life, Times, and Work*, p. 478: 'Canton Vernacular. Two Vols. With Chinese Illustrations. Translated by the Rev. G. Piercy, of the Wesleyan Mission, 1870–1.'
38. Brown, *John Bunyan*, p. 479.
39. M. Godolphin, *The Pilgrim's Progress, in Words of one Syllable* (1869), and S. P. Day, *The Pilgrim's Progress, In Words of one Syllable* (1872), as listed in Brown, *John Bunyan*, p. 482. In the appendix to the tercentenary edition of Brown's work, Frank Mott Harrison lists 32 different versions for children, published between 1825 and 1921, including two in 'picture cards' and one in braille, p. 482. Two phonetic editions are listed, and two others in braille, p. 483. Eight editions '*de luxe*' are listed, p. 483.
40. See James F. Forrest and Richard L. Greaves, *John Bunyan*, pp. 6 on; Hill, *A Turbulent, Seditious and Factious People*, pp. 373–4.
41. For a description of Wesley's editions of Bunyan's writings see Isabel Rivers, *Reason, Grace, and Sentiment: a Study of the Language of Religion and Ethics in England 1660–1780. Volume I: Whichcote to Wesley.* (Cambridge and New York: Cambridge University Press, 1991), pp. 218–19.
42. See Richard L. Greaves, 'Bunyan through the centuries: some reflections', *English Studies*, 64 (1983), p. 114.
43. Mary Anne Burges, *The Progress of the Pilgrim Good-Intent, in Jacobinical Times* (London: John Hatchard, 1800), p. viii. See Forrest and Greaves, *John Greaves*, p. 25.
44. Robert Southey (ed.), *The Pilgrim's Progress, with a Life of John Bunyan* (London: John Murray and John Major, 1830).
45. Among those who commented favourably on text and/or author were Thomas Macaulay, George Eliot, Robert Browning, John Ruskin, Robert Louis Stevenson, George Bernard Shaw, Louisa May Alcott, Nathaniel Hawthorne and Teddy Roosevelt. For more details see Greaves, 'Bunyan through the centuries: some reflections', pp. 114–16.
46. See Christopher Hill, 'John Bunyan and his publics', *History Today*, 38 (October 1988), p. 19.
47. Keeble, *The Literary Culture of Nonconformity*, p. 135.
48. Bunyan, *Some Gospel-truths Opened, Misc. Works, Vol. I*, p. 8.
49. Bunyan, *Grace Abounding*, p. 1.
50. Ibid.
51. Ibid.
52. Hill, *A Turbulent, Seditious, and Factious People*, pp. 153, 179, 246, 284–91.
53. Bunyan, *Grace Abounding*, pp. 9, 10.
54. Ibid., p. 10.

55. Bunyan, *The Pilgrim's Progress*, p. 6.
56. Ibid., p. 7.
57. Ibid.
58. Ibid.
59. Keeble, *The Literary Culture of Nonconformity*, pp. 128, 134.
60. Bunyan, *The Pilgrim's Progress*, p. 169.
61. Ibid.
62. Ibid., pp. 169, 170.
63. Ibid., p. 170.
64. Ibid., p. 172.
65. Ibid., p. 173.
66. Margaret Olofson Thickstun, *Fictions of the Feminine: Puritan Doctrine and the Representation of Women* (Ithaca and London: Cornell University Press, 1988), p. 1.
67. Ibid., p. 4.
68. See Roger Sharrock, 'Women and children', in R. Sharrock (ed.), *The Pilgrim's Progress: A Casebook* (London: Macmillan, 1976), pp. 174–85.
69. Thickstun, *Fictions of the Feminine*, p. 92.
70. Ibid., p. 98.
71. Ibid., p. 104.
72. Bunyan, *The Pilgrim's Progress*, pp. 9, 10.
73. Ibid., p. 23.
74. Ibid., p. 29.
75. Ibid., p. 30.
76. It is the character Charity who questions Christian about his family and his behaviour towards them. She asks a series of 'leading' questions which elicit properly pious responses from Christian who is finally assured of the rectitude of his decision to leave his family when Charity presents their behaviour as analogous to that of Cain. Ibid., pp. 50–52.
77. Ibid., pp. 53, 56.
78. Ibid., pp. 68, 69.
79. Ibid., p. 81.
80. Ibid., p. 84.
81. J. Bunyan, *The Life and Death of Mr Badman* (Oxford: Oxford University Press, 1988), p. 2.
82. Ibid., pp. 66, 69.
83. Ibid., p. 145.
84. Bunyan, *Christian Behaviour, Misc. Works, Vol. III*, p. 35.
85. Ibid., pp. 35, 36.
86. Ibid., p. 36.
87. Bunyan, *The Life and Death of Mr Badman*, p. 73.
88. Ibid., pp. 78–9.
89. Ibid., p. 79.
90. Ibid., p. 147.
91. Ibid.
92. Ibid., p. 125.
93. Ibid.
94. Ibid.
95. Ibid.
96. Ibid., p. 128.

97. N. H. Keeble, '"Here is her Glory, even to be under him": the feminine in the thought and work of John Bunyan', in Laurence, Owens and Sim (eds), *John Bunyan and His England 1628–88*, p. 140.

98. Bunyan, *The Pilgrim's Progress*, p. 196.

99. See Keeble, '"Here is her Glory"', pp. 142–3.

100. Bunyan, *The Pilgrim's Progress*, p. 134.

101. Bunyan, *The Holy War*, p. 5.

102. Valentine Cunningham, 'Glossing and glozing: Bunyan and allegory', in Keeble (ed.), *John Bunyan: Conventicle and Parnassus*, p. 219.

103. Cunningham, 'Glossing and glozing', p. 236.

104. Ibid., p. 227.

105. Bunyan, *The Holy War*, p. 5.

106. Cunningham, 'Glossing and glozing', p. 236. Christopher Hill writes on the role played by marginal notes in the Geneva Bible in radical political deployments of scriptural material in *The English Bible and the Seventeenth-Century Revolution*, pp. 62–4. He suggests that the political dimensions of many of the glosses in the Geneva Bible may both have contributed to attempts to suppress the text on the part of the Established Church and have offered the grounds for limited resistance. He also notes that the Authorised Version was produced without marginal notes. Bunyan refers to both texts in his writings.

107. See John Morgan, *Godly Learning: Puritan Attitudes towards Reason, Learning and Education 1560–1640* (Cambridge and New York: Cambridge University Press, 1988).

108. Bunyan's association of classical and university-based learning with hypocrisy and carnality is typified by a reference in *A Few Sighs from Hell* (1658) to the godly who 'are not gentlemen, ... cannot, with Pontius Pilate, speak Hebrew, Greek and Latin', *Misc. Works, Vol. I*, p. 304. In the same text, however, he dissociates himself from the extreme scepticism about Scriptural authority or the importance of knowledge of the Word which characterised Ranters and other antinomian groups by ascribing to a damned soul in hell the view that the Scriptures were 'written by some politicians on purpose to make poor ignorant people submit to some religion and government', ibid., p. 343. This point is made by Christopher Hill in *A Nation of Change and Novelty*, p. 175.

109. Keeble, *The Literary Culture of Nonconformity*, p. 156.

110. Bunyan, *A Book for Boys and Girls*, *Misc. Works, Vol. VI*, p. 190.

111. Ibid., p. 191.

112. Ibid., p. 192.

113. Ibid.

114. Michel Foucault, *The Order of Things* (London and New York: Tavistock/Routledge, 1989), p. 56.

115. Bunyan, *A Book for Boys and Girls*, *Misc. Works, Vol. VI*, p. 193.

116. Ibid., pp. 194–6.

117. Ibid., p. 196.

118. Ibid., p. 194.

119. Ibid.

120. Tiyo Soga, *Uhambo Lo Mhambi, owesuka kweli liwe, waye esinga kwelo lizayo* (Lovedale: Lovedale Institution Bookstore, 1902), pp. xv–xvi.

## Conclusion: Bunyan @ large

1. Information from British and US editions of *Books in Print* (1996).

# Bibliography

## Editions of Bunyan's writings cited

*Grace Abounding to the Chief of Sinners*, R. Sharrock (ed.) (Oxford: Clarendon Press, 1962).

*The Holy War*, R. Sharrock and J. F. Forrest (eds) (Oxford: Clarendon Press, 1980).

*The Life and Death of Mr Badman*, J. F. Forrest and R. Sharrock (eds) (Oxford: Clarendon Press, 1988).

*The Miscellaneous Works of John Bunyan*, R. Sharrock (gen. ed.) (Oxford: Clarendon Press, 1976–89) comprising:

*Vol. I*, T. L. Underwood (ed.) (1980); *Vol. II*, R. L. Greaves (ed.) (1976); *Vol. III*, J. S. McGee, (ed.) (1986);

*Vol. IV*, T. L. Underwood (ed.) (1989); *Vol. V*, G. Midgley (ed.) (1986); *Vol. VI*, G. Midgley (ed.) (1980);

*Vol. VII*, G. Midgley (ed.) (1989); *Vol. VIII*, R. L. Greaves (ed.) (1979); *Vol. IX*, R. L. Greaves (ed.) (1981); *Vol. X*, O. C. Watkins (ed.) (1988); *Vol. XI*, R. L. Greaves (ed.) (1985); *Vol. XII*, W. R. Owens (ed.) (1994); *Vol. XIII*, W. R. Owens (ed.) (1994).

*The Pilgrim's Progress*, J. B. Wharey and R. Sharrock (eds) (Oxford: Oxford University Press, 1960).

## Other works consulted

Abelove, H. (1990), *The Evangelist of Desire: John Wesley and the Methodists*, Stanford: Stanford University Press.

Baldick, C. (1983), *The Social Mission of English Criticism 1848–1932*, Oxford: Clarendon Press.

Belsey C. (1985), *The Subject of Tragedy: Identity and Difference in Renaissance Drama*, London and New York: Methuen.

Berg, C. and Berry, P. (1981)'"Spiritual Whoredom": a essay on female prophets in the seventeenth century', in Barker, F., Bernstein, J., Coombes, J., Hulme, P., Stone, J. and Stratton, J. (eds), *1642: Literature and Power in the Seventeenth Century*, Colchester: University of Essex Press, pp. 37–54.

Birrell, A. (1928), 'Links of empire – books (IX): *The Pilgrim's Progress*', *Empire Review*, 47, February, pp. 79–87.

*Books in Print* (1991), New York: R. R. Bowker.

Borough of Bedford Public Library (1938), *Catalogue of the John Bunyan*

*Library (Frank Mott Harrison Collection)*, Bedford: Borough of Bedford Public Library.

Brink, A. (1975), 'Bunyan's *Pilgrim's Progress* and the secular reader: a psychological approach', *English Studies in Canada*, 1, pp. 386–405.

Brown, J. (1928), *John Bunyan: His Life, Times, and Work*, London and Glasgow: Hilbert Publishing.

Bruce, S. (1990), *Pray TV: Televangelism in America*, London and New York: Routledge.

Burges, M. A. (1800), *The Progress of the Pilgrim Good-Intent, in Jacobinical Times*, London: John Hatchard.

Camden, V. (ed.) (1992), *The Narrative of the Persecutions of Agnes Beaumont*, East Lansing: Colleages Press.

Carlton, P. J. (1984), 'Bunyan: language, convention, authority', *English Literary History*, 51, pp. 17–32.

Carroll, P. N. and Noble, D. W. (1988), *The Free and the Unfree: a New History of the United States*, Harmondsworth: Penguin.

Collmer, R. G. (ed.) (1989), *Bunyan in our Time*, Kent, Ohio and London: Kent State University Press.

Crawford, P. (1993), *Women and Religion in England 1500–1720*, London and New York: Routledge.

Cunningham, V. (1988), 'Glossing and glozing: John Bunyan and allegory', in Keeble, N. H. (ed.), *John Bunyan: Conventicle and Parnassus*, pp. 217–40.

Delany, P. (1969), *British Autobiography in the Seventeenth Century*, London: Routledge and Kegan Paul.

Derrida, J. (1976), *Of Grammatology*, G. C. Spivak (trans.), Baltimore and London: Johns Hopkins University Press.

Dunn, K. (1994), *Pretexts of Authority: The Rhetoric of Authorship in the Renaissance Preface*, Stanford: Stanford University Press.

Fell, M. (1979), *Womens Speaking Justified*, Los Angeles: Augustan Reprint Society.

Forrest, J. F. and Greaves, R. L. (1982), *John Bunyan: A Reference Guide*, Boston: G. K. Hall.

Foucault, M. (1977), 'What is an author?', in D. F. Bouchard (ed.), *Language, Counter Memory, Practice*, Oxford: Basil Blackwell, pp. 113–38.

———— (1986), 'The subject and power', in H. L. Dreyfus and P. Rabinow, *Beyond Structuralism and Hermeneutics*, Brighton: Harvester.

———— (1988) 'Politics and reason', in L. D. Kritzman (ed.), *Politics, Philosophy, Culture: Interviews and Other Writings 1977–1984*, New York and London: Routledge, pp. 57–85.

———— (1989), *The Order of Things*, London and New York: Tavistock/ Routledge.

Furlong, M. (ed.) (1978), *The Trial of John Bunyan and the Persecution of the Puritans*, London: Folio Society.

Graham, E. (1990), 'Authority, resistance and loss: gendered difference in the writings of John Bunyan and Hannah Allen', in Laurence, A., Owens, W. R. and Sim, S. (eds), *John Bunyan and his England 1628–88*, London and Ronceverte: Hambledon Press, pp. 115–30.

Graham, E., Hinds, H., Hobby, E. and Wilcox, H. (eds) (1989), *Her Own Life: Autobiographical Writings by Seventeenth-Century Englishwomen*, London and New York: Routledge.

Greaves, R. L. (1974), 'A John Bunyan signature', *Baptist Quarterly*, 25.

———— (1983), 'Bunyan through the centuries: some reflections', *English Studies*, 64, pp. 113–21.

———— (ed.) (1985), *Triumph over Silence: Women in Protestant History*, Westport and London: Greenwood Press.

———— (1988), 'Conscience, liberty, and the spirit: Bunyan and nonconformity', in N. H. Keeble (ed.), *John Bunyan: Conventicle and Parnassus*, Oxford: Clarendon Press, pp. 21–43.

———— (1990), 'Amid the Holy War: Bunyan and the ethic of suffering', in Laurence, A., Owens, W. R. and Sim, S. (eds), *John Bunyan and his England 1628–88*, London and Ronceverte: Hambledon Press, pp. 63–75.

Harrison, G. B. (ed.) (1930), *The Narrative of the Persecution of Agnes Beaumont in 1674*, London: Constable and Co.

Herreshoff, D. (1989), 'Marxist perspectives on Bunyan', in R. G. Collmer (ed.), *Bunyan in Our Time*, pp. 161–85.

Hill, C. (1988), *A Turbulent, Seditious, and Factious People: John Bunyan and his Church*, Oxford: Oxford University Press.

———— (1988), 'John Bunyan and his publics', *History Today*, 38 (October), pp. 13–19.

———— (1990), *Antichrist in Seventeenth-Century England*, London and New York: Verso.

———— (1990), *A Nation of Change and Novelty: Radical Politics in Seventeenth-Century England*, London and New York: Routledge.

———— (1993), *The English Bible and the Seventeenth-Century Revolution*, Harmondsworth: Allen Lane.

Hobby, E. (1988), *Virtue of Necessity: English Women's Writing 1649–88*, London: Virago.

Keeble, N. H. (1987), *The Literary Culture of Nonconformity in Later Seventeenth-Century England*, Leicester: Leicester University Press.

——— (ed.) (1988), *John Bunyan: Conventicle and Parnassus*, Oxford: Clarendon Press.

——— (1990), '"Here is her Glory, even to be under him": the feminine in the thought and work of John Bunyan', in Laurence, A., Owens, W. R. and Sim, S. (eds), *John Bunyan and his England 1628–88*, London and Ronceverte: Hambledon Press, pp. 131–47.

Laurence, A. (1990), 'Bunyan and the Parliamentary army', in Laurence, A., Owens, W. R. and Sim, S. (eds), *John Bunyan and his England 1628–88*, London and Ronceverte: Hambledon Press, pp. 16–29.

Laurence, A., Owens, W. R. and Sim, S. (1990), *John Bunyan and his England 1628–88*, London and Ronceverte: Hambledon Press.

Morgan, J. (1988), *Godly Learning: Puritan Attitudes towards Reason, Learning and Education 1560–1640*, Cambridge and New York: Cambridge University Press.

*National Union Catalog* (1983), Washington: Library of Congress.

Noyes, A. (1928a), 'Bunyan – a revaluation', *Bookman*, 75, October.

——— (1928b), 'Rejoinder', *Bookman*, 75, November.

Nussbaum, F. (1979), 'Introduction', in M. Fell, *Womens Speaking Justified*, Los Angeles: Augustan Reprint Society.

——— (1982), '"By these words I was sustained": Bunyan's *Grace Abounding*', *English Literary History*, 49, pp. 18–34.

——— (1989), *The Autobiographical Subject: Gender and Ideology in Eighteenth-Century England*, Baltimore and London: Johns Hopkins University Press.

Obelkevich, J., Roper, L. and Samuel, R. (eds) (1987), *Disciplines of Faith: Studies in Religion, Politics and Patriarchy*, London and New York: Routledge and Kegan Paul.

Offor, G. (1860), *The Works of John Bunyan*, 3 vols, Glasgow and Edinburgh: Blackie and Son.

Packenham, T. (1991), *The Scramble for Africa*, London: Abacus.

Pooley, R. (1990), '*Grace Abounding* and the new sense of self', in Laurence, A., Owens, W. R. and Sim, S. (eds), *John Bunyan and his England 1628–88*, London and Ronceverte: Hambledon Press, pp. 105–14.

Purkiss, D. (1992), 'Producing the voice, consuming the body: women prophets of the seventeenth century', in I. Grundy and S. Wiseman (eds), *Women, Writing History 1640–1740* (London: B. T. Batsford, 1992), pp. 139–58.

Quiller-Couch, A. T. (1908), *John Bunyan: Selections*, Oxford: Clarendon Press.

Raleigh, W. (1894), *The English Novel: Being a Short Sketch of Its History from the Earliest Times to the Appearance of Waverly*, London: John Murray.

Rivers, I. (1991), *Reason, Grace, and Sentiment: A Study of the Language of Religion and Ethics in England 1660–1780. Volume I: Whichcote to Wesley*. Cambridge and New York: Cambridge University Press.

Said, E. W. (1993), *Culture and Imperialism*, London: Chatto and Windus.

Sasek, L. A. (1961), *The Literary Temper of the English Puritans*, Baton Rouge: Louisiana State University Press.

Schapera, I. (ed.) (1959), *David Livingstone: Family Letters 1841–1856*, 2 vols, London: Chatto and Windus.

Sharrock, R. (1976), 'Women and children', in Sharrock (ed.), *The Pilgrim's Progress: A Casebook*, London: Macmillan, pp. 174–85.

Simson, J. (1858) 'Was John Bunyan a gipsy?', *Notes and Queries*, 5, April.

Smith, N. (1989), *Perfection Proclaimed: Language and Literature in English Radical Religion 1640–1660*, Oxford: Clarendon Press.

Soga, T. (1902), *Uhambo Lo Mhambi, owesuka kweli liwe, waye esinga kwelo lizayo*, Lovedale: Lovedale Institution Bookstore.

Southey, R. (ed.) (1830), *The Pilgrim's Progress, with a Life of John Bunyan*, London: John Murray and John Major.

Stachniewski, J. (1991), *The Persecutory Imagination: English Puritanism and the Literature of Religious Despair*, Oxford: Clarendon Press.

Tambling, J. (1990), *Confession: Sexuality, Sin, the Subject*, Manchester and New York: Manchester University Press.

Thickstun, M. O. (1988), *Fictions of the Feminine: Puritan Doctrine and the Representation of Women*, Ithaca and London: Cornell University Press.

Tindall, W. Y. (1934), *John Bunyan: Mechanick Preacher*, New York: Columbia University Press.

Trevett, C. (1991), *Women and Quakerism in the 17th Century*, York: Sessions Book Trust.

Underwood, T. L. (1988), '"It pleased me much to contend": John Bunyan as controversialist', *Church History*, 57, pp. 456–69.

Wagner, R. G. (1982), *Re-enacting the Heavenly Vision: the Role of Religion in the Taiping Rebellion*, Berkeley: Institute of East Asian Studies, University of California.

Whalley, G. (ed.) (1980), *The Collected Works of Samuel Taylor Coleridge: Marginalia I*, London: Routledge and Kegan Paul.

# Index